THE MAKING OF

MODERN ADVERTISING

THE
MAKING
OF
MODERN
ADVERTISING

DANIEL POPE

Basic Books, Inc., Publishers

New York

Table 2.4, Column 3 reprinted with permission from Harold Barger, *Distribution's Place in the American Economy* (Princeton, N.J.: Princeton University Press for the National Bureau of Economic Research, 1955), p. 70. Copyright, 1955, Princeton University Press.

Library of Congress Cataloging in Publication Data

Pope, Daniel, 1946-
   The making of modern advertising.

   Includes bibliographical references and index.
   1. Advertising. I. Title.
HF5821.P64   1983   338.4'76591   82–72404
ISBN 0–465–04325–9

For Barbara

CONTENTS

ACKNOWLEDGMENTS

M ANY PEOPLE contributed to the making of *The Making of Modern Advertising*. Stuart Bruchey was an ideal advisor for my dissertation at Columbia University that was my first attempt to understand the history of advertising. He has been unfailingly generous and encouraging since then as well. William Leuchtenburg and Walter Metzger were helpful members of my dissertation committee.

For reading and commenting on drafts of all or parts of this book, I want to thank my colleagues at the University of Oregon History Department: Val Lorwin; Jack Maddex; Louise Wade; and Allan Winkler. Bill Toll has been a good friend and the source of much intellectual stimulation. Other scholars working on advertising and related subjects have also been helpful. These include Stuart Ewen, Frank Fox, Roland Marchand, Richard Pollay, and Richard Tedlow. At Harvard Business School, Alfred D. Chandler, Tom McCraw, and David Mowery all read my work and offered useful suggestions. I also wish to thank Professors Chandler and McCraw for broadening my understanding of business history while I held the Harvard-Newcomen Postdoctoral Fellowship in Business History in 1980-81. Erica Liederman, my office-mate at Harvard Business School, applied her literary talents to editing some of the rougher pages of my manuscript and offered friendly encouragement as well.

René Olivieri, now at Basil Blackwell Publishers, was a kind supporter of this project as well as an intelligent critic. Martin Kessler and many others at Basic Books have been consistently responsive and extraordinarily helpful.

For assistance in typing the manuscript I am most grateful to Enid Scofield, Violet Crowe, and to the Harvard Business School's Word Processing Office under Rose Giacobbe.

Many librarians and archivists made my tasks easier. Although I cannot list them all by name, I am grateful to each of them. I would especially like to thank the reference, interlibrary loan, and special collections staff of the University of Oregon Library, the librarians at Harvard Business School's magnificent Baker Library, and Cynthia Swank and Annamarie Sandecki of the J. Walter Thompson Company Archives.

My mother, Edith Pope, provided love and support. Stephanie Pope, age eight, is something of an expert on advertising herself, and she is wise and wonderful in many other ways as well. Barbara Corrado Pope deserves my thanks for more than this book could ever reveal.

THE MAKING OF
MODERN ADVERTISING

1

Introduction: "The Age of Advertising"

ADVERTISEMENTS, commented *Harper's Weekly* in 1897, "are now part of the humanities, a true mirror of life, a sort of fossil history from which the future chronicler, if all other historical monuments were to be lost, might fully and graphically rewrite the history of our time."[1] It was in the late nineteenth and early twentieth centuries that advertising became an institution emblematic of American society and culture. An exuberant advertising man in 1915 predicted, "When the historian of the Twentieth Century shall have finished his narrative, and comes searching for the subtitle which shall best express the spirit of the period, we think it not at all unlikely that he may select 'The Age of Advertising' for the purpose."[2]

Of course, advertising predated the era of American industrialization. Advertising men have long delighted in finding allusions to their craft in biblical passages; a few have even contended that cave paintings were precursors of advertisements. Strained as these interpretations may be, signs over shop entrances did exist in biblical and classical antiquity. Criers in ancient Greece announced goods for sale as well as public edicts. This oral advertising reappeared in medieval fairs and markets and flourished in the new European cities. Retailers' signboards were common in Europe by the late Middle Ages. Printed handbills made their entrance not long after Gutenberg in the 1400s. By the seventeenth century, newspapers printed announcements from merchants. In the American colonies, the first newspaper advertisement was published in May 1704, in the *Boston News-Letter*. Two of the three notices under the heading "Advertising" concerned goods stolen from the advertisers. The third offered real estate for sale in New York.[3] On both sides of the Atlantic, advertising burgeoned during the eighteenth century. Benjamin Franklin's *Pennsylvania Gazette* was printing illustrated advertisements before 1750. Other publishers displayed ads in novel ways and used large type faces. By 1759, Dr. Samuel Johnson took note of these developments: "The trade of advertising," he wrote, "is now so near to perfection that it is not easy to propose any improvement."[4]

In America, there was indeed little improvement for the next century. Although the volume of advertising increased, the early nineteenth century saw a retrogression in technique. Innovations in display were few; advertisements were small and usually set in an eyestraining six-point type. Most newspapers depended on subscriptions for their revenues, so prices were high and circulations low. Steam-powered rotary presses, introduced in the 1830s and 1840s, and the growth of cities made possible the rise of one- and two-cent daily newspapers, but few advertisers before the Civil War responded to this opportunity to reach large audiences with attractive and persuasive messages.

The announcements of tradesmen and the blandishments of promoters which, therefore, constituted the bulk of advertising before the late nineteenth century were far different from most modern advertisements. Shopkeepers and artisans notified readers of the arrival of goods or the availability of new items. Advertising was almost entirely local; manufacturers who sold in wider markets rarely produced branded goods for sale to consumers. Advertising was closer to the classified notices in newspapers than to the product promotion in our media today.

The *Harper's Weekly* article of 1897 neatly summarized the difference between the announcements of advertisers only a few years earlier and the bold new displays beginning to make their mark. "Once we skipped [advertisements] unless some want compelled us to read, while now we read to find out what we really want." The larger shift which precipitated the remarkable transition in American advertising in the late nineteenth and early twentieth centuries was the development of national markets for the branded, standardized products of large-scale manufacturers. Striking innovations in technology and corporate organization resulted in mass production; selling quantities of goods so produced to millions of consumers often required intensive advertising.

The circumstances that led businesses to advertise branded products in the mass media required, in turn, the creation of an advertising industry that specialized in preparing, placing, and distributing advertising messages. At the time of the Civil War, the industry was virtually nonexistent; agencies in the modern sense were unknown. Trade associations and other bonds of occupational solidarity were lacking. Advertising men had done nothing to explain or justify their work to the public or to most businessmen. With few exceptions, advertisements themselves were crude announcements of goods on hand—perhaps seasoned with a few offhand superlatives. Nobody made a living writing advertisements.

By World War I, advertising expenditures had passed a billion dollars annually. The largest American advertisers, including such companies as Proctor & Gamble, Goodyear Tire, and Quaker Oats, each spent over a million dollars on magazine advertising alone in 1920. Advertising agencies performed functions not too different from the ones they handle today. Practitioners had created a network of institutions to handle common problems and had begun to propagate a vision of advertising as a force that would energize, stabilize, and moralize American business. Advertisements themselves, no longer the afterthoughts of local merchants, were now elements in campaigns based on marketing strategies. Quaint as many of the ads may seem now, advertising had come close to justifying the industry's claim that it was truly an applied science of persuasion. By 1920, American advertising had more in common with its counterpart today than with the advertising of a generation earlier.

This book describes the making of modern national advertising. In the next two chapters, the preconditions for the growth of national advertising in the late nineteenth and early twentieth centuries are analyzed, and the consequences of that growth for American business are discussed. The development of advertising agencies and related organizations as responses to the demands of the ascendant national advertisers are considered in chapter 4. I treat, in chapter 5, the emergence of ethical standards and the beginning of an ideology of advertising. Here, again, the large national advertisers, and the agencies and media that served them, set the tone. Chapter 6, on the advertisements themselves, shows how advertising appeals and styles changed to fulfill marketing roles and how the theories of consumer behavior and human nature held by advertising practitioners reflected business conditions. Finally, in chapter 7, advertising around 1920 is compared with its counterpart today. Now, as before, the principles and practices of American advertising are molded to fit the marketing needs of national advertisers. Institutionally and ideologically, modern advertising had taken shape by 1920. Yet the growth of electronic media and new patterns of consumer behavior have themselves altered marketing strategies and advertising campaigns.

This book tells the story of advertising as an aspect of business history. This approach differs from most other works on the subject. Some scholars have seen advertisements as works of art, others as expressions of national character. A few have treated advertising as a systematic manifestation of our underlying mental structures for apprehending the world. It is not my intention to quarrel with such approaches. All of them have provided insights. The fundamental assumption here, however, is that advertising responds to business needs and opportunities. As one ebullient advertising man insisted half a century ago, "There is just one justification for advertising: Sales! Sales! Sales!"[5] This, of course, oversimplifies motives, but in almost all cases the advertiser and the agency must keep their eyes on the cash register and the profit-and-loss statement. We may or may not get the kind of advertising we deserve; we most certainly get the kind of advertising corporations require. Businesses do not spend more than fifty billion dollars a year to create works of art or to undertake psychological experiments or to bring the deep structures of our psyches to the surface. My approach may risk the accusation of economic determinism. To this charge I plead no contest. Certainly

7

advertising men and women have responded to other forces. External pressure for reform, legal regulation, their own social backgrounds, and their ethical and esthetic beliefs all left marks on the work they did. I have tried to show how these factors came into play. Nevertheless, it seems most important to explain the evolution of modern advertising in terms of the business needs it fulfilled.

This book also differs from most previous work on the history of American advertising because it emphasizes changes occurring before the 1920s. Other studies tend to concentrate on more recent years. My contention, however, is that the rise of national producer advertising brought with it transformations—largely complete by 1920—in the structure of the advertising business, the values it espoused, and the work it did. Although change since then has often been striking, the institutional context has remained surprisingly stable. Moreover, many of the themes that scholars have noted in advertising in the 1920s—a quest for professional respect, ambivalence toward government regulation, an expansive faith in advertising's power, and a desire to use it for social control—can also be discerned in the Progressive Era earlier in the century.

The dynamic element in the emergence of modern advertising was the growth of national advertising by manufacturers. In the first place, it was national advertising that necessitated the growth of advertising agencies and dictated their activities. Retail advertising usually was, and often still is, handled in house by the retailer's own staff. Advertising men at the turn of the century called this local advertising "store news." National advertising was something more than news. It tipped the balance in advertising from information (however specious much of it had been) to persuasion (however benign and useful much of it may be). It was also national advertising that underwrote the growth of national media, in particular, the mass-circulation magazines and, later, radio and television.

Finally, it is national manufacturer's advertising that stands before the bar when we assess the economic, social, and esthetic complaints against advertising. The critic who calls advertising wasteful is concerned about the campaigns of rival oligopolists who produce similar products. The observer who judges advertising to be perniciously manipulative is complaining about national advertising campaigns, not the flyers of local grocers.

In advertising's garden, humble species like the classified newspaper notice grow alongside more wondrous blooms like thirty-second televised mini-dramas for beer or designer jeans or long-distance telephone calls.[6] Local advertising has, since the late 1960s, commanded a growing share of total expenditures. Between 1945 and 1965, national advertising accounted for about three-fifths of all outlays; in 1980, the figure had declined to about 55 percent.[7] However, retail advertising cannot receive detailed attention here; storekeepers' selling problems have been vastly different from those facing manufacturers. American advertising abroad also merits more attention than it receives in this book, but, with few exceptions, it did not begin in earnest until after World War I. Nonprofit organizations with nothing to sell, government agencies, candidates for office, and corporations expounding their points of view all advertise too. Such publicity deserves discussion but center stage must belong to the promotion of products for sale.

Although we have no satisfactory comprehensive history of advertising, the available sources are plentiful.[8] Richard W. Pollay's useful guide to *Information Sources in Advertising History* lists over sixteen hundred printed items, and there are countless other ephemeral publications. Most of these works come from within the advertising industry, and many of them reflect the perpetual uncertainty about advertising's true effects. An old chestnut, attributed both to the British soap manufacturer Lord Leverhulme and to the American department store magnate John Wanamaker, sums up the anxiety: "Half of the money I spend on advertising is wasted, and the trouble is I don't know which half."[9]

Because there is so much money at stake and because there are no simple formulas for success, prescriptive and evaluative studies abound. As we shall see, rudimentary market research and advertising testing followed closely upon the heels of modern advertising itself. In the past sixty years or so, researchers have amassed an imposing arsenal of hypotheses and techniques. For the most part, however, their work focuses on a small number of ads or campaigns. The emphasis is on measuring individual perceptions, attitudes, and behavior. Most importantly, the purpose of advertising research is almost always to create more effective advertising, not to discern the implication of mass promotion in a consumer society. Methodologically ahistorical and motivated by thoroughly practical interests, these sources are the raw material for the historian's work, not substitutes for it.

Not so abundant, but better known to the public, is another genre of advertising literature: commentaries on the social implications of advertising. The authors of these works tend to cull from contemporary advertisements portfolios of ads that support their general themes. In the hands of such talented critics as Marshall McLuhan or Erving Goffman, the cultural implications of advertisements unfold with often striking results.[10] However, some read into advertisements more than meets the unaided eye. Although their extrapolations can be provocative, the cultural critics sometimes press too hard on the rather flimsy and evanescent material they are scrutinizing. Too often, they divorce advertisements from the business conditions and marketing strategies behind them.

Few advertising men of the late nineteenth and early twentieth centuries had much interest in reflecting upon the cultural consequences of mass commercial persuasion. They were too busy going about their daily tasks of selling products. But when they did stop to consider the social impact of their activity, a few hinted at the theory that Daniel Boorstin has recently articulated so subtly and provocatively. For Boorstin, mass consumption is the great democratizing force in modern America; democracy is "a set of institutions which aim to make everything available to everybody."[11] Advertising, then, has become the herald of that democracy. Abundance allows us to choose what kind of person we want to be; advertising displays the alternatives before us and imbues them with meanings. Advertising proclaims our liberation from the dictates of scarcity and invites us to enter into "consumption communities." These collectivities are based on choice, not on the vagaries of geography or the bonds of craft or workplace. Unlike the early advertising men who eagerly and uncritically identified advertising with democracy, Boorstin recognizes the pathos behind the process. In the quest for more of everything, previous choices lose their charms; the meanings we once imputed to them become blurred. Today's promises expunge yesterday's claims, but they too will give way to tomorrow's enticements. The particularities of time, place, and culture are often lost. Differentiated images replace diverse realities. In order to promote a desire for the new, advertising subverts our attachment to the old.

Progressive Era advertising men had neither the time nor the taste for such paradoxes. They counterposed their persuasive missions to the compulsion that authoritarian rulers exercised and contrasted their openness to the deviousness of corrupt back-room power brokers. However, they also claimed that their skills could unify American society. This theme became more insistent during World War I. Advertising could—democratically—replace feckless exhortation with scientific persuasion. According to one editorialist, "In the dim and distant days before the war, reformers were wont to say, 'Oh, if the people would only do so and so!' Under the rigorous prod of Mars, they have learned to say, 'The people *must* do this and that—go out and advertise and make them come through.'"[12]

In the Progressive Era, advertising leaders implicitly recognized that the promises of democratic mass consumption could not yet be fulfilled. The mines, mills, and factories producing the nation's output demanded new forms of hierarchy and subordination. Migrants from European cities and from farms and villages on both sides of the Atlantic ultimately accepted, and adapted to, their proletarian condition here, hoping that they or their children would eventually do better. But, as labor historians have shown us, workers resisted the new disciplines of managers and machines. They struggled to carve out territories that they could themselves control. Thus, the freedom that mass consumption might bring depended upon authority and discipline in the workplace. Advertising might foster social harmony, but mass production created conditions of conflict and endemic resistance.

Moreover, although advertising men envisioned a society of mass consumption of brand-named merchandise, they knew in their day-to-day work that they faced a mosaic of markets, not a unified bloc of consumers. The distribution of income had crept toward greater inequality since the Civil War. Standards of living had, of course, risen for those at the bottom of the distribution, too, but the nation was not yet wealthy enough for all to partake unstintingly at the feast that advertisements portrayed. Advertising campaigns rarely directed overt appeals to particular social classes or ethno-cultural groups, but admen were aware of social distinctions. Seeking to mute conflict, advertising leaders in the Progressive Era could not ignore diversity. Not until more recently, however, did the industry embrace heterogeneity and recognize that market segmentation—targeting consumer sub-groups—could be profitable.

In the final analysis, advertising negated its own democratizing pretensions. The growth of the advertising industry implicitly challenged the models of human thought and behavior underlying nineteenth-century democratic individualism. First, persuasive advertising threatened older notions of free will. Even the most sanguine advertising expert knew that his persuasive powers were finite, but he and his colleagues also assumed that consumer choices were the results of external influences, not the unconstrained manifestations of an autonomous will. In the words of Chicago's leading advertising agency, Lord & Thomas, advertising was "literature which compels Action . . . [and] changes the mind of millions at will."[13]

Second, individual rationality, which nineteenth-century democrats used to justify both personal liberty and popular sovereignty, lost some of its meaning in the era of mass advertising's rise. As consumers, men and women were supposed to apply a rationality of means, not ends. They were to use their expenditures to satisfy their desires as well as possible. As to the reasonableness of those desires, advertising remained agnostic. Advertising intended to create more wants, not necessarily better ones. Thus, early advertising men expounded a radically subjective theory of value: "The value of a thing is what you get for it," wrote the man who managed the advertising of Shredded Wheat. "This . . . will kick to death all pretty theories about Value."[14] Still bolder was the nineteenth-century nostrum manufacturer who happily boasted, "I can advertise *dish water* and sell it, just as well as an article of merit. It is all in the advertising."[15]

Even in the domain of choice, rationality was circumscribed. Consumers were not infinitely malleable, but national advertisers and their agencies increasingly favored nonrational, even irrational buying appeals. Writings by advertising experts depicted consumers who were reactive, suggestible, and impulsive. By the 1920s, psychologists were bringing the new gospel of behaviorism to the study of advertising.[16] The challenge to reason was not merely the corollary of changing fashions in psychological theory; it resulted quite naturally from efforts to differentiate fundamentally equivalent products in oligopolistic markets and to cultivate brand loyalty through intensive publicity.

Finally, massive national advertising of branded products, as it widened the boundaries of "consumption communities" and promised ordinary Americans the chance to define their own life-styles, vitiated its own offer of inclusion. The earliest advice on writing advertisements had suggested a fundamental equality between advertiser and reader. Advertising was to be like a personal letter or a conversation between friends. By the Progressive Era, suggestions about advertising rhetoric had changed in recognition of the fundamental asymmetry in the relationship between big business and its customers. Advertising theorists had come to understand that their messages were spread broadcast from a relatively small number of producers to many thousands or even millions of consumers. Their purpose was to incite action and get results. Advertising could hardly pretend to be a part of a dialogue between equals.

To be sure, there is a utopian aspect to these criticisms of advertising. National advertising in the late nineteenth century and the early decades of the twentieth was not designed to eradicate free will, reason, and egalitarian social relations, nor in any case could it have accomplished these nefarious deeds. Crude notions of the consumer as marionette were no more realistic than the earlier ideal of the fully autonomous individual. Moreover, the intellectual challenge to liberal democratic ideology antedated the rise of national advertising in the United States. The corrosive impact of Marx, Darwin, and Freud had little or nothing to do with the mundane pursuits of advertising men. Finally, despite their occasional flights of fancy, advertising experts had neither the tools nor the sophistication to "change the mind of millions at will." In the preelectronic era, lacking such modern techniques as public opinion polling and projective testing, admen were in no position to be omnipotent persuaders. Even their better-armed descendants today are well aware that their powers are limited. Nevertheless, new, potentially antidemocratic, doctrines were implicit in the advertising industry's pretensions of guiding individual choice for corporate profit.

Although these historical reflections on the social implications of the growth of national advertising suggest harsh judgments on the persuasion industry, studying those who peopled the advertising business early in this century may be somewhat reassuring. Advertising men (and the few women whom custom permitted to make a mark in the field) were far more often guilty of philistinism than of totalitarianism. In common with many other small businessmen (and, it would appear, with a newer middle class of salaried managers and professionals), advertising men espoused the verities and commonplaces of American democratic capitalism. They favored competition (modified and mitigated by oligopoly and by advertising itself), individualism (circumscribed by the "infinite power of advertising"), and freedom (from overtly authoritarian compulsion). Almost always, advertising practitioners were trying to sell their clients' products, not to peddle ideology. They seldom had cause to consider the implications of massive advertising of consumer products; when their thoughts did turn to such matters, they found little reason to doubt that the effects were felicitous.

Thus, my strictures are not advanced in order to rake the muck of the advertising business in its formative decades. There is no real need for a retrospective exposé of fraud and deception or a blast against not-so-hidden persuaders long since departed. The evils of our own time, after all, are sufficient for us to combat. That early advertising men were often shallow and narrow, and that they balked at contemplating the consequences of their labors, is understandable. There was little in their daily work or in the objections of outsiders that would have fostered introspection and promoted a broader vision.

Even those who attacked advertising most vocally in the Progressive Era failed to offer a thoroughgoing critique. Most of them concentrated on dishonesty, and on this issue advertising leaders could convincingly point to their own zeal for truthful publicity. They were making real progress in ridding the most prominent campaigns of factual misstatements. Other objections to advertising smacked of a sour asceticism which had little appeal in a nation not yet rich enough to doubt the desirability of wealth.

Yet those who analyze and criticize advertising today would do well to look at its formative decades. No doubt it would be good to have advertising be less intrusive, tasteless, and manipulative than much of it is now. No doubt, too, there is potential for improvement and reform. However, there are reasons why we have the kind of national advertising we do today, and they have their roots in the evolution of business needs and advertising responses in the last century. The task of this book is to trace that evolution and explore its implications.

When the historian of the Twentieth Century shall have finished his narrative, and comes searching for the sub-title which shall best express the spirit of the period, we think it not at all unlikely that he may select "The Age of Advertising" for the purpose.

Every advertising man knows how the functions of advertising have expanded during the last twenty years ... That expansion, we are convinced, has only begun—we have taken only the first steps in learning to use and control the power we are working with. The man who would set any limits to the influence of advertising would be presumptuous indeed.

Printer's Ink,
27 May 1915

2

Industry's Demand for Advertising

FIRMLY enshrined in the mainstream of American historiography, and of common belief as well, is the idea that the United States, sometime around 1900, passed from an era of competition to one of big business. Decried and resisted by small businessmen and their allies, considered by most Marxists as a stage in the maturation and eventual crisis of capitalism, and viewed by Weberian sociologists as one aspect of our entrapment in the iron cage of modernity, the decline of competition has been treated as a well-established fact of American history. Few would fully agree with John Kenneth Galbraith's contentions that big business has managed to supersede the market entirely or that corporations have created, willy-nilly, a privately planned economy, but most would probably admit that economic models based on the competition of small-scale entrepreneurs fail to capture the essence of the American economy in the twentieth century.

From the work of some economists and economic historians, however, a rather different picture emerges. These scholars find "big business" and industrial concentration compatible with effective competition. They maintain that achieving monopoly power is difficult and maintaining it is even more arduous. If they have thrown away the diagrams of introductory economics textbooks, they have nevertheless carefully preserved a basic principle: the invisible hand will work when firms and individuals are free to seek their own advantage by buying and selling in an unregulated market. If market power is to be exerted successfully, these scholars contend, government regulation must almost invariably be the cause. For these economists, governmental intervention is the most effective (and harmful) way to regulate entry into an industry, raise transaction costs, increase uncertainty, inhibit the proper specification of property rights, or block the flow of information.[1]

Contemporary capitalism, then, is said to offer a reasonable approximation of the results, if not the structure, of a competitive market—at least when government does not intervene. Meanwhile, several lines of historical investigation have clouded the image of nineteenth-century American capitalism as pristinely competitive. First, the role of government in the nineteenth-century economy has been subjected to continual reassessment. One result has been to limit sharply, if not eradicate, the years in which government is believed to have pursued a genuinely laissez-faire policy. We know, for example, that states and localities in the pre–Civil War years frequently acted as developers, so that 73 percent of expenditures on canal construction came from public funds between 1815 and 1860, as did about 30 percent of investments in railroads.[2] Second, some studies have noted how barriers of transportation, communications, and law hindered the flow of goods and information in the nineteenth century. Attempts to reconstruct estimates of manufacturing profits indicate that rates of return were quite high, a finding consistent not with vigorous atomistic competition but with local monopoly and protected markets.[3] If America in its first century of independence was indeed a nation of "island communities" (to use historian Robert Wiebe's phrase), this insularity would be expected to present formidable obstacles to the operation of a competitive national market.[4]

This reassessment of the structure, conduct, and performance of the nineteenth-century economy has been more fragmentary and less purposeful than the reappraisal of the modern economy. There is, however, a significant convergence between the two endeavors, and the result may be a reshaping of common ideas about American economic history. However, it should be noted that the differences between the two points of view outlined here are grounded in theory and ideology as well as in fact. Data alone are unlikely to indicate which view is more fruitful.

In each of these approaches, advertising plays an important, if often unacknowledged, role. Although it may be omitted from their narratives, historians recounting the decline of competition and the growth of big business implicitly or explicitly consider advertising both as a weapon that was wielded against competitor and consumer alike and as a sign of the waning potency of competitive forces. On the other hand, if market forces prevailed, then advertising may have been a more benign influence, invading the bastions of local monopoly with news of new and better products, filling

the information gaps that resulted from social and technological change, and offering a way for creative entrepreneurs
to combat the market power of entrenched interests. Here,
too, major theoretical and ideological differences separate
the two positions. One simple way to state the issue is to ask
if advertising was fundamentally persuasive or informative? If
it was (and is) essentially persuasive, designed to alter tastes
and preferences, then it is easy to see the power to persuade
as complementing other forms of corporate power developing in industrial America. If it is information (albeit occasionally misinformation), we can maintain that it helped consumers seeking to maximize their welfare by offering more and
better choices for their money.

Before we can begin to judge the respective merits of the
positions which see advertising as monopolistic and competitive, we must discover what data are available on advertising
in the late nineteenth and early twentieth centuries. Although the results presented here are somewhat discourag-
ing, the situation is not hopeless. Admittedly, for almost all
the questions which economists ask about advertising today,
statistical information from the pre–World War I era is simply not available. Yet the scattered figures we have are better than nothing at all, and some progress may be made by
studying them.

Even today, data on advertising are often incomplete or
inaccessible. Not all media measure and report the volume
of advertising they carry; not all firms readily publicize their
advertising budget figures; not all other variables with which
advertising may be associated (such as profits) are measured
in ways well suited for analysis. Statistics of advertising volume compiled by the advertising trade press go back only to
1935; we have estimates ranging back to the Civil War, but
their usefulness is questionable. Apparently, L. D. H. Weld,
an economist with the McCann-Erickson Advertising Agen-

cy, constructed an annual index of general advertising activity and applied it to the 1935 figure (which had been constructed from actual expenditure reports) to estimate expenditures for earlier years.[5]

Regarded highly enough to be included in the Census Bureau's *Historical Statistics of the United States* volumes, the pre-1935 advertising expenditure estimates nevertheless do not inspire great confidence. Since they have been widely accepted, however, we may begin our discussion with them, accompanied by relevant gross national product (GNP) figures (see table 2.1).

Several curiosities may be noted. First, Weld's estimates are identical for 1914 and 1915 and for 1916 and 1918. One is tempted to say that this is literally too good to be true. Second, the trend of the ratio of advertising to GNP is, if anything, slightly downward. The notion that advertising today plays a less quantitatively important role in the American economy than it did in our grandparents' and great-grandparents' generations seems counterintuitive. One reason for the declining trend in recent decades, however, is the rising proportion of government expenditures in GNP. Since most of the goods and services produced in the public sector are not sold in the market, they are rarely advertised. Similarly, since advertising to ultimate consumers is our concern here, it might be more appropriate to compare advertising to disposable personal income rather than more inclusive measures of output or income.

With thousands of national advertisers and hundreds of thousands of potential local advertisers, and with approximately twice as many newspapers as there are today, the turn-of-the-century advertising space market consisted of literally millions of small transactions along with a much smaller number of large sales. Most transactions took place without an advertising agent, and in many cases, the price paid

Industry's Demand for Advertising

TABLE 2.1
*Advertising Volume and
Gross National Product, 1880–1970
(L. D. H. Weld Advertising Estimates)*

Year	(1) Advertising	(2) GNP	(3) Advertising as Percentage of GNP
1880	200	N.A.	N.A.
1890	360	13.1	2.7
1900	542	18.7	2.9
1904	821	22.9	3.6
1909	1,142	32.2	3.5
1914	1,302	36.4	3.6
1915	1,302	38.7	3.4
1916	1,468	49.8	2.9
1917	1,627	59.9	2.7
1918	1,468	76.2	1.9
1919	2,282	78.9	2.9
1920	2,935	88.9	3.3
1929	3,426	104.4	3.3
1935	1,690	72.2	2.3
1945	2,875	211.9	1.4
1955	9,194	398.0	2.3
1965	15,255	684.9	2.2
1970	19,600	974.1	2.0

SOURCES: Column 1: U.S. Bureau of the Census, *Historical Statistics of the United States Colonial Times to 1970*, (Washington, D.C.: Government Printing Office, 1975), pp. 855–856. Figures in millions of current dollars. Column 2: U.S. Department of Commerce, Bureau of Economic Analysis, *Long-Term Economic Growth 1860–1970* (Washington, D.C., 1973), pp. 182–183. For 1880–1929, figures are from Series A7; from 1935–70, figures are from Series A8. Figures in billions of current dollars. Column 3: Column 2 divided by Column 1.

was far from the one stated on the publication's rate card. Indeed, barter arrangements were very common. The famous copywriter Claude Hopkins recalled that his father, who owned a small-town newspaper, received goods for most of the advertisements he printed. "Our home became a warehouse of advertised merchandise. I remember that at one time we had six pianos and six sewing-machines in stock."[6] In short, any effort to measure advertising outlays before the

1930s directly is fruitless, and indirect measurement is likely to yield unreliable results.

The Weld figures make no attempt to distinguish between the sum spent on retail advertising and that devoted to national (also called "general" or "foreign") advertising by manufacturers. One 1893 volume did profess to catalogue the advertising efforts of about four thousand general advertisers (defined as those who "advertise outside of [their] own city, village or hamlet; who seek to reach the general public away from [their] immediate home").[7] The book contains information of uncertain quality and detail, but figures seem to jibe with other estimates of advertising spending in the 1890s. Based on a sampling procedure, we estimate the mean advertising outlay per firm at slightly over $9,300 in 1893, which would suggest total expenditures for firms listed in the book at about $38 million. If *America's Advertisers* is reasonably inclusive and accurate, a comparison with the Weld estimates for 1890 indicates either of two possibilities: If Weld's figures are correct, then general advertising as measured by this sampling technique represents only about 11 percent of the total advertising expenditure of 1890. The other possibility is that Weld's estimates are simply too high. In every year for which we have direct measurements of advertising costs (that is to say, since 1935), expenditures for national advertising have been greater than for local advertising. Although national advertising played a smaller role in the 1890s, it is unlikely that it constituted as small a proportion as comparison of *America's Advertisers* and the Weld figures would indicate.

A second indirect method of estimating advertising volume also suggests that the Weld figures are overstated. This makes use of the Census of Manufactures which, since 1880, has required newspapers and periodicals to apportion their revenues between sales and subscriptions, on the one hand,

and advertising on the other. The figures are not strictly comparable to the Weld series, in that they do not include production costs or advertising agency commissions and fees. For the post-1935 years, they are approximately three-quarters the size of the Weld estimates for newspapers and magazines. In these more recent years, the Weld series for newspapers and magazines shows that these media received approximately half of advertising outlays on all media excluding radio and television. If we assume that the proportion of all advertising that went to newspapers and periodicals before 1920 was the same as the post-1935 proportion, we can then estimate total advertising outlays for the earlier years by adjusting the Census of Manufactures figures twice:

1. Multiply the census figure by 1.33 (to correct for the underestimate of newspaper and magazine advertising relative to the Weld data);

2. Multiply this product by two (on the assumption that newspaper and magazine advertising was about half of total advertising; see table 2.2.).

One notes immediately that this method of estimation provides much lower figures for total advertising expenditures. Obviously two major assumptions are at issue here. First, are the Census of Manufactures data reasonably accurate? For recent years, they probably are; they correspond closely to the figures compiled by Weld and to other industry sources. For the late nineteenth century and the first decades of the twentieth, the information is less reliable but still plausible. The trend of advertising revenue as a proportion of total publishers' receipts is upward, as we might expect. No strong statements of doubt or uncertainty accompany the statistics in the Census Bureau reports. In an era without corporate or personal income taxes, publishers would have little incentive to understate their incomes. Thus, while not above suspicion, the Census data for the advertising receipts

TABLE 2.2

*Revised Advertising Volume Compared with Earlier
Estimates and with GNP, Selected Years, 1880–1935*

Year	(1) Census of Manufacturing Publications Ad Receipts	(2) Revised Advertising Estimates	(3) Column 2 as Percentage of Weld Estimates	(4) Column 2 as Percentage of GNP
1880	39.1	104	52	N.A.
1890	71.2	190	53	1.5
1900	95.9	256	47	1.4
1904	145.5	388	47	1.7
1909	202.5	540	47	1.7
1914	255.6	682	52	1.9
1919	528.3	1,409	62	1.8
1929	1,120.2	2,987	87	2.9
1935	686.1	1,830	108	2.5

SOURCES: Column 1: 1880–1904, U.S. Bureau of Census, *Census of Manufactures,
1905*, III, p. 720; 1909, *Thirteenth Census, 1910*, X, *Manufactures*, p. 781; 1914–19,
Biennial Census of Manufactures, 1921, p. 623; 1929–35, *Census of Manufactures,
1947*, II, pp. 353, 356. Figures in millions of dollars. Column 2: Column 1 × 2⅔. See
text for explanation. Column 3: Column 2 divided by table 2.1, Column 1. Column
4: Column 2 divided by table 2.1, Column 2.

of newspapers and periodicals make some sense. The second
assumption of our method of calculation is that newspaper
and periodical advertising accounted for at least as large a
share of total advertising (excluding radio and television) in
the Gilded Age and Progressive Era as they have since 1935.
Here the situation is complicated. Some advertising methods—in particular, the distribution of handbills and outdoor
billposting—were probably more important near the turn of
the century than they are today. On the other hand, direct-
mail advertising and point-of-sale advertising displays were in
their infancy at the turn of the century. There is no way of
being certain, but we might conjecture that these trends cancel each other out and that newspapers' and magazines'
share of total advertising did not rise sharply in the years
after 1935.[8]

If we look for guidance to estimates offered by contemporaries, we learn little. It is not surprising that most seem little better than stabs in the dark. Charles Austin Bates, a well-known advertising man around the turn of the century, put the sum spent on advertising at $300 million in 1896. For 1902, a *Printers' Ink* editorial estimated only about $100 million. Two years later, a newspaper article asserted that half a billion dollars were spent for advertising, but *Printers' Ink* continued to maintain that outlays were really far below that. Only six months later, however, the same publication raised its estimate to one billion dollars, and its claim went undisputed. By the second decade of this century, statistics seem better grounded. By totaling up approximate figures for the various media, figures of $616 million for 1911 and $651 million for 1916 were reached.[9] An almost contemporaneous estimate of advertising volume can be found in J. George Frederick's 1925 book, *Masters of Advertising Copy*.[10] Frederick had been an advertising trade journal editor and wrote extensively on advertising topics. His estimates are shown in table 2.3 and correspond roughly with our revised estimates in table 2.2.

With this morass of conjectures, we may find ourselves sympathizing with one writer in 1918 who contended that calculating advertising expenditures was futile, though a

TABLE 2.3
Estimates of Advertising Volume
from Masters of Advertising Copy

Year	Amount (in millions of dollars)
1880	30
1890	80
1900	200
1910	600
1920	850
1925	1,200

SOURCE: J. George Frederick, *Masters of Advertising Copy* (New York: Frank-Maurice, 1925), p. 32.

"fine exercise for gasolineless Sundays" during the War.[11] Nevertheless, the preponderance of the evidence does indicate that the frequently cited Weld series overstates advertising volume during the Gilded Age or Progressive Era.

By itself, a series showing a lower total amount of advertising before the 1920s tells us very little. Beyond the problems of accuracy, the figures beg some important questions. For example, Neil Borden, in his seminal book, *The Economic Effects of Advertising,* stressed that advertising costs were only about 7 percent of total distribution costs in 1935. If distribution did cost too much, as many complained, Borden contended that advertising could hardly be the main culprit. Borden also pointed out that more money in 1935 was spent for personal selling than for advertising.[12] Advertising men as early as the 1870s had portrayed advertising as a modern, more efficient alternative to salesmen. For the economists dealing with issues of aggregate demand or discussing market power, the distinction between advertising and other selling costs is secondary. They want to know what determined the size of promotional expenditures and their relationship to market power. Was advertising, as its boosters put it in the pre-radio years, the "silent salesman," substituting for personal contact? Or did it complement other marketing activities? The data do not allow us to answer the question definitively. A recent survey of the literature on the economics of advertising concludes that advertising may, in fact, substitute for direct selling, but that this probably occurs most frequently in the firms where advertising accompanies a strategic change in distribution channels. For the early twentieth century, unfortunately, information on other sales costs is even more fragmentary than data on advertising outlays. However, if we crudely measure distribution costs as the sum of wholesaler and retailer value added in those industries that sell at least some of their products through retail outlets, it appears that the ratio of advertising to these costs grew during our period[13] (see table 2.4).

TABLE 2.4
*Advertising Volume and Distribution Costs,
Selected Years, 1880–1929*

Year	(1) Ad Volume Historical Statistics Estimate	(2) Ad Volume Revised Estimate	(3) Distribution Costs	(4) Column 1 as Percentage of Distribution Costs	(5) Column 2 as Percentage of Distribution Costs
1880	200	104	1.7	12	6
1890	60	190	2.6	14	7
1900	542	256	3.5	15	7
1909	1,142	540	6.5	18	8
1919	2,282	1,409	16.8	14	8
1929	3,426	2,987	21.2	16	14

SOURCES: Column 1: See table 2.1, column 1. Figures in millions of current dollars. Column 2: See table 2.2, column 2. Figures in millions of current dollars. Column 3: Harold Barger, *Distribution's Place in the American Economy* (Princeton, N.J.: Princeton University Press, 1955), p. 70. Figure equals the sum of retailer and wholesaler value added for industries which sell at least part of their output through retail outlets. Figures in billions of current dollars. Column 4: Column 1 divided by column 3. Column 5: Column 2 divided by column 3.

Perhaps the earliest effort to judge the role of advertising in marketing was a study made for the Association of National Advertisers in 1931. The study of distribution expenses for 312 manufacturers indicated no significant correlation ($r = .02$) between advertising and direct selling expenditures in nineteen consumer goods industries. (If office equipment and supplies are omitted from the list of consumer goods industries, the correlation rises to .16.)[14] The study thus indicates that, at this level of aggregation, advertising did not replace manufacturers' outlays on personal selling. Certainly, for many firms, advertising did eliminate traveling salesmen and other personal sales workers, but for others, advertising became part of a broader marketing system that continued to rely on other methods of reaching potential customers.

Murky though the quantitative picture of advertising may be for the Gilded Age and Progressive Era, we may safely state several conclusions. First, advertising increased at a rapid pace. By World War I, many more firms advertised than had done so a generation earlier. The largest among them spent sums that were unheard of in previous decades. New media for advertising—streetcar cards, direct mail, and, most significantly, mass-circulation national magazines—and increasing receptiveness to advertisements in older media gave Americans a sense of the ubiquity of commercial persuasion. In 1880, for example, 44 percent of the receipts of American newspapers came from advertising. By 1890, the figure approached 50 percent, and by the 1919 *Census of Manufactures,* 66 percent, or almost two-thirds, of all newspaper revenues came from advertising. The figure for periodicals was about the same, 65 percent. Finally, and for our purposes perhaps most important, the lead in advertising had passed to manufacturers of nationally distributed, brand-named goods. There is no way to determine the balance of local and national advertising for the early years of national advertising, but virtually all observers agreed that national advertising was the dynamic force, reshaping the purposes and methods of advertising and calling forth an industry—some chose to call it a profession—to perform its persuasive tasks.

What, then, explains the growth of national advertising in the late nineteenth and early twentieth centuries? And what consequences did this growth have for the American economy? These are the broad questions we shall address in the rest of this chapter. Although our answers cannot be framed with the precision that economists usually strive for, the investigation should offer insight into institutional and strategic changes of great magnitude in American business.

Advertising men, as we have said, enjoy tracing the origins of advertising back to biblical times, or even beyond, but whatever cravings for professional stature or the dignity of antique precedents this may fulfill, it is poor anthropology and poorer history. National advertising of manufactured, branded products was a nineteenth-century creation. So, too, was the retail advertising that bears comparison to that dominating newspapers today. Earnest Elmo Calkins and Ralph Holden were correct in 1905: "Advertising, as we understand it, is a development of the past half century . . ."[15]

Not surprisingly, when we seek the reasons for the growth of advertising and especially the virtual invention of national advertising, we must invoke the key economic and social trends of the era: industrialization, urbanization, and the revolutions in transportation and communications. Beyond that, however, we must examine the activities of businesses that undertook advertising campaigns in the late nineteenth and early twentieth centuries. Advertising depended upon the socioeconomic preconditions, but it also was a policy chosen by business executives in the context of particular manufacturing and marketing conditions.

It is said that when Abraham Lincoln tended store at Old Salem, Illinois, in 1833, Walter Baker's Chocolate was on the shelves, the only packaged and branded product in the store. Shopkeepers in more settled areas might carry a few more items, but only a sprinkling of canned specialty goods, an occasional import, and some patent medicine concoctions carried a manufacturer's brand. Manufacturing in pre–Civil War America did not, for the most part, produce goods suitable for national advertising, nor, of course, was there a network to distribute those goods throughout the nation. The most important industries in mid-nineteenth century America—flour and grain milling, lumber and saw milling, even the relatively advanced textile and footwear industries—were, for the most part, processing the nation's abundant raw materials and agricultural products into materials which consumers themselves would then fashion into items of utility—bread from flour, buildings from boards, clothing from textiles. In this stage of economic development, there was little room for manufacturers to advertise their goods widely. It would be hard to conceive of developing a consumer allegiance to the flour of a local grist mill or the lumber of a particular saw mill.

The era of industrialization from the mid-nineteenth century through the 1890s was marked by qualitative change as well as staggering quantitative increase. Coal replaced wood and water as the major source of industrial energy. Abundant anthracite from the mines of Pennsylvania also paved the way for the growth of the iron and steel industry whose output in turn built the machines and the rails for the industrial and transportation revolutions to follow. New machinery—reapers, sewing machines, industrial machine tools— engendered new products and enabled older products to be made by radically new processes. The scale of operations greatly increased in manufacturing; the largest factory of the pre–Civil War era, the Merrimack Textile Mill, employed perhaps two thousand workers in 1854, but in 1900, Daniel Nelson lists seventy plants with at least that many workers.[16] Equally significant was the more rapid pace of newer industries. Materials flowed through these factories at unprecedented rates. The economies of speed, as Alfred Chandler calls them, portended the monumental changes in industrial organization in the late nineteenth century and in the earliest decades of this one.[17]

From the Civil War to World War I, the growth of manufacturing was marked by increasingly capital-intensive means of production. The value of capital per production worker in manufacturing increased steadily from $1,764 in 1879 to $5,565 in 1914 (in constant 1929 dollars). Capital-to-output ratios also increased. The book value of manufacturing capital was 1.38 times as high as value added in 1879, but 2.21 times as high in 1914.[18]

In consumer goods industries, the growing prevalence of mass production under conditions of capital-intensivity and high fixed costs impelled manufacturers to seek ways to ensure the sale of their output on satisfactory terms. These more "roundabout" production methods meant that industrialists had to invest resources in machinery and in finished products before customers had ordered their goods. Machinery that lay idle in the face of seasonal or unpredictable fluctuations in demand would cost these producers dearly. Advertising could be a strategy to match demand to the conditions of capitalist production required by the new technologies.

Did high (or rapidly increasing) ratios of fixed to variable costs occur in industries that advertised most intensively? Since there is no valid way to ascertain the ratios of advertising to sales for industries during the Gilded Age or Progressive Era, there is no definitive answer. There were heavy advertisers in industries such as soap and chocolate and cocoa, where fixed costs were relatively low, just as there were capital-intensive consumer products like sugar for which advertising was virtually nonexistent. Nevertheless, it seems likely that increasingly capital-intensive production impelled manufacturers in such industries as tobacco, brewing, and some processed foods to promote their products.

Advertising men in these early years did not speak the economists' language of fixed and variable costs, but they were aware that high-volume, capital-intensive production could mean heavy advertising. Harry Tipper, advertising manager of Texaco, noted that the introduction of mass production required that consumers "be taught to use more than they formerly had used, and to discriminate between different sellers or sections in order to control the market." When, as a 1915 textbook commented, "continued improvement in the machinery of production, transportation, communication, etc." increased the volume and variety of output, "the problem of disposing of these goods became, consequently, more important." Indeed, high-volume production with low-unit profits was "the order of the age," and advertising was to usher in this new order.[19]

If concentration and capital-intensive production provided motives for businessmen to advertise, the development of a communications and transportation network was a necessary condition for the development of national advertising. In some cases, it may have been possible to advertise to increase demand in a territory, thereby decreasing unit transportation costs through volume discounts or other economies of scale. In most instances, however, the growth of a railroad network, declining costs, and technological advances in transportation and storage preceded penetration of new markets and made entry possible. Before the completion of the nation's railroad network in the late nineteenth century, few products were advertised nationally. Among those that were promoted widely, intangibles and goods with an unusually high price per unit of weight or volume were most common. Thus, early advertisements often sold information by mail: books, recipes, medical and other self-help material had few transportation cost barriers to surmount. Patent medicines and other drugs also usually sold at markups that made transportation a minor part of the price. On the whole, life insurance companies relied on personal selling, but national advertising emerged early as a supplementary selling device. Finally, railroads and steamship lines themselves could advertise their services throughout the area they covered and beyond.

As America industrialized, it moved to the city. A nation

four-fifths rural in 1860 was more than 50 percent urban in 1920. Directly and indirectly, the growth of cities called forth more advertising. National advertisers could find receptive customers for their goods and suitable media for their appeals, as could the most innovative and aggressive retail advertisers, the great department stores of the era.

Urbanization may lead to increased national advertising by broadening the market. Growing population density may be associated with declining unit costs of physical distribution; at some point, a manufacturer will be able to enter a market he formerly viewed as unprofitable. He may then choose to promote his products through advertising. Second, cities have more diversified and specialized advertising media than smaller communities. Outdoor advertising and streetcar cards thrived in the growing cities. Media designed for special groups in the population, such as the foreign-language press, offered opportunities to advertisers who sought that particular market segment. The jargon of today's advertisers was unknown in the late nineteenth century, but the principle of aiming one's message at a distinct group was well understood. Third, cities allowed new specialized distribution institutions to emerge. These could provide the proper facilities for manufacturers of technically complex goods or other products requiring intensive service along with the sale. Companies that needed, for example, repair facilities or cold storage would be most likely to find their markets (and hence do their advertising) in cities.

Not only did urbanization alter the ways manufacturers could distribute goods and advertising messages, it also affected the nature of demand for both products and information about them. The yeoman farmer and his family, independent and self-sufficient, never were typical of America's rural residents. The search for cash crops, specialization and speculative gains seems to have begun shortly after settlers arrived at Jamestown and Plymouth Rock. Progressive Era lamentations about the decline of the American family as a productive unit tell us as much about cultural anxieties as economic realities. Nevertheless, urbanization and industrialization in the late nineteenth and early twentieth centuries meant that Americans would purchase more goods and services from strangers and make fewer of them at home. As the scope of commodity production expanded, advertising sometimes stepped in to fill the gap between production and consumption. For example, only about 10 percent of the bread eaten in the United States in 1850 had been baked commercially, and certain specialty items accounted for most of this share. The figure increased to 25 percent by 1900 and about 60 percent in 1930.[20] Ready-made clothing for men similarly replaced production in the home or by the local tailor. For women's clothing, branded and advertised paper dress patterns themselves became an industry by the 1870s.[21] Less direct forms of substitution of marketed commodities for home production also provided bases for advertising campaigns. Home appliances tended to substitute capital for household labor—at least in the manufacturers' campaigns. Thus, for example, washing machines were sometimes advertised as alternatives to older washtub methods and unsanitary washerwomen. Electric irons would reduce the labor of ironing clothes. Central heating would eliminate the arduous task of stoking wood stoves.

These new products, and new versions of older products, of course appealed to rural Americans as well as to city dwellers, but their main impact was in urban markets. In the cities, consumption patterns changed most markedly. Life insurance, for example, made more sense for a city worker whose family's income rested on his employment than for a farmer who owned salable land. Cigarettes gradually became the preferred addiction of the urban smoker; pipes, chewing tobacco, and cigars were ill-suited to the city's pace and crowds. An affinity existed between urban society and nationally advertised consumer products.

There is scattered support for the idea that urbanization itself led to increased advertising. One economist has found that per capita advertising outlays do tend to increase with the size of cities. The most populous receive the most advertising dollars per resident.[22] One rough measure of the connection between advertising and urbanization is the correlation between newspaper advertising revenue in a state and its level of urbanization; for 1900, the correlation coefficient between newspaper advertising per dollar of personal income and the urban proportion of a state's population was .40; for 1919, $r^2 = .167$.[23]

Despite these indications, for advertising men the pull of the urban market sometimes was outweighed by the attractions of advertising to rural dwellers. Products like patent medicines and the sort of media exemplified by religious magazines and the so-called mail order magazines, which wrapped pulp fiction around mail order advertising, were naturally deemed more suitable for rural than urban audiences. An "experienced advertiser" in 1870 recommended country weeklies over city dailies because the former were more closely read and more fully believed. "Country people consume the greater portion" of patent medicines, he hastened to add. E. C. Allen, publisher of a group of mail-order magazines which achieved a circulation of over a million in the 1880s and early 1890s, asserted that his magazines "go to the great mass of the middle and better class country population . . . who are more easily influenced by advertising than the like classes in the cities." For city dwellers, he noted, shop window displays might substitute for print advertising. Sears, Roebuck's mail-order selling also typified a form of advertising particularly suited to rural America. As Sears executive Louis Asher defined it in 1905, "We are a supply house. We deal in necessities. Our constant effort is to furnish these necessities at the lowest possible prices, so that the farmer at a distance can get his goods from us . . ."[24]

Despite these voices, by the turn of the century, advertising men were increasingly adopting an urban perspective. The transition can be noted in such matters as the increased attention paid to advertising to immigrants and industrial workers. While *Printers' Ink* continued to advise businessmen to "advertise among farmers; they are more evenly prosperous than city folks, perhaps," it also noted in 1903 that city newspapers' circulations in rural areas were on the rise. With the coming of interurban trollies, automobiles, and telephones, more and more farmers were in reach of urban marketing outlets. Farm-oriented publications struck an increasingly defensive pose in touting their value as advertising media. As one Iowa publisher complained in 1915, "Some of you advertisers act as if you didn't think the farmers wear coats or shoes. Why, do you know that fifty percent of all farmers wear garters?"[25]

As a shorthand expression for the economic changes in post-Civil War America, it is tempting to call advertising the child of American affluence. David Potter, who contended that advertising was the quintessential institution of American abundance, put it this way: "Advertising is not badly needed in an economy of scarcity . . . it is . . . when abundance prevails that advertising begins to fulfill a really essential function." Julian Simon, in his *Issues in the Economics of Advertising*, shows a strong positive correlation between the proportion of a nation's gross national product spent on advertising and that nation's national income per person.[26] Although we have recently come to realize that long-run per capita growth in national income has not been exceptionally high in the United States (in comparison to other advanced industrial nations), rising personal incomes and growing sums available for discretionary purchases have been an almost constant fact of American life. Thus, the argument goes, advertising seeks the dollars that Americans need no longer devote to necessities.

The logic here is attractive, but the catch-all of abundance raises as many questions as it answers. The evidence from international comparisons is inconclusive; one recent study, for example, indicates a remarkable variation in advertising levels in less developed nations today. Thus, for example, Peru, with a per capita national income of $468 had an advertising-to-GNP ratio of 0.83 percent; Greece, with national income at $2,019 per person, maintained a ratio of only 0.25 percent. Regressing per capita income on advertising as a percentage of national product revealed a fairly low r^2 of 0.31.[27] For the United States, we have suggested a marked but irregular rise in advertising's share of GNP from the Civil War through the 1920s. On the other hand, from World War II through the mid-1970s, despite unprecedented increases in consumer spending power, advertising remained a roughly constant proportion of national income. Such ambiguities in the quantitative data suggest that looking at as broad a category as affluence to explain the growth of advertising is insufficient. After all, needs themselves are both psychologically and socially defined; sharp distinctions among various human necessities cannot survive close scrutiny. Even in the poorest societies, some consumption serves purposes beyond simple survival. Indeed, the notion that advertising exists only to sell the products we don't "really" need fails to stand up to examination. Most Americans, for example, would define such items as toothpaste and soap as necessities of daily life; yet these are among the most actively advertised products, while others which might be considered luxuries (for example, high-fashion clothing) receive relatively little advertising. We must, then, go beyond affluence to explain the growth of American advertising in the decades before World War I.

Enumerating the social and economic preconditions for the rapid expansion of national advertising provides at best a partial explanation of its rise. Then as now, advertising was a *policy* of some (though certainly not all) businesses, not the unintended outcome of impersonal social forces. To go beyond taxonomic generalities, we must look at advertising as an element of business strategy. What kinds of companies decided to sell, make, and advertise brand-named consumer products? What industries were they in? What were the goals they hoped to accomplish?

Two problems with this perspective come to mind. First, it might be said that the notion of a business strategy is an anachronism, applicable to the professionally managed, multiproduct, multinational firm of the 1980s, but to only a few exceptional companies at the turn of the century. The objection has some weight, especially considering the evidence of rudimentary and haphazard advertising policies. Decisions about whether to advertise, how much to spend, and where and how to advertise tended to be personalized, ad hoc, and, in large measure, stabs in the dark. Agencies' injunctions to "Keep Everlastingly At It" or advice that advertising was "Salesmanship in Print" hardly amounted to a carefully wrought marketing plan.

The first objection suggests a second. If advertising decisions were so idiosyncratic, would not enumeration of individual firms' choices mean, in effect, abandoning generalization in favor of anecdotes? What explanatory power could a diverse set of narratives of firms' early advertising campaigns have in accounting for the overall growth of advertising in the age of big business?

The first objection is meritorious if it reminds us not to

read current business theories and terminology back into the activities of businessmen three and four generations ago. Still, especially by the second decade of this century, advertising decision making was far from casual. As we shall see, service-oriented advertising agencies that espoused ideals of skilled professionalism advised most major national advertisers on their campaigns. Advertising men formulated plans which considered advertising's relationship to other aspects of production and distribution. Advertising was more and more a part of marketing, and businessmen's understanding of marketing was progressing beyond the level of physical distribution and dealer relations. Like Molière's "bourgeois gentilhomme," advertising men of the era might have been surprised to find that they had been practicing marketing strategy all along.

The second query casts doubts on the appropriateness of concentrating on firms' advertising strategies to obtain useful generalizations. In fact, however, patterns do emerge. The kinds of companies that became important national advertisers, the kind of advertising they did, and the links between advertising and other corporate policies all can tell us something about the nature of American business in the Progressive Era.

To analyze the characteristics of large-scale national advertisers, it is first necessary to identify them—a more difficult task than one might think. For our purposes, we have chosen a group of fifty-eight firms; these companies spent over $100,000 for advertising in major national magazines in any one of the years 1913, 1914, and 1915, according to a tabulation by the Crowell Publishing Company.[28] The computations purport to include advertising in magazines with 90 percent of the total circulation of nationally distributed periodicals. The 1913–15 years are the earliest for which these figures are available. Although relying on this data alone omits some important national advertisers, such as patent medicine makers and distillers and brewers who were not allowed in most national magazines, the information in other respects seems superior to the guesswork about advertising budgets that can be culled from other sources for the era (see table 2.5).

A glance at table 2.5 will reveal many familiar names. The large national advertisers of the pre–World War I years were, for the most part, big businesses at that time; many remain in the front ranks of American industry. Twenty-one of the sample (or their corporate descendants) remain among the hundred leading national advertisers of 1979. Procter & Gamble, the leading magazine advertiser in 1913 and 1914, ranks first today in national advertising. It is only sixth among magazine advertisers, but the $40.6 million it placed in magazines in 1979 is, nevertheless, about sixty-three times its annual outlays from 1913 to 1915.[29] In other words, although the major advertisers have remained strikingly consistent, the quantity of their advertising has skyrocketed.

The largest advertisers were also the leading firms within their industries. There are exceptions, of course: Henry Ford would have sooner painted a Model T chartreuse than have undertaken a major national advertising campaign. Dodge, Maxwell-Chalmers, Studebaker, Hudson, Cadillac, Hupp, Reo, and Willys-Overland are the auto manufacturers on our list. Cudahy appears, but not its larger oligopolistic competitor, Swift. Nevertheless, companies on the list often dominated their markets—Eastman Kodak, Campbell Soup, Procter & Gamble, Nabisco—or ranked among the largest firms—Goodyear, U. S. Rubber, and B. F. Goodrich in tires and other rubber products; Kellogg, Cream of Wheat, and Quaker Oats in breakfast cereals. There is no way to discern whether these leading companies spent a larger proportion of their revenues on advertising than did their smaller competi-

TABLE 2.5
Largest Advertisers in National Magazines, 1913-15

Standard Industrial Classification (SIC) of Most Heavily Advertised Product	Rank by Size of Assets 1917	Rank by Amount of National Magazine Advertising		
		1913	1914	1915
SIC 20—Food and Kindred Products (14 firms)				
Armour & Co.	4	31	32	—
Borden's Condensed Milk Co.	103	—	41	45
California Fruit Growers' Exchange	—	—	—	28
Joseph Campbell Co.	442	15	11	9
Coca-Cola Co.	212	34	27	36
Cream of Wheat Co.	—	17	15	13
Kellogg Toasted Corn Flake Co.	—	11	12	17
National Biscuit Co.	76	22	29	—
Postum Cereal Co.	—	3	5	14
Quaker Oats Co.	134	2	2	1
Van Camp Packing Co.	—	40	18	24
Washburn-Crosby Co.	279	33	27	59
Welch's Grape Juice Co.	—	39	46	47
William Wrigley Jr. Co.	246	24	21	—
SIC 21—Tobacco Manufactures (4 firms)				
American Tobacco Co.	18	10	3	4
Liggett & Myers Tobacco Co.	44	45	30	6
P. Lorillard & Co.	81	8	42	26
R. J. Reynolds Tobacco Co.	146	12	14	11
SIC 23—Apparel and Related Products (4 firms)				
Bellas Hess & Co.	—	26	22	30
Chalmers Knitting Co.	—	57	—	34
Holeproof Hosiery Co.	—	38	31	29
National Cloak & Suit Co.	235	23	61	—
SIC 24—Lumber and Wood Products, Excluding Furniture (1 firm)				
Aladdin Co.	—	—	—	31
SIC 28—Chemicals (9 firms)				
Bon Ami Co.	—	54	33	33
Channel Chemical Co.	—	27	54	—
Colgate & Co.	—	6	10	12
Cudahy Packing Co.[1]	79	13	8	10
N. K. Fairbanks[2]	126	35	57	32
Andrew Jergens Co.	—	42	34	21

TABLE 2.5 (continued)
Largest Advertisers in National Magazines, 1913–15

Standard Industrial Classification (SIC) of Most Heavily Advertised Product	Rank by Size of Assets 1917	Rank by Amount of National Magazine Advertising		
		1913	1914	1915
Palmolive Co.	—	58	55	40
Pompeian Manufacturing Co.	—	37	53	75
Proctor & Gamble Co.	83	1	1	3
SIC 29—Petroleum Refining and Coal Products (1 firm)				
Barrett Manufacturing Co.[a]	—	—	52	38
SIC 30—Rubber Products (4 firms)				
Firestone Tire & Rubber Co.	97	36	44	57
B. F. Goodrich Co.	22	21	47	—
Goodyear Tire & Rubber Co.	65	14	7	7
U.S. Rubber Co.	9	18	20	19
SIC 32—Stone, Clay, and Glass Products (1 firm)				
Johns Manville Co.	337	—	35	39
SIC 34—Fabricated Metal Products (2 firms)				
American Radiator Co.	201	41	66	72
American Safety Razor Co.	—	—	38	64
SIC 35—Machinery, Except Electrical (2 firms)				
Oliver Typewriter Co.	—	16	—	—
Remington Typewriter Co.	182	—	37	—
SIC 36—Electrical Machinery (3 firms)				
Columbia Graphophone Co.	290	19	25	20
General Electric Co.	11	25	17	22
Victor Talking Machine Co.	174	4	4	5
SIC 37—Transportation Equipment (9 firms)				
Cadillac Motor Co.	30[4]	—	28	27
Dodge Brothers Motor Car Co.	99	—	—	23
Hudson Motor Car Co.	484	32	16	18
Hupp Motor Co.	—	43	39	56
Maxwell-Chalmers Motor Car Co.	98	20	19	15
Reo Motor Car Co.	—	30	36	—
Stewart Warner Speedometer Co.	331	9	24	35

TABLE 2.5 (continued)
Largest Advertisers in National Magazines, 1913–15

Standard Industrial Classification (SIC) of Most Heavily Advertised Product	Rank by Size of Assets 1917	Rank by Amount of National Magazine Advertising		
		1913	1914	1915
Studebaker Corp.	78	74	16	18
Willys-Overland Co.	41	5	6	2
SIC 38—Instruments and Related Products (1 firm)				
Eastman Kodak Co.	80	7	9	8
SIC 39—Miscellaneous Manufacturing Industries (2 firms)				
International Silver Co.	303	29	26	25
Oneida Community Silver Co.	—	28	56	51
SIC 48—Communications (1 firm)				
American Telephone and Telegraph Co.	—	46	40	57

[1] Cudahy's most heavily advertised product was Old Dutch Cleanser.
[2] N. K. Fairbanks in 1917 was owned by American Cotton Oil Company.
[3] Barrett's major advertised products were roofing and road surfacing materials.
[4] Firm size rank for Cadillac is that of General Motors.
SOURCES: Firms listed are companies that spent more than $100,000 in national magazine advertising in 1913, 1914, or 1915. Expenditures are listed in Crowell Publishing Company, *National Markets and National Advertising 1922* (New York: Crowell, 1923), pp. 52–53. Rank by asset size in 1917 from Thomas R. Navin, "The 500 Largest Industrials in 1917," *Business History Review*, XLIV (Autumn 1970): 360–86. Rank by amount of national magazine advertising from *National Markets and National Advertising 1922* lists of the seventy-five largest advertisers annually. Thus, for example, Armour was the thirty-first largest spender in 1913, the thirty-second in 1914, and ranked below seventy-fifth in 1915.

tors; as we shall see, even if this proved to be the case, its significance would be disputable. Still, heavy advertising was a strategy the biggest firms in an industry were likely to pursue.

The products on this list contrast sharply with the most publicized products of a mere twenty years earlier. Among about 104 firms, which, in 1893, were said to spend over $50,000 on national advertising, more than half were patent medicine manufacturers.[30] Only seven of the companies on the 1893 list were among the later sample—Quaker Oats,

Armour, Cudahy, American Tobacco Company, P. Lorillard, Remington Typewriters, and Procter & Gamble. In two decades, not only had advertising expenditures of manufacturers grown rapidly, but the advertising industry had replaced its overwhelming reliance on medicines with a far wider (and more savory) range of products to sell. In fact, among leading national advertisers, there was far more turnover in the twenty-five years before World War I than in the nearly seventy years since then.

Although the range of advertised goods expanded, the largest advertisers in the Progressive Era were clustered in a few industries. Of the fifty-eight in our sample, fourteen were food producers, nine made automobiles or auto accessories, and nine sold chemical products (mostly soap and cosmetics). Adding four tire manufacturers and another four tobacco companies indicates that over two-thirds of the firms were in these five industries.

What distinguished these companies from other consumer products firms—including quite a few large ones—that advertised very little was their opportunity and their willingness to invest in selling their products, not simply in making them. The opportunity was not readily available to all firms. The nature of the product and the behavior of consumers limited the possibilities of employing an advertising-oriented marketing strategy with success.

Although enthusiasts in the Progressive Era ardently believed that advertising could sell any kind of product and warmly welcomed all newly advertised products to the fold, more dispassionate observation reveals that the character of demand for some products makes them more "advertisable" than others. The persistently large variations in advertising intensity among industries and products suggest that not everything can be marketed successfully through mass advertising.

Industry's Demand for Advertising

Marketing research reveals that consumers rely more on advertising when there are few alternative sources of information about the product under consideration. Where the buyer can appraise the value of a product before buying—by trying on clothing, for example—advertising is unlikely to determine the purchaser's decision. When a product's price is a large proportion of the consumer's budget, she or he will have good reason to search actively for other more objective sources of information. Where the psychological or economic risks of buying an unsatisfactory product are great, consumers will shop around and seek more personal advice. In particular, where retailers' salespeople can offer important advice about how a product is made, how it works, and how to use it, the store assumes a larger share of the task of differentiating one maker's product from another. In these cases, national advertising by manufacturers is likely to be diminished and to have a smaller effect on the manufacturer's profits. On the other hand, if the consumer is willing to buy without "shopping around" (or if opportunities to get other information are limited and costly), national advertising will probably be more intensive and more closely related to manufacturers' profits. In the phrase of Michael E. Porter, these are "convenience goods."[31]

Admittedly, these consumer behavior considerations do not account for the entire roster of heavy national advertisers. In particular, the auto and tire manufacturers on the list, as well as companies like Remington Typewriter, Oneida Community Plate, and Victor Talking Machines sold costly products; in some of these cases, too, consumers could judge the product before they bought it. Of the largest advertisers, only about half were selling groceries, soaps, toothpastes, cosmetics, and tobacco. We can in part explain the nonconvenience items by pointing out that many of them were rather new products, where advertising is customarily high to build consumer awareness and introduce the novel items. Of those pre–World War I national brands that have remained heavy advertisers for over six decades, roughly two-thirds are convenience products.

Thus, the chance to differentiate and market goods with a strong manufacturer's brand identification was not available to all producers. Moreover, even within the categories where advertising was heaviest, manufacturers had to be willing not only to spend money on publicity but also to recast their marketing strategies in new ways. Some examples from the Progressive Era will indicate the kinds of changes that these firms introduced.

The National Biscuit Company's marketing of the U-needa Biscuit is perhaps the clearest example of how advertising and marketing could be reshaped. Crackers and cookies in nineteenth-century America were commodities, generic products sold loose, without brand identification, from an often-dirty cracker barrel. As soon as the National Biscuit Company emerged from the competitive warfare of bakeries in the 1890s, its president, Adolphus Green, decided to standardize and market a brand-named, nationally advertised soda cracker.[32] He differentiated the product physically by cutting off the corners, giving it an octagonal shape. In the summer of 1889, Green met with Henry N. McKinney of the N. W. Ayer and Son advertising agency. The two mused over the choice of a brand name, considering, among others, Taka Cracker, Hava Cracker, Usa Cracker, and Wanta Cracker, until Green accepted McKinney's suggestion of Uneeda. Packaging was the next step; after some months of experimentation, Green's law partner devised a method of wrapping the crackers in a wax paper lined cardboard box. Meanwhile, Green himself closely supervised everything from baking formulas to package lettering styles. A year after the Uneeda Biscuit (a supposedly more dignified synonym for cracker) was introduced, the company was selling ten million packages a month. A staff of salesmen and a network of company-owned branch sales offices soon followed to ensure that the crackers would reach the customer fresh and unbroken and to convince grocers that they could not shun a product with Uneeda's consumer appeal, despite its low profit margin.

Capping the company's new marketing strategy was an unsurpassed advertising campaign. Although the figures are unreliable, National Biscuit is said to have been the first company to appropriate one million dollars in a year for advertising. A coordinated "teaser" campaign of ads containing the single word "Uneeda" appearing in newspapers and on billboards and streetcar cards proclaimed the arrival of the new biscuit in a marketing area. Even the watertight packaging was promoted in ads featuring a little boy in a raincoat carrying a box of the biscuits through a storm. The paid publicity itself engendered others' promotional efforts; retailers sponsored biscuit eating contests in store windows, and toy manufacturers offered miniature copies of the familiar National Biscuit Company delivery wagons.

The biscuit "trust" never could attain a full-fledged monopoly on cracker and cookie production; the nature of the baking process, the varied nature of the products, and the difficulties of physical distribution prevented that. In fact, the company repeatedly denied its intention to take over the entire market. Nevertheless, its size offered definite advantages for the marketing course it pursued. It inherited some brands that were well known regionally before 1898, such as the Fig Newton (named after the Boston suburb), and developed others, like ZuZu ginger-molasses cookies, to meet retailers' demands for a broader product line and to use its distribution network more efficiently. Within a decade, there were forty-four items on the National Biscuit Company's product list.

The success of Uneeda and the In-er-Seal box led one advertising periodical to announce in 1900 that "the package is the very keynote of modern advertising."[33] In the case of many food products, this was apt enough. For other manufactured goods, however, national advertising sometimes entailed creating an entirely new product, not just packaging a familiar one. Such was the case with George Eastman's transformation of photography from a professional pursuit to an amateur pastime. Eastman and his associates in the late 1880s manufactured what was still the staple product of the industry—glass photographic plates—and also made the newer roll film. In neither line was the company exceptionally successful, although it had profitable operations making photographic printing paper and enlarging pictures. What distinguished Eastman's approach in each segment of the photographic supply business was his commitment to mechanized, high-volume production methods. His firm, for example, was the industry's leader in devising machinery for applying light-sensitive emulsion to glass plates, in manufacturing photographic papers by a continuous-strip process, and in coating paper-backed negative film in the same high-volume fashion. Even the enlarging and printing department was, by 1886, using a large automatic printing press capable of turning out five to ten thousand prints each day.[34]

By about 1887, Eastman's experiences gave him a crucial insight into the photography industry and permitted him to shape its future. He recognized that a system requiring photographers simply to expose the film, while the manufacturer performed the complex chemical tasks of developing and printing it, was now technologically possible. With his record of investing heavily in high-volume manufacturing facilities, Eastman was well situated to act on this insight. "The mere mechanical act of taking the picture, which anybody can perform, is *divorced* from all the chemical manipulations . . . which only experts can perform," his company explained. By 1888, the firm had not only a new camera, which Eastman named the Kodak, but a new system of photography which "any person of ordinary intelligence [could] . . . learn in ten minutes."[35] Eastman sold the Kodak preloaded with enough film for one hundred photos. After taking the pictures, the customer would mail the entire camera back to the Rochester factory. There, the pictures would be processed, the camera reloaded, and both shipped back to the user. Here was a new technology, a new method of physical distribution, and a new market all in one. Clearly, these changes dictated a new promotional strategy, and Eastman Kodak (as the firm became known in 1892) soon became an advertising leader.

Domestic sales in 1893 were still less than half a million dollars, but one estimate put newspaper and magazine advertising for that year at about $30,000, with additional thousands spent on circulars, instruction booklets, and other promotional material.[36] By the end of the decade, when Eastman Kodak sales were $2.3 million, *Printers' Ink* cited an estimate that the firm spent $750,000 on advertising.[37] However, this figure does seem implausibly high.

The Kodak advertising slogan, "You press the button and we do the rest," was a singularly pithy description of the system's most appealing feature. As early as 1892, the Kodak slogan was said to be "probably the most imitated and adapted of any." The company's advertising manager, Lewis B. Jones, joined Eastman that year; he attained positions of influence both within the firm and in the advertising business, serving as president of the Association of National Advertising Managers. Early advertising for Kodak offered more than just a clever catch-phrase. Since dealers as well as consumers had to be taught the virtues of the new cameras and films, and since retailers could influence consumers' choices, Kodak began to award prizes and bonuses for retailers' promotional efforts.[38]

The cigarette industry offers another example of the relationship between innovation in production and new paths in marketing and advertising. Until the 1880s, cigarettes were rolled by hand for sale to a small number of well-to-do smokers and Eastern European immigrants. Even as late as 1904, the value of cigar production was nearly thirteen times that of cigarettes.[39] Yet the cigarette industry in the 1880s contained two "secret ingredients" which were to remake it within a matter of a few years: a new cigarette machine and, in the person of James Buchanan Duke, a man who would aggressively market the output which the machines poured forth.

Duke had taken over this father's firm in 1880, when it was valued at only about $70,000. After a brief period of manufacturing smoking tobacco, Duke realized that Bull Durham, the most prominent rival brand, had literally painted its trademark on the barn walls and billboards of rural America. "My company is up against a stone wall. It cannot compete with the bull. Something has to be done and that quick. As for me, I am going into the cigarette business," Duke decided.[40]

Duke went in with a gusto previously unknown in the cigarette business. He knew the importance of enticing dealers. In 1884, he sent 400,000 chairs, each with his advertisement on the back, to the retail tobacconists of the nation. With such devices, sales reached about $600,000 in 1885. That was the year Duke acquired rights to the newly developed Bonsack cigarette rolling machine for a royalty of twenty-four cents per 1,000 cigarettes. Equally significant was the provision that guaranteed Duke that his royalties would remain 25 percent lower than those charged his competitors. Since the machine could produce 120,000 cigarettes a day, whereas a hand roller could turn out only about 2,500, manufacturing costs fell about 50 percent. Duke's pledge to use only the Bonsack machine had also won him an insuperable cost advantage. In retrospect, we can see his rivals' acquiescence to the 1890 merger that created the American Tobacco Company as inevitable.[41]

What is less obvious but equally important was Duke's impact on marketing. Even if he had not been so eager to promote his goods, the sheer volume of cigarettes spewed forth by the Bonsack machines would have necessitated major selling innovations. Even before the merger, Duke was spending about $800,000 on advertising out of sales of $4,500,000. Although his "Tobacco Trust" soon sold nearly 90 percent of the nation's cigarettes, it maintained, for most of its twenty-year life, a heavy advertising program aimed at both building loyalty to Trust brands and inducing more people to smoke cigarettes. Since the American Tobacco Company controlled such a preponderant share of sales, it did not have to entice smokers of other brands. It stressed coupons and premiums as its main promotional devices. During the 1890s, about four-fifths of the Trust's formidable advertising budgets (these averaged over 10 percent of sales between 1893 and 1910) appear to have gone into premiums and coupons.[42]

The Trust also began to distribute its own output. As production had soared in the 1880s, Duke had established branch offices and a network of salesmen who reached wholesalers and large retailers alike. The American Tobacco Company's aim was not to eradicate the wholesalers, who still had a useful function in physically distributing the goods, but to control them and reduce selling margins. Indeed, when a company salesman received an order from a retailer, he would hand it over to the appropriate jobber to fill. The Trust wielded a variety of rewards and threats in its dealings with distributors. Wholesalers found that the Tobacco Company often would offer higher margins if they would handle no independent brands, but that they would withdraw all of their goods from jobbers who refused this exclusive arrangement. Retailers were also dissuaded from selling rival goods and were pressured to report to the Trust on the strategies of independent salesmen. "The result is," noted the Justice Department in its argument for dissolving the Trust, "that dealers are subservient, anxious to win favor and larger discounts—a hope shrewdly held out to those who will do as bidden."[48] After about 1902, the American Tobacco Company also secretly controlled the United Cigar Stores, a powerful retail chain whose ability to buy at wholesalers' prices from the Trust and aggressive site selection policies threatened many smaller tobacconists. The Bureau of Corporations' study of the tobacco industry indicated that, on balance, distributors' margins on cigarettes slipped steadily from 1901 to 1910. It is hardly surprising. Heavy advertising and a sales department as resourceful as it was unscrupulous had converted the wholesaler into little more than a deliveryman and the retailer into little more than a changemaker.

Among the leading advertisers of the Progressive Era, these scenarios could be duplicated with only minor variations. For example, Ferdinand Schumacher's new milling methods for oats created a situation where manufacturers could make twice as much oatmeal as the limited markets of the mid-1880s could handle. At the time, consumers generally scorned oatmeal as a food for invalids and for a few Scottish immigrants—whose taste for oatmeal was said to show their dour, parsimonious nature. Excess capacity and competition led to the merger in 1888 of the seven largest mills to create the American Cereal Company. It was not the production-oriented Schumacher who seized upon the possibility of making oatmeal into a branded, nationally advertised breakfast food, but his former rival Henry Parsons Crowell. Even before the American Cereal Company, Crowell was packaging his oats in twenty-four ounce boxes with the already familiar picture of the black-coated Quaker on the label. Marketing techniques advanced after consolidations. As the chronicler of the history of Quaker Oats puts it, Crowell used "every device of the advertiser's art . . . between 1890 and 1896" to promote the company's cereals.[44] For example, in the summer of 1891, the company ran a fifteen-car freight train from its Cedar Rapids, Iowa, factory to Portland, Oregon. An actor dressed in Quaker garb entertained spectators along the way, and the train carried exhibits of the cereals. In Portland, every household received a half-ounce sample of Quaker Oats. In 1893, the firm was reported to be spending about $100,000 for advertising in newspapers, magazines, trade journals, and street car and elevated railway posters, in addition to the "liberal sum" given to other promotional methods. *Printers' Ink* noted in 1898 that "one result of the extensive advertising of Quaker Oats is that exceedingly few people now buy oatmeal in bulk."[45] Again, consumption patterns were transformed.

The case of the Gillette Safety Razor Company illustrates a slightly different pattern. Here the marketing strategy even antedated the product itself. King C. Gillette, a curious combination of master salesman, impractical tinkerer, and utopian reformer, was working for the Crown Cork & Seal Company in the early 1890s; William Painter, president of the firm, had invented a metal and cork cap that could be crimped over the top of beer and soft drink bottles. In conversation one day, Painter remarked, "King, you are always thinking and inventing something. Why don't you try to think of something like the Crown Cork which, when once used, is thrown away, and the customer keeps coming back for more—and with every additional customer you get, you are building a foundation for profit."[46] The suggestion soon took root in Gillette's mind. He later claimed that he decided to concentrate his inventive energies on razors and razor blades while shaving one morning in 1895. Six years later, his company was formed, and in 1903 the Gillette Safety Razor kit was first marketed. As with other new products that entailed changes in purchasing and consumption habits, heavy advertising proved essential. At first, Gillette appropriated about twenty-five cents per kit for advertising, or about 5 percent of the five dollar retail price. By 1905, the allocation was doubled to about fifty cents a razor. The ads, which had at first appeared in business periodicals, moved into general interest magazines and were aimed at consumers, "to get the user to demand of the dealer that he supply him with the article," as an executive later put it.[47] At the same time, Gillette took an increasingly active role in other aspects of marketing. Initially, the company sold its entire output to a wholesaling firm, Townsend & Hunt, but as Gillette's sales grew, Townsend & Hunt gave up its other lines of business and became the Gillette Sales Company, a subsidiary of the manufacturer. As advertising expanded, Gillette became increasingly concerned with maintaining retail prices; large, low-overhead retailers were cutting prices on the razors, and smaller merchants, unable to meet their competitors, were reluctant to stock the product. The Gillette sales staff relentlessly pursued price cutters and removed razors from their stores. The changing sales mix affected marketing strategy as well. Blade sales grew more rapidly than razor sales, as the advertising message that the blades were disposable sank in. Gillette consumer advertising needed the complement of a growing sales force who could get the blades into convenience stores as well as the jewelers, hardware stores, and cutlery outlets where the razor was first sold. When King C. Gillette noted in 1912, *"the whole success of the business depends on advertising,"* he was only partially correct.[48] Advertising was but one element in a strategy of differentiating a product and implementing new ways to market it.

In marketing an intangible—life insurance—advertising played a quantitatively small but nevertheless important role both in controlling channels of distribution and in marketing a new kind of product. In relation to the volume of business transacted by the great life insurance companies, advertising outlays were almost negligible; fundamentally, life insurance rested on personal salesmanship. As one company remarked in 1857, "Few, if any, are ever influenced by a mere newspaper advertisement to take a policy."[49] Yet the "Big Three" of the Gilded Age life insurance business and their rivals did use advertising to centralize control over marketing operations. At the same time, the newer companies specializing in low-cost, low-benefit "industrial insurance" for urban workers employed advertising to create a corporate image and proclaim their product's distinctive qualities.

The insurance firms which emerged from the depression of the 1870s at the top of the industry amassed pools of capital and built organizational structures whose size was practically unparalleled in the American economy. The Equitable Life Assurance Society, Mutual of New York, and the New York Life Insurance Company each had over a billion dollars of insurance in force by 1900 and each sold through a network of general agents and salesmen throughout the nation. These immense companies found that neither the individual policy salesman nor the prosperous general agents could be easily controlled. As Morton Keller explains, "For a society of mature, institutionalized corporations, the domains of the general agents became as much an irritant as the fiefs of the great lords had been to rising national monarchs."[50]

Advertising was part of the companies' drive to centralize power in several ways. First, companies frequently recruited agents through advertising. The ads attempted to screen out undesirables by specifying that temperate, respectable, and honest men were needed and by warning that agents who would rebate part of the insurance premium to a customer in order to win sales need not apply. Second, the firms attempted to make sure that agents used only material prepared at or approved by the central office. This advertising literature itself attempted to discourage rebating: "No discrimination [in premium rates] is permitted or practiced," stated an 1889 sales brochure which notified readers that any agent caught rebating would be summarily fired.[51] Insurance company headquarters also tried—without great sincerity or success, for the most part—to use advertising to counteract misleading and exaggerated claims for their policies which over-enthusiastic agents might make.

Life insurance advertising did more than curb the discretion of the companies' selling forces. The firms also used it to reinforce their images and to focus attention on certain sales appeals. From the 1870s until New York State's Armstrong Commission investigation in 1905, the leading companies emphasized life insurance as an investment, not as family protection. As Equitable instructed its agents in 1901, "Get the idea out of your own head, and keep it out of the investor's head, that you are simply *assuring his life* . . . You are selling a block of Bonds—that is the first idea. To that you add the idea of insurance. Insurance of what? Why, insurance of the *investment*."[52] For the Big Three and their lesser competitors, $1,000 was generally the smallest policy they would write, and premiums had to be paid annually or semi-annually. The policies themselves generally rewarded longevity with high dividends and treated those who died or whose premium payments lapsed less than generously. For these reasons, life insurance advertising emphasized financial calculations and promised favorable returns. Advertising men criticized this kind of publicity; it was "based on old-world notions . . . hedged in with conservatism, and bounded with precedent."[53] Surely, appeals to the customer's cupidity and bombastic promises of high returns were not the stuff of sprightly advertising, but these advertisements fit the policies and the purchasers of ordinary life insurance before 1905.

For the millions of Americans unable to afford ordinary life insurance, "industrial" life insurance rapidly began to fill the gap. John F. Dryden, a New Jersey insurance agent, observed the success of the Prudential Assurance Company of Great Britain, which sold small policies to industrial workers and their families, did not require a medical examination, and collected premiums each week. By the mid-1890s, Dryden's American Prudential Insurance Company had become the sixth largest life insurance company in the United States, and its main rival in industrial insurance, Metropolitan Life, stood in fourth place. By 1898, over a billion dollars of industrial life insurance was in force.[54]

The Metropolitan and, especially, the Prudential became major advertisers in the 1890s. Late in the decade, Prudential was consistently spending as much as or more than the Big Three for advertising—well over $100,000 per year. Prudential's rise followed a chance meeting in 1895 between President Dryden and free-lance advertising writer Charles Austin Bates, who convinced the insurance man that the firm should adopt modern selling methods. Soon thereafter, a young representative of the J. Walter Thompson Agency approached Dryden and won the account. A Thompson executive, Mortimer Remington, designed a vivid symbol for the company and coined its trademark, "The Prudential has the strength of Gibraltar." The theme continues in Prudential advertising to this day. Its force and simplicity won advertising industry approval. By 1905, the landmark had become "inseparably associated with the Prudential, or the Prudential with it, in the minds of the American people."[55] As industrial insurance had tapped a new market for life insurance, the Prudential tailored an advertising campaign that reflected its novel marketing needs.

The paths to national advertising of branded products were varied. Some manufacturers actively sought out products and markets amenable to national advertising, as did George Eastman and King Gillette. Others, like John Dryden and Henry Crowell, altered what they sold enough to reach new markets. This was especially true of many food and beverage products sold initially on the basis of hygienic or curative powers. Coca-Cola, for example, had touted its tonic qualities and its temperance virtues; Welch's Grape Juice was originally intended by its Methodist manufacturers as a substitute for wine; C. W. Post had promoted his hot beverage, Postum, by trumpeting the dangers of coffee; and Walter Baker Chocolate had stressed the hazards of cocoa made by other processes. In each of these cases, modern advertising in the early twentieth century repositioned the product, offering it not only to the chronic dyspeptic or the occasionally ill, but to a mass audience of potentially steady customers.

Finally, some large national advertisers reacted defensively and hesitantly to changes in marketing environments. Ferdinand Schumacher, for example, resisted Henry Crowell's urgings to advertise Quaker Oats actively. Procter & Gamble had to witness the success of other wrapped and branded soap bars before they introduced and advertised Ivory. When Campbell Soup awarded its first advertising appropriation in 1899, the company's secretary turned to the treasurer and remarked, "Well, we've kissed that money goodbye!"[56]

Despite the varying situations and motives of these firms, national advertising appeared and flourished only under certain conditions. For most large-scale national advertisers, heavy investment in plant and equipment made demand fluctuations costly and price competition perilous. Advertisers, too, needed to be able to deliver to the consumer a distinctive, differentiated product, one that promised real or imagined advantages over rival brands or unbranded goods. Moreover, for advertising to play a large part in the marketing strategy, consumers had to be willing to accept this kind of self-interested persuasion as a tolerable substitute or complement to more objective product information.

To its most enthusiastic boosters, the growth of national advertising seemed unstoppable. "If they are put up in distinctive packages—and advertised—demand may be created for the most ordinary and commonplace articles," they proclaimed. "This is a golden age in trademarks. . . . In ten years at the farthest, perhaps in five or less, every commodity of large consumption will have its trademarked leader, firmly entrenched through advertising."[57] Advertising was not, in fact, omnipotent; however, its power, when combined with other innovations in manufacturing and distribution, was real enough. Manufacturers found in advertising a method of rivalry well suited to a wide range of oligopolistic consumer markets. Their decisions to market their products with intensive advertising campaigns engendered a series of usually unforeseen consequences for themselves, for merchants, and for consumers. We shall now turn to those effects.

3

Advertising's Effects
on Industry

NATIONAL ADVERTISING developed when businessmen in several important industries decided that branding and promoting their products would be profitable. Their decisions had ramifications beyond the firms themselves. Here we shall consider the impact of national advertising on industrial structure and performance, examining its effects on market structure, on distribution channels, and on consumer welfare.

Advertising's Effects on Industry

MARKET STRUCTURE

The rise of national advertising at the turn of this century accompanied a set of changes that drastically reshaped the American business scene. Beginning around the 1880s, mass production of goods in large batches and continuous-flow processing of liquid or semiliquid commodities induced manufacturers to integrate forward to handle the physical distribution of their increased output. These firms found themselves performing more and more of their required marketing activities. Later, some of these companies obtained control of raw materials as well to ensure that their new capital-intensive machinery would not be idled by material shortages. Faced with excess capacity and destabilizing price competition, industrialists sought refuge in horizontal combinations, at first through informal pools and price-fixing agreements, then through various degrees of administrative consolidation. The merger wave of 1898–1902, which swallowed up 2,653 independent firms, brought forth 269 consolidated companies, so-called trusts, with $6.3 billion of capital.[1] With remarkable swiftness, large-scale corporate capitalism had appeared. Yet, as Alfred D. Chandler has emphasized, the merger wave brought about enduring big businesses only when rationalization of production and centralization of management followed legal consolidation. Quite quickly, these firms saw the advantages of taking on marketing and purchasing functions to coordinate the rapid flow of materials and products. A few large firms, vertically integrated and increasingly run by professional managers, dominated in food, petroleum, tobacco, rubber, chemicals, and machinery manufacturing. At the other end of the industrial spectrum, however, where new technologies and demand patterns did not threaten older modes, big businesses were rare. The industrial groups of apparel, furniture, and printing and publishing contributed no firms to the hundred largest industrials of 1917; only one firm each from the textile, lumber, and paper groups appeared on the list. The industrial classification of the nation's largest businesses has shown remarkable stability since the Progressive Era.[2]

Not remarkably, the largest firms also usually possessed large shares of the markets where they operated. Size and market concentration were closely linked, and big businesses typically competed in oligopolistic, not atomistic, markets.

One searches in vain in the early writings of advertising men for any serious examination of advertising's impact on these phenomena. In the era of the growth of big business and the great controversies regarding its economic and moral values, advertising men in general seemed uninterested in the possibility that advertising might be playing an important role in these dramatic changes. Persuaded that the trusts would continue to advertise, even when they dominated their existing markets, advertising men rarely considered whether advertising had helped bring about concentration.

Jonathan Cutler, writing in 1899, pointed out that if trusts stopped advertising, they would soon find smaller rivals encroaching upon local and regional markets with their own advertising campaigns. A month later, an officer of a newly formed bicycle combination told readers of *Printers' Ink,* "We are going to keep the quality and quantity of our advertising at a high standard. It will be just as aggressive as formerly." A prominent advertising textbook explained that monopolists would still have cause to advertise to inform customers of new products and to "stimulate new needs not already felt to be urgent." There was "no basis for alarm in the concentrating tendency of modern industry."[3]

Later observers have paid more attention to the converse question: Does advertising increase concentration? Nicholas

Advertising's Effects on Industry

Kaldor remarked in 1949 that "there is a general presumption that advertising promotes industrial concentration," basing his contention on the superior "pulling power" of heavy advertising campaigns over smaller ones.[4] In other words, Kaldor postulated increasing returns to advertising. A second approach, pioneered by Joe S. Bain, linked advertising to concentration through its role as a barrier to entry.[5] Bain suggested that if firms have used advertising to establish reputations in their industry, a potential entrant's unit selling costs would exceed those of older firms. Alternatively, the entrant may have to counter consumers' loyalty to established brands by pegging his price lower than his rivals'. These barriers might hold even if there are no increasing returns to advertising. If advertising is an investment in future, as well as current, sales, the potential entrant might face a situation where his advertising outlays would eventually win as many sales per dollar as those of existing firms, but where he would have to match the older companies' pre-existing investments in advertising goodwill. This could mean a capital requirements barrier to entry, exacerbated because suppliers of capital are likely to be dubious about lending for investments in anything as intangible as advertising. Thus, firms' past investments in advertising may make it hard for new companies to enter, causing concentration and excess profits for the established companies.

In recent years, economists have sharply attacked these purported links between advertising and concentration as theoretically untenable and empirically questionable. The hypothesis of increasing returns to advertising, some argue, violates most economists' sense that an efficient entrepreneur would use the most effective units of a productive factor (in this case advertising) first, and that diminishing returns must obtain when an industry is in equilibrium. That many oligopolists choose to split their advertising expenditures among several branded products in the same industry suggests further that they see no increasing returns from putting their advertising eggs into one large basket. A second line of attack has been to point out that increasing advertisement sizes and frequencies seldom brings a proportionate rise in responses. Last, the possibility that media offer quantity discounts to heavy advertisers, giving them cost advantages, has been hotly disputed.[6]

Likewise, the barriers to entry proposition has come under fire. Richard Schmalensee points out that any fixed stream of returns from past investments in advertising cannot in itself be a barrier to entry as long as the potential new firm's advertising is as effective as the advertising of the established companies. Returns from past outlays for advertising are, writes Schmalensee, "like a bond in that it is fixed income, the level of which has no effect on the returns from any action and thus can have no influence on any rational decision maker." Empirically, Harold Demsetz has recently contended that once profit rates are corrected for the bias imparted by treating advertising as a current (not capital) expense, the statistical basis for considering advertising a barrier to entry disappears.[7]

Finally, as we have noted, virtually all participants in the debate over advertising and concentration have conceded the desirability of investigating a two-way relationship. If oligopoly itself induces firms to favor advertising rivalry over price competition, then it is fallacious to measure the impact of advertising on concentration without considering the reciprocal influence of concentration on advertising. Once again, cause and effect are intertwined, creating thorny statistical problems.

Defenders of the hypothesis that advertising does increase industrial concentration have in turn replied to these objections, and the controversy shows no signs of abating. The statistical evidence is mixed. Although most of the studies cited by Stanley Ornstein in his survey of the literature on advertising and concentration indicate a positive impact for advertising, there are exceptions. Coefficients in regression equations are often insignificant, and the problems of interpretation which we have mentioned persist. Yet the balance of evidence does suggest a causal link. A recent investigation of changes in concentration among 167 industries finds that the industry's volume of advertising as a percentage of sales was the single most powerful variable in explaining increases in concentration between 1947 and 1972. Another investigation indicates that even when feedback influences of high profit margins and concentration are taken into account, advertising "leads to greater concentration." A third study sought to ascertain which variable was "causally prior" to the other and indicated that the chain of causation ran from advertising to concentration.[8]

Advertising men have not been consistent in judging the relative efficacy of large and small advertising budgets. In the Progressive Era, most of them were willing to base their judgments on unsure foundations in psychological and economic speculations. Off-the-cuff observations and unsubstantiated hunches abounded. Nevertheless, most advertising men in the early twentieth century apparently believed there were increasing returns to advertising. Most recommended large advertisements as drawing proportionately better than small ones, although potential advertisers were often urged to start small. An advertising campaign that did not reach a threshold of visibility was not likely to succeed. In 1873, one agency's magazine recommended that advertisements show "a quiet courtesy and modest unobtrusiveness," but by the twentieth century such advice was outmoded.[9] Large headlines, white space surrounding the copy, and prominent illustrations became the hallmarks of effective advertising. Clearly, this required outlays not all could make. As an article by Edwin G. Dexter, Professor of Education at the University of Illinois, put it, "The modern advertisement is not intended for the man who wants the thing already. It is for the one who don't [*sic*] in order to make him." Size was an important way to catch the reader's attention: "The cathedral builders of the Middle Ages knew something about it," Dexter noted. On the other hand, Seymour Eaton, a well-known copywriter, asserted that "an advertisement should be big enough to make an impression but not any bigger than the thing advertised."[10] Such oracular advice indicates the shaky footing of advertising expertise of the era.

The most vociferous opponent of the doctrine of increasing returns was William A. Shryer, a Detroit publisher, mail-order advertiser, and advertising researcher. Shryer insisted, "The law of diminishing returns . . . is the real law of advertising, and not cumulative value."[11] His contention rested on detailed analyses of the inquiries and orders from mail-order advertisements. These could be "keyed" (coded) to permit the advertiser to determine which advertisement had brought a consumer's response. Yet other advertising commentators of the Progressive Era paid little attention to Shryer's findings. Daniel Starch, then commencing a long career in advertising research, answered Shryer by pointing out that results for mail-order advertising were not likely to hold true for other kinds of advertising campaigns.[12] In mail-order advertising, the entire inducement to buy must be packed into a single advertisement. In other campaigns, cumulative appeals reinforced by other kinds of publicity and salesmanship might work quite differently.

Advertising men at the turn of the century believed that a judicious and skillful campaign could establish a product differentiation entry barrier. (Of course such terminology was then unknown.) They frequently observed that advertising should be looked upon as an investment, creating goodwill that newer entrants would not be able to match. They hoped to rewrite the rules of accounting to legitimate treating advertising as a capital expenditure—an unrealized aspiration even today.

Advertising-created goodwill sometimes did become a marketable asset. In the 1880s, for example, Henry L. Pierce, who had purchased the Walter Baker Chocolate Company, was reputedly paying a $10,000 royalty to Baker's widow for rights to the Baker name and trademark. More often, estimates of the value of brand reputations were impressionistic at best. Royal Baking Powder's goodwill in 1905 was said to be $5 million—"a million dollars a letter." Three years later, another advertising man estimated, "At least fifty percent of the advertising being done today is for the purpose of creating *property in trademarks.*" In sum, advertising men shared the faith that they could create "reputation monopolies" through advertising.[13]

Admittedly, large firms with ready access to large sums of capital and reputations of their own to carry with them ought to be able to vault any advertising-created barriers to entry with some ease. In the second decade of this century, advertising men began to note this potential and to urge big firms to extend their product lines and carry trademarks into new fields. For some of the large food processors, in particular, such a strategy may have intensified competition in certain industries. Heinz, of course, prized its product diversity so much that H. J. Heinz chose to make it a key selling theme for the firm's publicity, placarding and painting the nation with his "57 Varieties" slogan. Presumably, a firm like Heinz would have little trouble matching established firms in food lines it chose to enter, but even here the continuing dominance of Campbell relegated Heinz to a small share of the soup market. In general, pre–World War I firms were confined to one product line. Diversification was the exception, not the rule, for even very large firms, and pioneers in adding new products were most likely to be selling to other producers, not consumers. Only four of the largest ninety manufacturers in 1919 were operating in ten or more industries.[14] These firms—Union Carbide, U.S. Steel, General Electric, and Westinghouse—were not primarily consumer goods manufacturers. Therefore, the likely entrants into competition with large national advertisers in the early decades of the century were not the widely diversified giants we see today. The impact of product differentiation entry barriers may have been larger then than now. Those who recommended advertising as a strategy to stave off new competitors had a persuasive, if not proven, case.

PRICES, PROFITS, AND CONSUMER WELFARE

To conclude that national advertising created barriers to entry and raised industrial concentration does not necessarily imply that it increased monopoly power to the detriment of consumer welfare. In some instances, at least, the performance of oligopolistic competitors may approximate the optima of perfect competition. However, if advertising-induced brand loyalty lowered advertised brands' elasticity of demand, their manufacturers could charge prices higher than marginal costs. The differential between price and costs is a commonly used measure of market power and misallocation of resources. Alternatively, if oligopolists found it practical or necessary to restrain price competition and instead engage in rivalry through advertising, such spending would likely be socially wasteful and prices unjustifiably high, even if the firms' revenues were dissipated on advertising costs.

Once again, however, there is no consensus today among economists on the validity of the logic behind or evidence for the proposition that advertising yields market power and harms consumer welfare. Some economists maintain that better-managed or luckier firms may profit from the introduction of better products or cheaper processes of production or distribution. These firms may grow, capture economies of scale, and achieve higher profits than their less adept or fortunate rivals. According to this line of reasoning, it is fallacious to equate the profits from superior performance with excessive market power. Since advertising may be one means of achieving these economies, there may be a correlation of profit rates with advertising intensity, but both variables reflect the underlying skill or good fortune of the successful firms.[15]

If this account of business success appears excessively sanguine, it is nevertheless true that a second conceptual problem should stop us from too readily accepting the hypothesis that advertising causes monopoly profits. Under the plausible assumption of diminishing returns to advertising, a profit-maximizing firm would increase its advertising outlays as its market power increased. Therefore, high profits can themselves cause intensive advertising.

The case for seeing advertising as creating market power is best elaborated in the research of William S. Comanor and Thomas A. Wilson. They find, for forty-one consumer goods industries, that variations in industry advertising intensity accounted for a significant portion of the variation in industry profit rates. A related investigation concluded that large firms in industries that advertise heavily have greater advantages in profitability over smaller competitors than do firms in which advertising is less prevalent. Their rough estimate of excessive consumer goods advertising and of production that is restricted or misallocated by market power suggests social costs of about $1.5 billion annually as early as the mid-1950s. In addition, another billion dollars or more was transferred from consumers to producers with market power based on advertising.[16]

Critiques of the Comanor and Wilson study have, on the whole, focused on technical matters concerning measurement of variables, the nature of their industry sample, and their interpretation of certain regression coefficients. At the same time, defenders of advertising as a procompetitive practice introduce a different group of studies. These argue, for example, that market shares and profit levels in industries with high advertising are not especially stable; thus, advertising is not a sure way to fend off rivals. Some direct efforts to measure the impact of advertising on price elasticity of demand suggest that it actually increases consumer responsiveness to price changes by providing more information about the range of choices available.[17] An investigation of prescription eyeglasses suggests that consumer prices were significantly lower where advertising was legal than in states where it was banned.[18]

If present-day economists' opinions of the effects of advertising on prices and competition are divided, early advertising writers were equally inconsistent on the subject. Although they rejected charges that consumers might be paying for advertising in the form of higher product prices, they also continually urged businessmen to use advertising as a substitute for price competition. An examination of their viewpoints will not provide a clear-cut answer to the questions we have posed about advertising's role in the competitive process, but it should offer some insights into how advertising men thought publicity functioned.

If advertisements provide honest information about a brand's price, it may help a buyer find the best bargain, facilitate brand comparisons, and increase the price elasticity of demand. Without some price information, advertisements are less likely to help consumers find the best buys. Almost all advertisers in the Gilded Age and Progressive Era faced the question of whether their ads should give price information. Most mid-nineteenth century retail advertisements had not mentioned prices. In some cases, general knowledge of customary prices might have reduced the need for publicizing them in print; in other cases, haggling and the absence of a one-price-for-all system made it virtually impossible to put prices in advertisements. Finally, where transportation cost barriers produced local mercantile monopolies, protected retailers did not need to proclaim prices as a competitive tactic. Later in the century, each of these factors limiting price advertising diminished in importance. As department stores in large cities adopted one-price-for-all policies, they began to proclaim prices in their ads. By the 1880s, it appears that stated prices were the rule, not the exception, in Macy's and Wanamaker's ads. At the time, these department stores were selling items without strong national advertising campaigns behind them. But by about 1900, as brand-named, nationally advertised goods gained more importance on their counters, "the incessant emphasis on mere price was lessened . . ." in Macy's advertisements.[19]

In 1892, advertising agent Artemas Ward contended that price might properly play a role in retail advertisements and store displays, but that manufacturers, in their national advertising, should "almost invariably seek to create a desire . . . before divulging the price." Occasionally thereafter, advertising experts would claim, "The price is the key to the ad." More often, the profession saw advertising as a substitute for price appeals. Even for retailers, according to Macy's advertising manager, "to attempt to create interest by prices alone is to walk in a circle, for the sensational effect is over in a day." *Printers' Ink* by 1908 was glad to note that even in mail-order advertising, where mentioning prices was obligatory, there was a new emphasis on product characteristics, not price.[20]

Aversion to printing prices in ads sometimes rose to the status of moral principle. Joseph Appel, advertising manager of Wanamaker's, contended that advertisements that compared prices were a form of unfair competition. A *Printers' Ink* editorial echoed these sentiments: "The policy of advertising comparative prices is responsible for many of the evils that have crept into department store selling." Advertising was all too often "price crazy," commented *Associated Advertising*: "Price is one of many factors. It is not the paramount issue."[21]

In fact, the proper task of advertising was to ensure that customers did *not* make the price the "paramount issue." "Advertising along quality lines is gradually abolishing the bargain counter and its cut price," noted *Printers' Ink* approvingly in 1903. "The day of deliverance ... is in sight." Price competition harmed seller and buyer alike: "Price cutting doesn't educate the public. Advertising does, and that means increased demand." Advertising agent John Lee Mahin insisted that "advertising is the only means that a businessman has of investing the goods that he handles with qualities or characteristics that exempt him from price competition." Mahin's vehement contention that "mere price competition logically ends in the debasement of those who practice it ..." indicates how advertising men could raise their aversion to price competition to the level of a moral principle.[22]

While advertising men were encouraging their audiences to substitute advertising for price competition, they also insisted that advertising could lower consumer prices. In general, they asserted that advertising would raise sales and, therefore, allow firms to obtain economies of scale in production.

Cost reductions would be shared, then, with the consumer through high-volume, low-margin marketing procedures. The experience of at least some major national advertisers seems to have borne out this rationale for consumer advertising. W. K. Kellogg, the cornflake magnate, pointed out in 1913 that he had begun breakfast cereal production in 1896, charging consumers 15 cents a box. By 1913, his packages were 15 percent bigger, and the price had declined to ten cents.[23] When an investigator interviewed the advertising manager of the Lowney Chocolate and Cocoa Company, the executive mentioned his plans to introduce a low-priced line of chocolates: "We want to put up a box to sell for fifty cents, but we have to wait until we have enough money to put the thing across by advertising."[24] Campbell Soup sold for only about one-third the price of less-promoted brands. National Biscuit held prices down to build volume. Kodak first made photography affordable for a middle-class, amateur public. Yet this sort of proof by example, which advertising men regarded as conclusive, is hardly sufficient for us. Surely not all the important examples of low-margin, high-volume manufacturing in the early twentieth century relied on heavy advertising to reach their positions. The Ford Motor Company did, "comparatively speaking, practically no advertising at all..." in 1913 as Henry Ford captured the economies of mass production and continually managed to increase sales and lower the Model T's price.[25] Other companies that sold consumer products also managed to grow without extensive advertising. Singer Sewing Machines, where personal selling, credit, and service dominated the marketing mix, and the major sugar refiners, offering a fundamentally undifferentiated product, are examples. Conversely, there were heavy national advertisers whose prices reflected either the absence of production scale economies or the presence of market power or both. Their prices did not fall as volume grew. In the case of the American Tobacco Company, cigarette manufacturing costs fell about 40 percent from 1893 to 1899; by 1907, however, costs had almost returned to their 1893 levels. Profit margins generally accounted for 30 percent of the manufacturer's selling price. During the years when the Trust's prices were rising, ironically its profit margins on cigarettes were slipping. Rising manufacturing costs tell part of the story, but so do rising advertising costs, which averaged 7.9 percent of selling prices between 1893 and 1900, but 13.2 percent from 1901 to 1910.[26]

Regrettably, it is impossible to measure the quantitative importance of these two counterposed forces. Either side of the debate can muster a plausible case. Certainly the consumer of 1920 was offered a far wider array of branded, packaged, and nationally advertised goods than could have been bought a generation earlier. Advertising men delighted in recounting the day of the gentleman who awoke to a Big Ben alarm clock, shaved with a Gillette razor, washed with Ivory Soap, breakfasted on Kellogg's Corn Flakes, and continued through his daily routines depending on advertised brands. The very ubiquity of these consumer goods implies that massively advertised products became affordable for millions of customers. Conventional economics contends that monopoly power results in restricted output and excessive prices in comparison with the competitive norms. Advertising no doubt induced these allocative distortions and permitted some firms to attain profits above a "normal" rate of return. Yet the most cogent critiques of advertising emphasize its squandering of productive resources in selling products that lack intrinsic advantages; advertising has been a fuel, not a fetter, for production.

Nevertheless, advertisers' desires to replace price competition with the "constructive" rivalry of advertising cannot be gainsaid. That they succeeded in profiting from advertising-induced brand loyalty is equally likely. Advertising men vindicated their work by pointing to the successes of mass production and distribution; however, in some industries these successes came without intensive advertising, and in others heavy advertising accompanied rising prices. When consumers compared prices and found themselves paying more for nationally advertised brands than for less publicized substitutes, advertisers replied that they were paying a premium for the advertiser's reliability and quality. Indeed, since consumers did frequently pay that premium, their behavior indicates they at least partially accepted this argument. At the same time, many must have feared that they were paying the bill for their own bamboozlement.

MANUFACTURERS, DISTRIBUTORS, AND NATIONAL ADVERTISING

Advertising was a cost that somehow had to be paid. It might indeed be paid by productivity savings elsewhere for the manufacturer or by lowering the costs of consumer search for information. Buyers might also avoid the burden of manufacturers' advertising outlays if the costs were absorbed in the process of distribution. National advertising may have made goods flow more efficiently through the channels of distribution, as the manufacturers contended; it may also have altered the power relationships in distribution so that retailers and wholesalers had to narrow the gap between what they paid for their products and the prices consumers faced.

As marketing specialists have pointed out, economic analysis of advertising has too often ignored this possibility. Frequently, models assume that distributive institutions are, in themselves, perfectly competitive and virtually "transparent," that they facilitate transactions between consumers and manufacturers without in any way altering those transactions.[27] These judgments would appear ludicrous to the businessmen of America in the Progressive Era. For them, there was a very real political economy of distribution, one that played itself out in myriads of bargains over terms of payment, shelf display, quantity discounts treatment of competitors' products, and advertising allowances, to name a few issues. Strategic decisions—what kinds of channels to use, whether to integrate forward into distribution, whether to establish exclusive franchises or consignment sales plans, and the like—were equally a part of advertisers' omnipresent concerns.

National advertising, then, was more than a method of altering consumer preferences and competing with rival producers. National advertising was an element in a complex of changing distribution patterns and struggles for control in Gilded Age and Progressive Era America. To understand advertising's role in horizontal competition (rivalry among manufacturers of similar products) and its effects on consumer welfare, its place in vertical competition (relations among institutions in the distribution channels) must be explored.

In the decades preceding the growth of giant integrated manufacturing firms, "The manufacturer stood on the merchant's doorstep begging him to buy his product. The merchant then was the King of Commerce, with the manufacturer groveling at his feet."[28] This, the judgment of a national advertiser looking backwards in 1915, was an appraisal many would have shared. In the mid-nineteenth century, the spread of a railroad and telegraph network enabled the skillful merchant wholesaler (one who purchased goods on his own account for resale to retailers) to deploy a sales force and ship his orders more quickly and cheaply than ever before. Specialized wholesalers could offer a full line of dry goods, hardware, groceries, or drugs to their shopkeeper customers and were well suited to evaluate retailers' needs and opportunities. Merchants also served as sources of capital, for both manufacturers and retailers; in an era when long-term capital needs were fairly slender, a prosperous merchant could extend much-needed book credit to reliable suppliers and customers. It is not surprising, all in all, that the great fortunes of antebellum America often came from mercantile sources; it was not until the later years of the century that manufacturing became the route to riches in America.[29]

Several changes curbed the power of the independent wholesaler. The same transportation network that facilitated the success of these distributors was soon used by producers like Gustavus Swift and John D. Rockefeller. Retained earnings and an increasingly rationalized capital market made manufacturers less dependent on credit from their distributors. Meanwhile, new methods of capital-intensive production made the wholesalers less able to meet the demands for huge pools of fixed capital investment. The growth of systematic industrial management allowed manufacturers to survey their environments and made them more capable of assuming risks instead of passing them on to merchants.

Paralleling these developments, the emergence of mass retailers, most notably urban department stores, mail-order firms, and, slightly later, chain stores, negated some of the wholesalers' control over retailers. Like the mass manufacturers, large-scale retailers threatened to assume some of the functions of wholesalers and could bargain for more favorable terms on those activities left to the wholesalers.

Prominent among the forces reshaping relations among manufacturers, wholesalers, and retailers was national advertising. When producers made unbranded, unadvertised goods, wholesalers could ignore them, could drive down prices, and could control which items reached the retailers' shelves. Retailers themselves could devote their sale efforts only to products carrying a high margin. Manufacturers' advertising campaigns might remedy this. "Once you create a demand by advertising," wrote an enthusiast in 1897, "you can compel the trade to handle it on your own terms."[30]

Advertising alone, however, was not likely to be sufficient to wrest power from the merchants. Publicity accompanied other investment by manufacturers in marketing facilities and instruments. These outlays ranged from full-scale forward integration into wholesaling and retailing to continued reliance on the merchant wholesaler and independent retailer. In general, national advertisers emphasized control of distribution channels on terms favorable to manufacturing interests rather than the elimination of independent merchants; they did not credit advertising with the ability to perform the services merchants had supplied. In some cases, however, ownership of distribution outlets seemed the proper strategy.

Selling directly to the consumer was not common for heavily advertised products, with the significant but idiosyncratic exception of mail-order advertising. The limiting condition for such products was that consumers had to be willing to buy them without physically inspecting them in advance. A few sizeable businesses thrived on direct-mail sales; these tended to be products whose attributes could be evaluated only after use. For example, the W. Atlee Burpee Seed Company, an early client of N. W. Ayer & Son Advertising Agency, specialized in mail-order sales, and other seed companies followed suit. Other successful users of mail-order advertising included some book publishers, especially those selling self-help material or sets of classic literature, and correspondence schools. In each of these cases, the direct costs of holding inventory were low for the manufacturer, buyers could wait to receive the goods they purchased, and there were no large apparent economies available from having independent intermediaries assume ownership, break bulk, or transport the products.

Those manufacturers who integrated forward into conventional retail stores generally did so cautiously. Several shoe manufacturers owned retail outlets, but most of their production probably went to independent storekeepers. A few clothing manufacturers also acquired stores. The Sherwin-Williams Paint Company, which advertised heavily in both consumer and business markets, established a small number of its own stores in areas where it had trouble persuading independent retailers to stock its paints.[31]

Another category of national advertiser selling directly to the ultimate user included firms that made complex durable goods, most notably agricultural equipment, sewing machines, and cameras. For such products, as we have noted, the need for credit, spare parts, repairs, and customer instruction impelled manufacturers to seek direct contact with buyers. Eastman Kodak, for example, maintained a small retail presence around 1914, with eighteen stores, primarily in the Midwest. These stores, it may be noted, sold other brands along with Eastman Kodak products.

Brewers, from the mid-1880s until Prohibition, often purchased saloons and sold their beer through these outlets. Again, defensive motivations predominated. Most breweries were still fairly small and sold in local or regional markets because of transportation and storage cost barriers. Because a tapped keg of beer was perishable, and since draft equipment was expensive, tavern proprietors could keep only one or two brands on hand. Since bottled beer sales were negligible at the time, saloon keepers' choices of what to serve were all the more crucial to the brewers. Independent tavern owners knew this and could play rival brewers off against each other to obtain substantial price concessions or other advantages, like bar furnishings, glasses, and calendars. Speaking of the Pabst Brewing Company, Thomas C. Cochran concluded, "Pabst's investment in saloons . . . helped to sell beer. But it was an expensive way to do it."[32] Management problems were severe, and the capital invested in retail properties might have been used more profitably elsewhere. On the other hand, direct sales to customers were probably necessary because brewers' advertising alone could not pull the product through independent retailer channels on terms satisfactory to the brewers. Apparently, drinkers chose their taverns without great concern for the brands of beer on tap.

Why were so few manufacturers interested in integrating as far as retailing? As one text put it, "The immediate causes of a manufacturer starting a chain of retail stores may be many, but the majority of them come down, in the end, to dissatisfaction with the methods of distribution." "It is probable," commented another text, "that scarcely any manufacturer desires to conduct his own distributive system if the service obtained from the regular channels is at all satisfactory."[33] Thus, most integration into retailing was defensive. Apart from managerial difficulties in conducting operations as disparate as manufacturing and retailing, we might suggest that advertising itself served as a partial substitute for vertical integration into retailing. If customer demand could make a dealer stock an item, and if manufacturer pressure could make him sell it expeditiously and efficiently, why duplicate effort by investing in a manufacturer-owned retail network? If an advertiser could achieve that degree of dealer control through his advertising to consumers, integration into retailing was unlikely to offer further advantages. The gains that usually accrued to vertical integration—superior coordination of material flow, reduction of transactions costs, and closer

surveillance of distributors—were more often than not outweighed by the difficulties of applying manufacturers' managerial, technical, and financial resources in the quite different
field of retailing.

An example of the perils of vertical integration can be
found in the experience of Rogers, Thompson, Givernaud,
manufacturers of R&T Silks. With some fanfare the firm
proclaimed in January 1912 that it was launching a retail silk
store in New York. In the previous year, the company had
acquired new mills and was for the first time "able to cover
every department of the broad silk field." Its store was to be
a prototype of manufacturer-owned silk retailers, offering
"large lines of representative silks . . . instead of the inadequate and unsatisfactory stocks now carried by retailers." By
late that summer, Rogers, Thompson, Givernaud had
thrown in their handkerchiefs. They couched the announcement of the store's closing in positive terms: the venture,
they claimed, had only been intended as a short-term publicity gesture. *Printers' Ink* contended that the store had in fact
failed, at least partially due to the implacable opposition of
other retailers. The plan's collapse, *Printers' Ink* implied,
would serve as a cautionary tale for other manufacturers contemplating their own chain stores.[34]

There are other morals to draw from the story. First, Rogers, Thompson, Givernaud intensely desired to alter the
terms of business between manufacturer and distributor. In
the silk industry, wholesale and retail margins were wide,
and producers, already faced with strong competition from
other manufacturers, found merchants dilatory about ordering. Merchants, in turn, were reluctant to commit themselves until consumers had indicated their fashion preferences. "This," noted *Printers' Ink,* "leaves the manufacturer
holding the bag."[35] Second, unsatisfactory though the traditional channels were, preempting them, in this and many

other cases, was no easy task. Although R&T Silks were branded and advertised and the store's opening was vigorously publicized, the firm's attempt at vertical integration proved unfeasible. In the presence of low capital barriers to entry, uncertain brand preferences, and shifting tastes in fashion, neither advertising nor vertical integration was likely to succeed.

Although integration into retailing was rare, several kinds of national advertisers assumed part or all of the wholesaling function. Forward integration by manufacturers and backward integration by mass retailers threatened the wholesalers' raison d'être. "The middleman is on the defensive; he is having a severer struggle for existence than the men either side of him," commented the New York *Journal of Commerce* in 1899. Perhaps overestimating the extent of vertical integration, Paul Cherington's popular text on advertising concluded, "And thus the jobber's business is not only whittled away at its most profitable end by direct dealing, but such as is left for him is also taken out of his control to a greater or lesser degree."[36]

Manufacturers took over part or all of the wholesalers' role when necessity or opportunity dictated. Selling new kinds of consumer goods through traditional marketing channels often proved difficult if not impossible. This impelled firms like Eastman Kodak, Gillette, and the National Biscuit Company to integrate forward. One witness at the United States Industrial Commission's hearings in 1900 reported that the National Biscuit Company bought the wagons of bakery salesmen who had formerly owned their own wagons and sold on commission; these men became salaried company employees.[37] Other firms with perishable products or items that required after-sales service or credit found existing channels inadequate as well. Except for very large firms, however, when the product itself was relatively inexpensive and sold in small quantities to individual users through many stores, the expense of maintaining a full-scale wholesaling operation was usually prohibitive. Only National Biscuit's enormous volume allowed it to send its wagons and trucks to the many thousands of grocers who stocked their crackers.[38]

As in the case of mail-order sales, assuming the jobber's role was sometimes also possible when a manufacturer's products were small in size relative to price, where physical distribution costs were low, and where retailers were willing to carry a substantial inventory of the products. Thus, for example, nationally advertised branded products like Parker Pens, Cluett Peabody collars, and Big Ben clocks often flowed from the manufacturers to the retailers' shelves. Even here, such a strategy made sense only when the firm was an industry leader with fairly high sales volume. Otherwise, the cost of acquiring a large sales force (as Parker did) or establishing warehouses around the nation (as Cluett Peabody did) would be prohibitive.[39]

In many other instances where firms sold some of their output direct to retailers, their motives were defensive and opportunistic. Pacific Coast Borax, for example, marketed almost all of its output through jobbers and considered them necessary for effective distribution; the firm's spokesman complained bitterly of the competition of mass retailers' private brands. Yet, he conceded, the firm did sell a small amount of its output to Sears, Roebuck for private label sales. Parke Davis, a drug manufacturer, also endorsed and employed the conventional wholesaler channel but admitted that it sold directly to large retailers who had the bargaining power to extract the wholesaler's price.[40]

In short, then, although national advertisers sought to control the distribution of their products, they generally preferred to exercise this control over administratively independent merchants; vertical integration was not a common strategy. The limited data indicate only a moderate decline in wholesaling's role. In 1879, and again in 1889, wholesalers handled about 70 percent of the nation's commodity output. The figure declined slightly during each ten-year interval thereafter, reaching 63 percent in 1919 and 60 percent in 1929. Value added by wholesalers as a percentage of retail value of commodities dropped from 9.6 percent in 1879 and 1889 to 8.5 percent in 1919 and 8.1 percent in 1929.[41] Since the census data on which these estimates are based count manufacturers' sales branches as wholesale facilities, the figures may overstate the persistence of wholesaling in these decades. Nevertheless, they belie the more apocalyptic predictions of those who forecast the eradication of the wholesaler.

By 1929, statistics are available for a rudimentary test of the relationship between manufacturers' advertising and vertical integration into distribution. Records of national advertising in thirty of the largest magazines in that year stand as a proxy for national advertising in general, since these magazines were still the single largest medium for national advertising. These thirty magazines reaped more than half of the total expenditures estimated by *National Advertising Records* for magazines. The 1929 *Census of Distribution* offers data on the distribution channels of manufacturing industries.[42] Matching the classifications used in compiling the advertising data with the census categories was not at all perfect, but it proved possible for thirty-four industries, ranging from automobiles and furniture to soft drinks and canned foods. Regressing the percentage of total sales that went to independent wholesalers (W) on the ratio of advertising to sales (A) showed that advertising intensity had a slightly positive relationship with wholesalers' share. However, the amount of variance in wholesalers' share explained by advertising is very low ($r^2 = .02$). The regression equation is

Advertising's Effects on Industry

$$W = 0.46 + 1.82A$$

$$W_i = \frac{\text{Sales of manufacturing industry } i \text{ to wholesalers}}{\text{Total distributed sales of industry } i - \text{Sales to large industrial users}}$$

In other words, by 1929, it appears that if there was any relationship at all, the national advertisers of brand-named goods tended to use independent wholesalers slightly more than firms in industries where national advertising was less prevalent.

What did advertisers hope to gain by controlling the channels of distribution? In the first place, they wanted to ensure that their distributors would sell *their* products and not substitute other manufacturers' brands or distributor-owned private label goods. This "substitution evil" was the bane of national advertisers, but advertising might also prove to be its cure. A loyal consumer might be the best defense against the substituting wiles of an artful retailer.

The problem of substitution first arose in patent medicines. Since the costs of manufacturing these drugs were low relative to their selling prices, druggists were severely tempted to concoct and sell their own remedies as substitutes for nationally advertised brands. The quasi-professional status of druggists may have helped them influence customers to buy their own medicines instead of the advertised ones. The drug manufacturers' Proprietary Medicine Manufacturers and Dealers Association had encountered the problem of retailer substitution since its founding in 1881, but controversy flared in the 1890s. Retailers claimed angrily that any substitution was defensive. They asserted that the manufacturers first shaved margins to the bone and then sold to large department stores and grocers who cut prices. Unable to match these cuts, the traditional pharmacist was, therefore, forced to substitute private brands. The growth of chain drug stores in the early twentieth century—there was one chain in 1896, but twenty-four a decade later—exacerbated the problem.[43]

In the 1890s as well, other national advertisers openly worried about dealer substitution. Its victims were, most notably, the very firms that had invested most heavily in creating brand loyalty through national advertising campaigns. The National Biscuit Company and Coca-Cola, for example, found themselves continually battling imitative private brands that infringed on their trademarks. Procter & Gamble found that storekeepers might sell other soaps as substitutes for Ivory, and Van Camp Pork and Beans was also menaced by dealer substitution. *Printers' Ink* and other advertising publications, by the early twentieth century, were campaigning vigorously against those who vitiated the impact of national advertising by substitution. They encouraged advertisers to scare consumers with tales of dangerous imitations of reliable branded products. *Printers' Ink* insisted that "part of the duty of the daily paper is to help suppress substitutors," and advised papers to run editorials each month denouncing the substituting scoundrels.[44]

In large measure, of course, substitution was a fraud and its suppression a step toward honest dealings with consumers. Manufacturers could legitimately complain that the retailer who deceived the customer with a look-alike product, package, or trademark, when the buyer had demanded a particular brand, was dishonest. Things were somewhat different, however, when the dealer offered a customer a private brand or a rival's brand and tried to persuade the buyer that it was a superior value. In this case, the campaign against substitution constituted an assertion that the manufacturer, not the retailer, had the right to mold consumer choices.

The nature of the substitution problem facing national advertisers shifted in the early twentieth century. Initially, substitutors had usually been portrayed as small retailers unwilling to accept the narrow margins offered on advertised products; the retailers therefore palmed off imitations or convinced customers that substitutes were just as good as the genuine article. However, during the Progressive Era, advertising men began to urge advertisers to treat such miscreants with sympathy; threats to substituting retailers might be destructive. In 1912, *Printers' Ink* noted, "The subject of substitution is one which wise manufacturers refuse to regard too seriously." The editors warned against destroying the loyalty of small retailers just to win a few extra sales. In opposing a legislative proposal to outlaw dealers' private brands, *Printers' Ink* confessed that campaigns in the 1890s against substitution had backfired, creating dealer resentment. Substitution was still disturbing, but it was "a problem for the *individual* manufacturer, rather than one which can be handled cooperatively." *Advertising and Selling,* another influential trade publication, counseled national advertisers to become more aware of the retailers' point of view. "Substitution will exist as long as the retail merchant desires to substitute—the only way to eliminate it is to eliminate the desire."[45]

What did incense advertising men was the kind of substitution that amounted to "an organized assault on advertised goods." For example, the American Druggists' Syndicate, a group of large wholesalers, manufactured and sold over-the-counter drugs to retailers at prices far below brand-named equivalents. Retailers, therefore, were eager to turn their customers to the Syndicate's products. This newer substitution peril rekindled rivalry for national advertisers from certain large jobbers and mass retailers. Large department stores often shunned advertised brands, used nationally advertised products as loss leaders, and sought to persuade customers to buy the store's private brands. For instance, although John Wanamaker in Philadelphia and J. L. Hudson's in Detroit were inclined to promote national brands, New York's Macy's and Chicago's Marshall Field were hostile to advertised products. Chain store retailers also failed to support nationally advertised items. When George Hartford of the Great Atlantic and Pacific Tea Company died in 1917, *Printers' Ink* commented that only in the most recent years had the A&P become willing to carry advertised products. Ad men also criticized mail-order houses. When a Rutland, Vermont, newspaper undertook a publicity campaign supporting local merchants in their struggles against the catalogue houses, *Printers' Ink* took enthusiastic notice. Similarly, small-town merchants gained sympathy from some advertising men when they fought a losing battle against the introduction of parcel post. *Advertising and Selling* pointed out that local retailer boosterism was welcome to manufacturers of advertised brands who saw Sears, Montgomery Ward, and other mail-order firms as their foes. Advertising men, who had once defined substitution as deception and palming off by smaller merchants, now focused their complaints on the activities of mass merchandisers who systematically played down national brands.[46]

Faced with common opponents, national advertisers and smaller, more traditional merchants were allied by necessity and convenience. The advertisers frequently professed a desire to cooperate with these dealers, but it was quite clear that the manufacturers were to be the dominant partners. According to a 1905 article, "The manufacturer selling an advertised trademarked article is absolutely independent. The only class to whom he is responsible is the consumer." A few years later, the Curtis Publishing Company spelled out the new balance of power between manufacturer and wholesaler: "We do not believe the jobber will ever be eliminated. . . . [But] it is for you to dictate to your jobbers by securing a constant demand for your goods."[47]

Advertising's Effects on Industry

Despite the imperious tone of such pronouncements, smaller merchants did prefer advertised brands. A study of retailers in Nebraska found that the larger the retailer's store and the larger the town he was in, the less favorable was his opinion of advertised products. Smaller, more rural store-keepers liked the advertised brands more. In Paul T. Cherington's words, "National advertising . . . is taking its place as a means of equalizing competitive conditions between the large and small retailer."[48]

If the independent merchant and the national advertiser were bound together, it behooved the advertiser to make the distributor handle his products more effectively. As we have noted, cooperation was the watchword—cooperation with the advertisers in the lead. By about 1910, naive early hopes of forcing distribution through advertising alone had subsided. "The day is rapidly departing when the retailer can be forced against his will to cooperate. . . . The retailer is part of the manufacturer's system. He must be strengthened; he must be educated," exhorted *Printers' Ink* in 1911. Wholesalers merited similar attention. "Manufacturers," stated one commentator, "will bend all their energies to remedy the backwardness of the jobber in rendering full cooperation."[49]

In practice, there were several facets to dealer cooperation with national advertisers. From the standpoint of the manufacturer, the advertising itself simplified the work of the merchants. "The retailer's service in the case of nationally advertised goods . . . becomes primarily a delivery service and not a selling service." Even in this diminished role, incompetent or recalcitrant sellers harmed advertisers, and assistance to retailers was needed. Promotional aids for dealers became a burgeoning field for advertisers. In-store displays, window-dressing service, signs, calendars, novelty premiums, and the like were offered to retailers. These aids were designed to speed merchants' turnover, help them offer customer service, and tie their personal selling to manufacturers' advertising. Similar objectives spurred the growth of company magazines, house organs that circulated to manufacturers' salesmen and to their customers. In-store demonstrators who exhibited products to local customers, preferably with attendant publicity and follow-up sales effort, constituted another dealer help. So-called "PMs" (probably an abbreviation for "push money") were payments to induce retail salespeople to stress a brand. Finally, what marketing experts term vertical cooperative advertising was beginning. This entailed manufacturer's allowances to retailers for local advertising featuring the maker's products. Although cooperative campaigns did not flourish until after World War I, there are references to such undertakings as early as 1869. A 1931 study found examples in campaigns for corsets and for automobiles dating from about 1902. By the early 1920s, a tenth of the national advertisers answering one poll paid the entire cost of newspaper space for dealers' ads that featured their goods; another 22 percent offered partial payment.[50]

The Associated Advertising Clubs and the local groups that composed it also worked to make the shopkeeper a better handler of advertised merchandise. In 1913, *Printers' Ink* recommended that advertising clubs poll local retailers on the cause of dissatisfaction with current conditions. In 1916, at a convention whose themes included "dealer efficiency," the Associated Clubs instructed a committee to devise and publicize an accounting system that would enable retailers to measure the value of advertising.[51]

The path toward dealer cooperation was not always smooth. Retailers were often less than grateful for the flood of in-store selling material they received. Complaining merchants tossed away useless displays, unreadable house organs, and other worthless material the manufacturers sent them. A survey in 1912 found that a majority of retailers considered dealer helps valuable, but fewer than half of them were willing to say they were worth the expense. Only six of about sixty respondents were pleased enough to say that all the assistance they received was useful. Significantly, a majority of the merchants would have preferred to see increased spending on consumer advertising instead of the house organs they were sent. Advertising men kept warning manufacturers that dealer helps were supposed to assist storekeepers as well as producers, and that they were to be supplied only on request. The frequency of these admonitions may indicate the limited effectiveness of manufacturers' gestures of cooperation.[52]

Eventually, even advertising allowances for dealers may have undercut the national advertisers' general strategy of supporting smaller, independent merchants. These payments turned into boons for mass retailers. Chains, especially in groceries and drugs, demanded allowances, which they then used to compensate themselves for price cutting or to cover nebulous "merchandising services." A 1931 study found that department stores showed a high correlation between sales volume and the amount of advertising support they received from manufacturers. Indeed, the belief that uncontrolled advertising allowances constituted a disguised form of price concessions for large retailers brought about sharp limitations on cooperative campaigns in the 1936 Robinson-Patman Act. Thus, the emphasis on dealer cooperation in advertising, initially part of a strategy allying national advertisers with traditional distribution channels may, in fact, have weakened the older outlets.[53]

The nub of the problem facing national advertisers who wanted their advertising to expand distribution and control channels was that distributor margins on advertised brands were consistently lower than on unadvertised items. Advertising might stimulate buyer interest, speed merchants' stock turnover, and reduce their selling expenses to compensate for these lower margins, but storekeepers did not always see things that way. As one speaker at the 1916 Associated Advertising Clubs convention observed, most retailers looked at margins, not promises of dealer cooperation or national advertising, when they decided which brands to carry. Even some of the largest national advertisers found this out the hard way. When Procter & Gamble launched Crisco Shortening with extensive publicity, free samples for the dealers, and prepared advertising copy for local campaigns, it met a disappointing response. Only when Procter & Gamble lowered its price to retailers to allow them a 20 percent margin did the brand achieve widespread distribution.[54]

In sum, the task of the national advertiser in the Progressive Era was twofold. He had to persuade consumers to buy his brand at the same time he convinced dealers that they could profit by stocking it. These dual ambitions were not easily realized, and advertisers were sometimes tempted to invest in their own selling outlets to rid themselves of the need to cajole and pressure dealers. Yet, as we have seen, this vertical integration itself was laden with difficulties that made most manufacturers draw back.

Seeking maximum control without excessive investments in marketing, many national advertisers turned to resale price maintenance. By fixing the price at which wholesalers and retailers sold their brands, national advertisers hoped to get their products on as many dealers' shelves as possible, induce storekeepers to offer customer services, combat price-cutting mass merchants, and associate their products with a set, stable price. In the second decade of this century, as the Supreme Court curtailed the legal basis of resale price maintenance, legislation for its reinstatement became a major focus of struggles over the control of distribution. Although subsequent observers have tended to neglect the importance

of advertising in these controversies, the movement for resale price maintenance in the Progressive Era relied heavily
on national advertisers. The cause (dubbed fair trade by its
supporters and price fixing by its foes) was fraught with social and ideological overtones; the intensity of advertising
men's concern with resale price maintenance suggests its importance. At first, one may wonder why a manufacturer
would care how much a distributor asked for goods which
had passed from the manufacturer's legal and physical pos-
session. Indeed, a manufacturer of an undifferentiated, unbranded commodity would have no reason to care about
price maintenance. Economist Lester Telser calls the interest of manufacturers in legalized price maintenance a "long-
standing puzzle to economists." In the words of a 1919 study
of resale price maintenance, "The problem of price maintenance is directly connected with the marketing of only
branded or trademarked goods." [55]

National advertisers usually advocated resale price maintenance because they feared the countervailing power of price
cutting mass retailers and wanted to offer some protection to
the traditional distribution outlets they employed. If mass retailers, playing upon the reputation a brand had acquired
through national advertising, cut prices sharply on Kellogg's
Corn Flakes or Eastman Kodak film or Ingersoll Watches,
bargain-conscious shoppers would flock to these stores.
Smaller retailers, lacking the ability to absorb short-run losses
and perhaps less efficient than their chain and department
store rivals, would not be able to match the cut prices. They
would feel pressure to substitute private brands or rival labels
rather than sell a national brand at a loss; eventually, the
smaller retailer might shun entirely the brand whose price
had been cut. In exchange for a brief flurry of purchases, the
manufacturer might lose his most trustworthy outlets and
find his trade in the hands of powerful and aggressive mass

merchandisers. Even if these firms were not able to extract a share of the producer's margin, a brand might be harmed by losing shelf space in the smaller and weaker stores. The mass marketers, too, would drop a brand after it had served them as a loss leader. Eventually, a brand might even perish for want of resale price maintenance. That this scene was seldom played out to its conclusion mattered little to the most earnest supporters of price maintenance. For men like the advertising manager of Kellogg's Corn Flakes, a great deal was at stake. "The thing really on trial in this controversy," he wrote in 1913, "is the recognition of advertising as a legitimate and economical selling force and of a trademark or brand as a tangible, valuable and protectable property."[56]

The burst of advertiser interest in price maintenance in the second decade of the twentieth century represents a reaction to a series of court rulings that severely limited manufacturers' methods of setting resale prices. In 1906, a Circuit Court ruled invalid a pact among drug makers, jobbers, and retailer druggists which had set forth an elaborate system of surveillance to stop price cutting. In 1911, the Supreme Court upheld a decision in *Dr. Miles Medical Co* v. *Park and Sons,* which found that contracts requiring purchasers to resell at prices established by manufacturers were unlawful restraints of trade. In the 1913 case of *Bauer* v. *O'Donnell* (referred to as the Sanatogen case, after the medicine involved), manufacturers were denied the right to set resale prices even on patented goods. Despite occasional court victories in the next few years, legal limitations on price maintenance were further tightened. By 1919, one scholar commented, "Seemingly, no dependable price-maintenance weapon is left in the hands of the manufacturers."[57]

After the Sanatogen decision, *Printers' Ink* asserted that the ruling would not stop manufacturers from advertising their brands. Meanwhile, however, they heeded the threats of the mass retailers and other price cutting merchants. "The time is close at hand," crowed a department store executive in 1914, "when there will be no manufacturers' brands, but the public will walk into our stores, look over the stock and choose goods on their merits as they appear to them. There will be no national advertising to bias their judgment. We ourselves—the retail trade—will do all the advertising."[58]

The editors of *Printers' Ink* proved nearer the mark than the apocalyptic merchant. National advertising, of course, continued to thrive despite the limits on price maintenance and the other triumphs of mass retailers. Yet the advertisers, along with established retailers, were frightened. In 1913, the United States Bureau of Corporations began an extensive investigation of resale price maintenance; in the next two years, agents queried representatives of over one hundred manufacturers, as well as a sample of jobbers and retailers. The interviews reveal the alarm of many national advertisers about the demise of resale price maintenance. George Eastman, for example, told the Bureau that, before the Sanatogen decision, "We never had very much difficulty with cut price retail dealers." The verdict, however, had left him "strongly in favor" of federal legislation to restore price maintenance. The Gillette Razor Company, also endorsing legislative remedies, noted that "cut prices are destructive for all concerned." The president of the Parker Pen Company greeted the Bureau's agent with the opinion that its investigation was "a ripping good proposition" and that price maintenance was "very vital to the successful existence of our company." Eaton, Crane, and Pike, the stationery manufacturer, complained that price cutting had "ruined our market" in some cities, threatened the "legitimate stationer" everywhere.[59]

Some manufacturers suggested that a clear legal recognition of the "right to refuse to sell [to price cutters] is all the protection a manufacturer needs." Yet others feared that discounters would go to extreme lengths to get a supply of price-maintained brands for loss leaders. "Jew brokers [*sic*] and large commission men in New York City made a regular practice for a time of going around among small retail dealers picking up goods for price cutters like Riker-Hegeman [a drug store chain]," according to the Dr. Miles company. One Chicago-based chain of photographic supply stores even boasted to the Bureau of Corporations investigator that it could obtain Kodaks "in a roundabout way," and that it had "the only stores in the world that have successfully and continually cut the prices on Eastman Kodaks . . ." Even where refusal to sell to price cutters was an adequate protection for advertisers, this method of controlling resale channels was soon to become legally risky. In 1915, the Cream of Wheat Company won a case where it had been sued for refusing to sell to A&P because the chain had cut prices, but comparable cases continued to be pressed against other national advertisers. Finally, in 1922, the Federal Trade Commission claimed that the Beech-Nut Packing Company had scouted out cut-price dealers for punishment so assiduously that it was an unfair method of competition. The Supreme Court upheld the FTC's ruling, and the producers' last line of defense had been breached.[60]

Few of the executives whom the Bureau interviewed trusted advertising by itself to counteract mass retailer price cutting. One manufacturer of branded hosiery did state that heavy advertising of his suggested retail prices adequately fended off discounters. However, other manufacturers admitted that they feared publicizing retail prices in their advertising copy because doing so would only encourage cutting by making bargains more evident to buyers. A small number saw consignment selling or an agency system as potential relief; systems in which manufacturers maintained title to their goods until final sale were legally permissible. The spokesman for Dr. Miles Medical Company asserted that "because we force the demand [through advertising]" the company could use a consignment system: "If our product was a staple, and less advertised, we would not be in such a strong position."[61] Nevertheless, consignment selling had many of the major drawbacks of full-scale vertical integration into distribution; it tied up capital, raising fixed costs of distribution, and demanded more managerial talent to move the goods through the channels. It was rarely an attractive alternative.

Of those manufacturers who opposed resale price maintenance or were indifferent to it, many were making producers' goods or unbranded consumer staples. Some apparel makers, where national advertising and brand identification were generally slight, found price maintenance untenable: "We couldn't adopt the resale price system, I don't believe, if we wanted to." A stove manufacturer who personally favored price maintenance legislation, nevertheless said that stove makers "will not be deeply interested" in the subject. A casket maker and a producer of industrial borax expressed the same opinion. A few national advertisers also had qualms about price maintenance legislation. The spokesman for Van Camp, a prominent canner, contended that resale price maintenance was unnecessary and led to monopoly; for his firm, price cutting was not a problem. Despite the fact that Van Camp was a major national advertiser itself, the executive contended that "not even in the majority" of instances were nationally advertised goods of superior quality. The Cudahy Packing Company, which extensively promoted Old Dutch Cleanser, nevertheless opposed legislation for price maintenance. It was not concerned with the price consumers paid and had encountered no serious difficulties with wholesalers' price cutting.[62]

Despite objections and uncertainty about price maintenance legislation, the Bureau of Corporations reports show that a clear majority of manufacturers surveyed advocated some form of price fixing. Collectively, national advertisers took the lead in pressuring for action. The catch-all business group working for price maintenance legislation was the American Fair Trade League, formed in June 1913. Majority control of the organization resided with those who paid dues of $100 annually to become general members. These were virtually all manufacturers of branded, advertised items. The Fair Trade League's statement of objectives underscored the connection between the price maintenance issue and national advertising. It aimed to "promote honesty in manufacturing, in advertising and in merchandising . . ." and to pass legislation to "(a) prohibit and penalize unfair competition; (b) prohibit and penalize dishonest advertising; (c) prevent the elimination of the smaller businessman by unfair methods."[63]

Just as fair trade advocates linked their cause to advertising, the advertising industry offered support for price maintenance legislation. In 1912, the Associated Advertising Clubs of America passed a convention resolution opposing a bill that would have curtailed price maintenance activity on the grounds that the law would harm small retailers as well as advertising manufacturers. The next year, the Associated Clubs called for "such legislation as will promote standard prices for standard brands."[64] Other advertising groups expressed the same opinion.

Supporters of resale price maintenance were not eager to have the dominant role of national advertisers publicized. The American Fair Trade League's Secretary, Edwin B. Whittier, told supporters in January 1915, "Up to this time we have succeeded in keeping the manufacturers' interest submerged and that the elements were the small independent retailers." That June, addressing the League's annual meeting, he announced: "We have been able to carry it so far as a retailers' fight and you won't hear in Washington a suggestion that this is a manufacturers' fight. The retailers have been in evidence and they are doing the obvious work, the work that is on the surface."[65] Indeed, the effort to camouflage national advertisers' interests was successful enough to persuade Louis Brandeis, a founder of the Fair Trade League and an ardent supporter of price maintenance, that industrial plutocrats opposed the cause and used price cutting to build monopoly power. Brandeis's position on fair trade must be seen as part of his willingness to favor the survival of independent competitors in business life even at the expense of the competitive process itself. Cushioning small shopkeepers against the pressures of mass distributors delivered them into greater dependency on mass producers.

Of course many retailers wanted to make that bargain. Surveys of retail tobacconists and hardware dealers, for example, indicated overwhelming support for price maintenance. It might also be added that where manufacturers were weaker, a legal price maintenance contract seemed to offer an opening for a retailers' cartel which would maintain their prices by suppressing competition. Wholesalers, except for those who made or controlled their own private labels, also tended to support resale price maintenance; their fate, too, was tied to preserving the traditional channels of distribution.[66]

On balance, businesses in the Progressive Era probably favored reestablishing resale price maintenance. The U.S. Chamber of Commerce conducted a referendum in 1915–16 among its member organizations on the proposition: "There should be federal legislation permitting the maintenance of resale prices under proper restrictions, on identified merchandise for voluntary purchase, made and sold under competitive conditions." The measure passed by a margin of nearly three to one. (A companion proposition concerning implementing price maintenance through the Federal Trade Commission barely failed to gain the two-thirds majority needed to make it official Chamber of Commerce policy.) About a decade later, a similar alignment was evident in a Federal Trade Commission report; close to three quarters of all manufacturers answering its survey advocated price maintenance. Among merchants, 93.6 percent of the wholesalers and 84.4 percent of the retailers endorsed it. A companion study indicated that manufacturers advocating fair trade were larger, more profitable, and heavier advertisers than their opponents. Conversely, among retailers, smaller and less profitable merchants backed price maintenance while larger dry goods, department, and chain stores were most often found in the opposition.[67]

Legislation permitting manufacturers to control resale prices was first introduced in Congress by Representative R. B. Stevens of New Hampshire in 1914. An almost identical measure, the Stephens-Ashurst Bill, was the chosen vehicle of price maintenance advocates during the next Congress. Both proposals attempted to hitch themselves onto the cause of truth in advertising. The Stevens Bill was entitled, "To Prevent Discrimination in Prices and to Provide for Publicity of Prices to Dealers and the Public." Even more explicitly, the Stephens-Ashurst Bill called itself a measure "To Protect the Public Against Dishonest Advertising and False Pretenses in Merchandising." Hearings in 1915, 1916, and 1917 before the House Committee on Interstate and Foreign Commerce featured supporting testimony from independent retailer organizations, consumer spokeswomen, and academic experts on marketing, while national manufacturers for the most part stayed in the background. It was more seemly for proponents of price maintenance to stress the injuries price cutting allegedly brought upon local merchants and consumers.

Counterattacks on price maintenance legislation were led by department store and dry goods interests. Statements from spokesmen for Macy's, J. L. Hudson's, Jordan Marsh, Filene's, and Marshall Field depicted price maintenance proposals as hostile to competition and unfair to bargain-conscious consumers. One foe of price maintenance even offered a bit of doggerel:

> The Stephens bill
> Is a poison pill
>   Coated with sugary language.
>
> Its words seem fair
> But when they're laid bare
>   They reek with monopoly's cunning.
>
> *   *   *   *   *
>
> It's a trust lawyer's fake
> Planned only to make
>   Millions pay toll to a few.
>
> Prices they'd fix
> Through legalized tricks
>   To bleed and oppress the poor.[68]

Congressmen, too, seemed less than sympathetic to the pleas of price maintenance supporters. Alben Barkley (Democrat-Kentucky) summed up one line of objection in a dialogue with Paul Nystrom, a marketing researcher who was an advisor to the American Fair Trade League. "This bill," Barkley stated, "makes the merchant an errand boy. He cannot do anything except by permission of the manufacturer. He is simply the agent of the manufacturer to do what the manufacturer tells him to do, and then can only sell it according to the terms the manufacturer provides."[69]

Ultimately, sentiments like these doomed the crusade of the fair traders until the era of the Great Depression. It was quite difficult, if not impossible, to persuade consumers that merchants needed to be protected by law from offering them lower prices. "Popular sympathy is with the price cutters," noted *The New York Times* in 1913, shortly after the Sanatogen decision. Paul T. Cherington, an instructor at Harvard Business School and supporter of price maintenance, admitted that consumer prices were "the one argument which still resists the logic and the skill of the fixed-price advocates... Whether this position of the consumer be sound or not, it is surprisingly general." Although we have no quantitative data on public opinion during this period, a poll of nearly two thousand consumers conducted by the Federal Trade Commission in 1928 found nearly three-quarters opposed to price maintenance legislation.[70] Combined with the very real antipathy of mass retailers and some newspaper publishers who relied heavily on department store advertising, consumer resistance was an insuperable obstacle to fair trade legislation, and the bills died in committee.

It appears that national advertisers' ardor for price maintenance was fading by the time the nation entered World War I. As early as 1916, *Printers' Ink* was warning its readers that the times were inopportune for pressure: "Any public agitation in favor of the bill just now will... inevitably react against price maintenance." Perhaps because of preoccupation with the war, perhaps because shortages and rapid price inflation limited the power of mass merchandisers to cut prices and substitute private brands, price maintenance was less prominent in the pages of advertising periodicals in the next few years. By the 1920s, many national advertisers seemed to lose interest in the issue. When demands for fair trade legislation grew more insistent in the 1930s, "Retailers and wholesalers [had] displaced manufacturers as active sponsors." The Miller-Tydings Act of 1937 exempted state resale price maintenance laws from federal antitrust action, but this measure owed more to the desperate plight of small retailers in hard times than to the pressures of large-scale national advertisers.[71]

What accounts for this waning interest of manufacturers in price maintenance? Lester Telser suggests that "resale price maintenance substitutes to some extent for impersonal national advertising," and he hypothesizes that the opening of new advertising media in the 1920s diminished manufacturers' need for "fair trade" legislation. Though this is an intriguing conjecture, Telser fails to account for the close attachment between national advertisers and the resale price maintenance movement in the Progressive Era. Advertising men in those years viewed advertising and price maintenance as complements, not substitutes. A more likely explanation for manufacturers' diminished enthusiasm is that some of them realized the futility of opposing the growth of mass marketing institutions. In contrast with the stagnant volume of wholesaler sales during the 1920s, grocery chain stores quadrupled their sales and apparel chains quintupled theirs. It is not surprising that national advertisers tried to make their peace with the rising mass distribution organizations and accepted the inevitability of coming to terms with them. On the other side, mass merchandisers may have increasingly realized, as *Printers' Ink* predicted in 1915, that it was "impolitic to substitute aggressively and unprofitable to substitute diplomatically . . ." and that too aggressive price cutting was dangerous. The concept of the "wheel of retailing" in which retail channels are likely to begin as aggressive price competitors and evolve toward an emphasis on service and standard brands may also explain the rapprochement between national advertisers and mass marketers. The Progressive Era alliance of national advertisers and traditional marketing institutions was indeed an affair of the purse, not of the heart, and as conditions changed the enthusiasm cooled.[72]

The failure of the movement for resale price maintenance in the Progressive Era indicates the limitations of national advertising as a strategy of marketing channel control. Alone, it was not sufficient to prevent distributors from cutting prices, substituting rival products, or even refusing to carry certain brands. Moreover, national advertisers and their allies lacked the political muscle to reinstate legalized price maintenance or otherwise seriously obstruct the growth of mass merchandisers. Should we then conclude that, in its vertical dimension—its impact on the channels of distribution and their control—national advertising lacked real power? Those who maintain that advertising is inherently informative and procompetitive might adopt this view. So, paradoxically, might a disciple of John Kenneth Galbraith, who has emphasized the countervailing power of large-scale distributors in checking the power of big manufacturing firms in concentrated industries.

From the standpoint of the consumer, the matter is quite important. If the market power of national advertisers is curbed by the buying power of mass retailers, the consumer may benefit from this stand-off. This is the situation which Robert Steiner has recently labeled the "mixed regimen." Here, national advertisers' appeals to consumers keep distributors' margins low, but merchants can also threaten retaliation with private brands or other competition and thus effectively prevent the manufacturers from taking too great a mark-up over costs. If not the best of all possible worlds, Steiner's mixed regimen appears to offer reasonably low prices through a distribution system that is both efficient and competitive. Where this stalemate does not emerge, however, Steiner suggests manufacturers' brand domination is a likely outcome. Here, advertising differentiates a product and creates entry barriers horizontally, but "increases in advertising outlays have lost most of the power further to narrow the brand's gross margin, improve its market penetration level, or shift out its consumer demand curve by raising per capita consumption."[73] In this scenario, the anticompetitive effects of product differentiation among brands outweigh any price reducing impacts of improving dealer competitiveness or efficiency. Steiner suggests that the "mixed regimen" is typical of many consumer goods industries today, and that advertising is often actually able to lower prices to consumers even while it raises them to retailers.

To those less sanguine about the coexistence of heavy consumer advertising and genuine consumer benefits, Steiner's conclusions may be too optimistic. For him, manufacturer's advertising makes the demand curves facing individual retailers more elastic, because brand-name promotion makes consumers aware that standardized products are widely available under roughly equivalent conditions. This increased consumer price sensitivity makes retailers cut their margins on heavily advertised items because they cannot get away with charging more than other stores for the same brands. This would account for the fact that retailers do feature many intensively advertised brands as sale items. If these forces, however, are outweighed by advertising's power to differentiate products and build brand loyalty, then the consumer demand curve may become less, not more, elastic. In this case, consumer prices may rise and remain high while manufacturers and retailers contend for the lion's share of the monopoly profits. This struggle would take place on terms increasingly favorable to the national advertiser. In other words, if shrinking distributor margins are merely transferred to the manufacturer, they will be of little value to the consumer.

It is also notable that Steiner's "mixed regimen" depends on effective intrabrand price competition at the retail level. National advertisers, as we have seen, frequently sought to mute this competition or to transform it into nonprice rivalry. Resale price maintenance was one device for this, as were consignment sales arrangements and exclusive territorial franchises for dealers. The provision of dealer aids and cooperative advertising allowances were also efforts to dissuade dealers from competing by cutting prices. That these measures sometimes failed in the marketplace and in the courts does not negate their significance.

CONCLUSIONS

To offer a provisional summary of national advertising's effects on consumer welfare in the Progressive Era, we must begin by making a distinction. In some instances, advertising campaigns helped manufacturers take their products through a strategic passageway. Cameras, breakfast cereals, and canned soups, for example, had been produced and sold in fairly small quantities to restricted markets at high prices in specialty retail outlets. Soaps, crackers, and flour were at first essentially commodities, unpackaged and undifferentiated, and sold in local or regional markets. But by the early twentieth century, these products were mass produced, advertised, and offered to all at convenient locations and affordable prices. Once this transformation had occurred, however, it is more plausible to see advertising as a method (and an expensive one at that) of maintaining market power and dealer control. In the first category, we might find advertising beneficial to consumer interests, although here we must suspend moral judgment about the desirability of these products as items of mass consumption. (The mass production and distribution of cigarettes is a case where the moral judgment might well be negative.) In the second category, where advertising was used to defend established market niches, advertising seems to have played an anticompetitive role.

In evaluating advertising's impact on the distributive system, we are faced with comparing the merits of efficiency and control. The diminished margins of traditional retailers selling advertised goods represented, at least in part, a genuine improvement in marketing productivity as manufacturer advertising took over some of the selling functions of the merchant and allowed him to perform other tasks more productively. In part, too, the margins reveal merchants squeezed between the aggressive horizontal competition of the new mass marketing institutions and the vertical pressure of national advertisers. As the history of antitrust has indicated, many Americans have traditionally placed a high value on the well-being of an independent local entrepreneurial class. Insofar as national advertising helped community retailers stave off the encroachments of chain stores and other mass merchandisers, it helped this group to survive. But survival came at a price; as national advertising brought local storekeepers under the sway of brand-name manufacturers who could dictate the conditions of mercantile success, the retailers' independence was compromised. In a more subtle way, too, the rise of national advertising abridged the autonomy of local merchants. National advertising was a new and potent method of instructing and advising millions of shoppers; with branded, packaged products, the storekeeper's role as guide and mentor was certainly diminished.

Advertising men, understandably boastful, frequently attributed revolutionary powers to their work. "Advertising—

especially general advertising—is the machine method of distributing goods as compared with hand methods. Its growth is sound; it has only the most beneficial effect upon business as a whole; it will continue to grow until practically all staples have been subjected to its influence."[74] This survey of the economic role of advertising in the Gilded Age and Progressive Era suggests the hyperbole in this typical assertion. The magnitude of advertising in those years has probably been overstated by past estimates. The vast changes in production and distribution which transformed the American economy occurred in industries where advertising was negligible as well as in those where it was extensive. It is hard to specify the effects that advertising had on the competitive performance of firms and industries. Finally, in attempting to alter and control channels of distribution, many national advertisers learned the limitations of advertising and the complexities of the vertical struggles for power and profits.

On the other hand, it would be a mistake to dismiss national advertising as a minor epiphenomenon of the nation's economic upheavals. In its domain, the marketing of mass-produced, branded consumer products, advertising was often potent indeed. Advertising was most effective when it was integrated with a broader marketing strategy. As one textbook writer observed in 1916, "Thirty years ago an advertisement was an advertisement. It was thought of as nothing more than a few words displayed on paper. . . . In these days it is not enough to advertise just for the purpose of selling goods. The merchandising plan which is the foundation of the advertising must first be carefully studied. . . . An advertising campaign without a purpose is like a ship without a destination."[75] When advertising was joined with a skillful and appropriate marketing plan, campaigns could create consumer preferences worth millions of dollars to the manufacturers. Combined with other innovations in packaging, labeling, physical distribution, and personal salesmanship, national advertising around the turn of the century helped surround the consumer with new products and helped invest older products with new functions and meanings. To many, these consumer goods were well worth the monetary cost and the power that national advertisers now wielded over consumer choices. That the power was checked by rival advertisers and the growing power of mass retailers must have further sweetened the bargain. However, even if consumers could consider themselves still sovereign, the advertisers were far more than mere courtiers seeking customers' favor. National advertisers were big businesses, themselves largely sovereign in the world of work and powerful (though not omnipotent) in the political arena. Many of these advertisers found themselves at the core of an economy they had fundamentally transformed. Their advertisements did more than entreat and inform the consumer. Singly, ads tried to persuade Americans to buy manufacturers' brands. Collectively, they presented an invitation and an injunction to partake in a consumer society.

4

The Agencies of
Persuasion

COMING to the end of a speech at the 1926 convention of the American Association of Advertising Agencies, Calvin Coolidge showered his audience with praise: "Advertising ministers to the spiritual side of trade. It is great power that has been entrusted to your keeping which charges you with the high responsibility of inspiring and ennobling the commercial world. It is all part of the greater work of the regeneration and redemption of mankind."[1] An address from the President of the United States exemplified the respectability which advertising men had achieved by the 1920s. The rise of national advertising for branded products had

invested advertising with new and important economic purposes; advertising agencies, changing to meet the demands
of American business, now offered an array of services to
national advertisers and prided themselves on their professional accomplishments. However, the survival and success
of the advertising agency business did not come easily.
Agency practices that had proven highly profitable to nineteenth-century advertising men quickly became outmoded
or unacceptable to the advertisers who paid the bills. At the
same time, agencies had to learn how to create advertising
campaigns and plan marketing strategies.

Advertising agencies of the nineteenth century owed their
existence to the staggering problems of coordinating the
needs of advertisers and media. By the 1890s, when the first
useful estimates appear, there were perhaps four thousand
entrepreneurs who wanted to advertise their goods and services beyond their own localities. Meanwhile the number of
daily newspapers grew from 254 in 1850 to 2,226 in 1900.
Weeklies increased at a comparable pace, from about 991 in
1838 to 13,513 in 1904. There was, it seems, a multitude of
those whom Horace Greeley called "those little creatures
whom God for some inscrutable purpose has permitted to
edit country newspapers."[2] The complexity of matching advertisers with media was magnified by the absence of reliable information about either party. As we shall see, until
1869 there was not even a trustworthy list of the nation's
newspapers, and until World War I circulation information
was generally unreliable. Publishers across the country would
have been hard-pressed to ascertain the credit-worthiness of
all the advertisers who wanted to use their columns. For
local merchants who were hesitant to pay their advertising
bills, personal contact might suffice, but what could a publisher in a small town do if an advertiser hundreds or thousands of miles away failed to settle his account?

To make matters still worse, there was no uniform measure of advertising space. Most mid-century newspapers sold space by the square, a block one column high and one column wide. As type faces changed, however, papers redefined the measure. The pioneering advertising agent, George P. Rowell, recalled that a "square at last became an arbitrary measure, differing in each office, and having a range of anywhere between four and thirty-two lines."[3] If space measurement failed to conform to the dictates of Euclidean logic, prices for newspaper space were even more irrational. Many newspapers offered elaborate systems of deep discounts for repeated advertisements or for purchases of large space. Some charged extra for preferable positions in the paper, for advertisements for particular kinds of products, or for ads placed under columns with headings like "Business Notices." Stated rates were uncertain and complicated enough, but almost no publisher stuck to his rate card. Even those who protested most strenuously that their rates could not be varied were usually ready to negotiate. Rowell liked to tell the story of the publisher who "devoted four full pages to impressing upon us the necessity of paying according to his schedule, said the price would be the sum he named, 'and not one d——d cent less' and added in a postscript, 'Now what will you give?'"[4]

The earliest advertising agents found their niches by reducing some of the transactions costs and risks inherent in the chaotic advertising space market. Volney B. Palmer, son of a Pennsylvania lawyer, is generally considered the first American advertising agent. Around 1842, Palmer's Philadelphia Real Estate and Coal Office announced the following:

ADVERTISEMENTS and subscriptions received for some of the best and most widely circulated Newspapers in Pennsylvania and New Jersey and in many of the principal cities and towns throughout the United States, for which he has the Agency, affording an excellent opportunity for Merchants, Mechanics, Professional Men, Hotel and Boarding-house keepers, Railroad, Insurance and Transportation Companies, and the enterprising business portion of the community generally, to publish extensively abroad their respective pursuits—to learn the terms of subscription and advertising, and accomplish their object here without the trouble of perplexing and fruitless inquiries, the expense and labour of letter writing, the risk of making enclosures of money &c,&c.[5]

By the end of the 1840s, Palmer operated offices in Boston, New York, Philadelphia, and Baltimore, and advertising had replaced real estate and coal selling as his main line of business.

Palmer's advertising agency was a far different creature from today's agency; indeed, it differed drastically from leading agencies of the early twentieth century. Palmer emphasized his ability to facilitate advertising transactions. For potential advertisers, he offered access to the media and a convenient method of payment, since his receipts were evidence that the advertiser had paid his bill. For newspapers, Palmer was a space salesman. His employee and eventual competitor, S. M. Pettengill, describes Palmer's sales technique:

He would march into the counting-room of the merchants, calling for the principal partner, and announce himself . . . with as much assurance as if he were a customer who was about to purchase a large bill of goods. . . . He would make a well-considered statement of the benefits of advertising in general and to the party he was addressing in particular. . . . He would show how he (the merchant) could easily double his business and profits by a like course. He would point out the places where he should advertise, and how he should do it. . . . He would end up by asking if he might be permitted to make out an estimate for the merchant's advertisement.[6]

Although evidence about Palmer's finances is scanty, he apparently received his compensation in the form of a commission paid him by the newspapers. The payment may have been 25 percent of the gross cost of the space. Paradoxically, although the functions of the advertising agency have changed almost beyond recognition, the commission method of compensation has survived unending controversy and sporadic campaigns to abolish it.

Palmer's services smoothed out the process of placing advertisements and won him, he asserted, the exclusive right to sell advertising for the papers he represented.[7] He claimed about 1,300 papers handled their advertising sales through him by 1849. However, despite testimonials fulsomely praising his services, Palmer encountered two problems. He refused to assume the risk of nonpayment by advertisers. If he could not collect from a businessman, the newspapers would not collect from him. S. M. Pettengill, after less than a year in Palmer's Boston office, determined to offer an equivalent service and to pay publishers' bills even when he could not collect from advertisers. Along with John Hooper and a few others, Pettengill began to compete with Palmer. Second, Palmer could not maintain the exclusive agreements with publishers that he had demanded. When he sent a circular to publishers warning them of the nefarious plans of Pettengill, he violated one of the maxims of later advertising men who advised colleagues never to mention their rivals' names. Pettengill's business boomed. S. R. Niles acquired Palmer's Boston office, and the Baltimore office was closed during the 1850s. With partners, Palmer continued his New York and

Philadelphia agencies until his retirement in 1862 or 1863, but he was no longer the dominant figure in an infant industry. Rumor—apparently false—had it that he died insane.

In the thoroughly disorganized market for advertising space of mid-nineteenth century America, it is not surprising that advertising agents should look for sources of profit beyond publishers' sales commissions. Most agents became, in the terms of Ralph Hower, space jobbers.[8] They sold advertising to businessmen and then purchased the necessary space on their own account. Space jobbers could profit from the differential between the rates they negotiated with publishers and the prices they charged advertisers. By 1865, George P. Rowell took a second step. Recognizing that New England country weeklies would generally sell him a column of space for a year for $100 and would also grant him a 25-percent discount on the sale, Rowell contemplated enormous profits from buying columns in advance and then selling smaller units of the space he had purchased to advertisers who needed only a few lines. Offering businessmen an inch of space in 100 newspapers for $100 a month, Rowell calculated that even if he sold only half of the space he had bought, he would net $5,500 on an investment of $7,500 or less. Within a few years, Rowell moved to New York and was buying space throughout the country. Businessmen could choose from a smorgasbord of Rowell's newspaper lists, targeting a region or a state, rural or urban publications, high- or low-priced newspapers. Rowell contended that his lists were necessary for successful relations between advertisers and publishers who were not in the same locality. He reprinted and endorsed a Denver newspaper article maintaining that publishers could not judge the honesty and credit-worthiness of the "foreign" (out-of-town) advertisers. Indeed, the article suggested, nine-tenths of those who ordered advertisements without using an agency were "humbugs or swindlers who cannot get their orders through responsible agencies."[9]

Local advertisers in newspapers had little if any inducement to place their ads through Rowell's agency or any other. Newspapers usually handled local advertising themselves. For magazines, however, it made sense to sell all their advertising space to an independent agent for a fixed sum. The agent then could resell it to advertisers at his own prices. This began in 1867 when the New York agency, Carlton and Smith, began to buy the right to place all advertising in certain religious magazines. Carlton and Smith became, in effect, advertising concessionaires. This represented a further increase in advertising agency risk-bearing and completed the transition of the advertising "agent" to the status of independent principal. Carlton and Smith soon dominated the religious magazine field—a substantial accomplishment, since there were about four hundred weeklies with an estimated circulation of five million by 1870. In 1878, a young employee, J. Walter Thompson, took over Carlton and Smith and moved the firm into general magazine advertising. The agency, which still bears his name, is one of America's largest today.[10]

Success in the agency business of the Gilded Age required a blend of audacity and persistence. Publishers had to be pressured into cutting rates to the bone and potential advertisers had to be cajoled into investing in publicity without any assurance of returns. Yet some agents apparently did very well indeed. According to Rowell, his 1865 newspaper list offer brought him a profit of $10,000 on sales of $27,000 worth of advertising. Pettengill's agency in New York was handling business worth about $400,000 in 1867. Three years later, a New York magazine stated that the city's two principal agencies (presumably Rowell's and Pettengill's) did over a million dollars of business annually, and Rowell the next year claimed that he handled advertising "of from fifty to one hundred thousand dollars per month."[11] N. W. Ayer & Son, in Philadelphia, netted a profit of about 15 percent of the value of the advertising it placed in 1875; today a net profit of 2 to 3 percent of total billings is common.[12] Considering the risks of trading space on one's own account, it is not remarkable that advertising agency profits could be high, but agents also benefited from their strategic position in the space market, where they could control market information of value to publishers and advertisers alike.[13]

Despite such opportunities, Gilded Age advertising men were almost prototypically small businessmen, operating on the periphery of American industry. If the advertised products of the era smelled strongly medicinal, the odor around the advertising agencies was likely to be printers' ink. Agents were, until the 1890s, adjuncts to the newspaper business. Media used them to solicit advertisements from firms and convey those ads to the publishers who sold advertising space. Advertising men usually had backgrounds in journalism. Volney Palmer's father and brother had published newspapers, and Palmer had worked with them. John Hooper, New York City's first advertising agent, began in the advertising department of Horace Greeley's *New York Daily Tribune*. George P. Rowell initially solicited advertisements for the *Boston Post*. Francis Wayland Ayer, founder of N. W. Ayer & Son, had sold space for the *National Baptist* magazine. Even around the turn of the century, advertising leaders like Albert Lasker and Charles Austin Bates entered advertising from newspaper work. Few advertising men had experience in manufacturing industries.

Agencies in the nineteenth century were perched in small offices near the headquarters of big-city newspapers. The largest cluster formed in New York, on and around Park

Row in lower Manhattan. Park Row was already known as the "Fleet Street of America." One veteran recalled the agencies when he started out, in 1877:

> The agencies were located up one flight in long narrow rooms, a few being in office buildings, and two in New York were located on the ground floor. When you opened the office door you were in the agency, right in the middle of it. . . . In one corner the boss sat at his desk. In the opposite corner the estimate man sat with his ponderous scrap books before him at a slanted top desk. The bookkeeper at his old style standing desk was close at hand.

This advertising man recalled "the odor of musty newspapers and printer's ink in an unventilated room" emanating from the files of newspapers that all agents kept on hand to show their customers and to check to see whether ads had been printed according to contract.[14] The proprietor, estimator, and bookkeeper, along with a checking clerk and an office boy, could staff one of the larger agencies of the 1870s and 1880s. Rowell, who had perhaps the largest agency of these years, apparently employed a staff of about seven workers.

These advertising agents were essentially in the business of buying a shadowy, uncertain commodity—advertising space—paying for it, and reselling it to businesses whose own products were often equally obscure. Rowell's dealings with E. C. Allen of Augusta, Maine suggest the rather ethereal nature of much of the era's advertising business. In 1869, Allen wrote to the agent asking the cost of inserting a small advertisement in all of the nation's best newspapers. When Rowell replied, quoting the price of all the lists he controlled, Allen wrote back to say that he wanted all the newspapers, not just Rowell's lists. After Allen sent a check for $1,800 as a token of his serious intentions, Rowell decided it was time to pay a mid-winter visit to Augusta. There Allen, who was only a teenager, explained his scheme to Rowell. He had a recipe for a washing compound intended for farmers' wives; his advertisement would offer to sell the slips containing the formula for ten cents apiece. Purchasers would be appointed as Allen's sales "agents" to resell the recipe and would solemnly promise not to divulge the formula to anyone who did not buy a slip. On such an insubstantial proposition, Allen was willing to stake $11,000, and Rowell, once he was sure that Allen would pay his bills, went skeptically along.

The next September Allen was back, ordering an eighteen-line advertisement in every newspaper in America; to Rowell's amazement, he paid $30,000 on the spot for this. Surprisingly, Allen's advertising campaign proved to be not the undoing of a naive adolescent but the start of a career that made him the largest magazine publisher in America before his death in 1891. A nation willing to buy the right to sell recipes for a cleanser from Allen was also a ready market for a host of similar offers. Targeted for the rural masses, Allen's mail-order magazines wrapped pulp fiction and inspirational prose around ads for patent medicines, investment "opportunities," household novelties, and self-help information. Potentially lucrative but economically marginal, Allen's advertising symbolized the peripheral position of American advertising and its practitioners.

Advertising agents who were profiting from the sale of one commodity—advertising space—looked eagerly for other products to trade as well. Like other small businessmen, a large part of their success depended on receiving prompt cash payment from their customers and delaying or reducing cash outlays to their creditors and suppliers. Where possible, agencies created a network of barter arrangements for obtaining advertising space. George P. Rowell appears to have been an exceptionally avid pursuer of these opportunities. In 1869, he started the *American Newspaper Directory,* which compiled publication and circulation data for all newspapers in the nation. Rowell sold the directory for five dollars but financed it as well by printing advertisements from newspapers beseeching advertisers to consider their publications. Each year the volume swelled with advertising, until Rowell printed 1,221 pages of ads in 1891. At seventy-five dollars a page or more, newspapers usually did not pay with cash; instead, Rowell's agency gained credit balances on the books of thousands of newspapers they could use for their clients' advertising.

Two other advertising-related ventures also attracted Rowell. From about 1869 onward, Rowell published a magazine aimed at the newspaper and advertising industries; early issues were essentially long advertisements for the virtues of the Rowell agency, but they were also vehicles for publicity from newspapers looking for advertisers. Rowell's first periodicals lapsed in the 1870s, but he recommenced publishing in 1888, this time with a magazine called *Printers' Ink,* "The Little Schoolmaster in the Art of Advertising," as it soon billed itself. *Printers' Ink* gradually became an informative and independent trade journal, but in its initial years it obviously served Rowell's need to promote his own advertising work. Rowell also invested in a printing supply company which allowed him to exchange ink, type, and other paraphernalia for advertising space. "Printers Ink Jonson," whose rambling advertisements appeared weekly in *Printers' Ink* magazine, was actually William Johnston, the foreman of Rowell's printing operations; Rowell wrote the advertising copy.

The advertising space he amassed through these ventures in turn induced Rowell to diversify his businesses still further. If he could not find enough advertisers to fill the space he controlled, he would apply these credits to a product of his own. Rowell explained: "I thought it most probable that what I wanted was a medicine, but I was not decided on that point. Anything would do that would meet a moderately common want. I prepared an advertisement: 'Wanted—To buy a trade-mark, a proprietary article—something that if advertised would command a sale.'"[15] After testing a syrup that "suggested that it had its origin from putting a portion of pulverized brick into a vial filled two-thirds full of muddy water," Rowell and a young medical student he consulted decided that the liquid could be converted into tablets. Doing so, they named the product Ripans Tabules. The neologism "Tabules" was itself Rowell's concoction, and Ripans was an acronym for the pills' six ingredients.

Some rivals bristled at George Rowell's potentially conflicting business interests. Artemas Ward, who achieved great success as the advertising manager of Sapolio soap powder, caustically referred to Rowell as "Mrs. Ripans," while the later assiduously publicized his pills each week in *Printers' Ink.* Newspaper publishers often took aim at the policies of the *American Newspaper Directory;* they contended that Rowell would reward papers that purchased pages in the volume with high circulation estimates and punish those that failed to advertise with low figures in the directory listings. Rowell insisted that directory listings were unaffected by advertising purchases and proudly pointed out that none of the many libel suits with which publishers threatened him ever reached court.

Most of Rowell's competitors resorted to similar business activities. At least eight other agencies issued newspaper directories and sold advertising space in them.[16] Several also operated printing supply companies; for example, J. G. Cooley, who operated a type foundry and had a business that manufactured wooden type, joined forces with an agent named Dauchy, and the two paid all their bills from newspapers with wooden type. Like Rowell, S. M. Pettengill had set out purposefully to enter the patent medicine business, but N. W. Ayer & Son's drug firm passed into the agency's hands when it was unable to pay them its advertising debts.[17]

Rowell, in the 1880s, jokingly told a publisher that advertising agents "as a class were little lower than angels."[18] Indeed, as individuals, late nineteenth-century advertising men sometimes earned the respect and affection of their business colleagues. According to the historian of N. W. Ayer & Son, Francis W. Ayer and Harry N. McKinney, the two most responsible for the agency's success, were men of probity and ability. George Rowell, though castigated by some of his competitors during his career, received plaudits from a spectrum of businessmen upon his retirement. John E. Powers, the pioneering copywriter, also seems to have been very much admired by his peers.

Credit bureaus generally looked favorably on advertising agencies of the Gilded Age. Of the thirty-two agencies that I have located in the January 1885, *Mercantile Agency Reference Book,* ten had a "high" credit rating, fourteen were rated "good," and only one small agency was given the lowest, "limited" rating. Size alone did not earn them these generally positive evaluations; only Ayer and Rowell were said to be worth over $200,000 in "pecuniary strength." (Dauchy was in the $75,000–$125,000 range.) Almost half the agencies whose assets were listed were worth from $10,000 to $40,000.[19] Comments in the records of R. G. Dun & Co. are generally positive but not uniformly enthusiastic. For example, the Dauchy partners in 1877 were "considered very honorable men" and in 1886 "continue in high repute." J. Walter Thompson's credit reports show a success story. Taking over from Carlton and Smith, Thompson was "said to be very reliable, straightforward and careful.... Means small, not thought to exceed three or four thousand but in good standing and credit." Within eight years, however, Thompson's personal worth was estimated at two hundred thousand dollars. Although the Dun reports worried that he had too many outside interests and did not devote proper attention to the advertising business, Thompson was a wealthy man and "thought to be safe." On the other hand, a few agents give the distinct impression of having been ne'er-do-wells. E. N. Erickson had formerly done business as Peaslee and Company, which failed in 1877. Erickson was described as having "no capital," not being "a desirable risk," and having "little or no responsibility, does not stand well with the fraternity." Both J. H. Bates and his partner David Locke (whose humorous writings were popular under the pseudonym Petroleum Nasby) were reputedly "active and energetic," but the credit agency described both as "inclined to drink," a judgment that was surely true for Locke, according to Rowell's memoirs.[20]

If the barbs nineteenth-century advertising men directed at each other contained even a small fraction of truth, the agency business must have attracted its share of charlatans and incompetents. Well-known advertising agents like Rowell and Ward traded charges quite freely. Ward, for example, accused Rowell of plagiarizing an article, and Rowell replied that Ward stole advertising ideas.[21] *Art in Advertising,* another agent's house organ, attacked them both; this journal also managed in one short paragraph to defame both the former and the current editor of a rival publication: "A. A. Reed, founder and for a long time editor of *Profitable Advertising,* now languishes in jail, charged with various misdemeanors and attempted suicide. The present condition of the periodical ... is said to be the cause of his fall from grace."²² Some important agents had prickly personalities. One old-timer recalled that S. M. Pettengill:

> Was as vain as a peacock, and easily flattered, entirely desti-
> tute of imagination, and had no real perception of the mean-
> ing of the Sermon on the Mount, and the writings and teach-
> ings of St. Paul were as much out of his reach as if they had
> never been translated.²³

David Locke, who was partner in the agency of Bates and Locke during the 1880s, left in his wake a swarm of anec-dotes about his contentious (and alcoholic) style.²⁴ George Batten, who founded a successful and well-regarded agency, gained a reputation of being "as erratic as an overwound cuckoo clock," according to a company executive many dec-ades later.²⁵

We may wish to discount the testimony here, since much of it comes from business rivals with their own scores to settle. However, it is clear that leading advertising men deeply regretted their inability in the nineteenth century to exclude the ignorant and dishonest "dilettantes" who called themselves advertising agents without any discernible busi-ness skills. One old-timer later reminisced about the "easy-money seekers, soldiers of fortune: colorful, strange, quaint, picturesque, bold, brainy and clever characters" who flocked to advertising just as adventurers rushed to the Klondike, but this exaggerates the case. Men like Ayer, Thompson, and Rowell, along with several of the best-paid copywriters, made fortunes in advertising, but more common was the struggling advertising man of indifferent ability and uncer-tain success. There were, wrote Nathaniel C. Fowler in 1897, "irresponsible agents" in every city whose numbers were on the rise, "disappointed bundles of self-conceit and feeders upon the credulous . . . contemptible hangers-on." A few years later, copywriter Charles Austin Bates admitted,

"It is a notorious fact that there has been so much trickery and dishonesty in the advertising business that a man engaged in it sometimes feels embarrassed when he is asked what business he is in."[26]

By about 1890, advertising agents were beset by diverse forces which, in less than a generation, would threaten and then transform the agency business. Dissatisfaction with agents among existing advertisers and publishers, changes in the ways advertising business could be transacted, and the emergence of new media and new kinds of national advertisers all worked to render the agent as space broker obsolete.

Advertisers in the Gilded Age who used agencies could not help wondering about the value they received. They hoped to acquire space through agencies at the lowest possible price and to have their advertisements put in the most suitable media. On neither count was the agent sure to be reliable. Agents were, after all, receiving a commission from the publishers on the space they sold and were also profiting by their own dealings in advertising space. Since agents dealt with publishers on their own and did not reveal to advertisers the terms on which they acquired space, advertisers might well wonder whether they were the beneficiaries or the victims of agents' negotiating skills. As for choosing the best publications, the agents were strongly tempted to steer advertisers into media where they received the largest commissions or the best price concessions, regardless of whether they were appropriate for the product being advertised.

Publishers were also unhappy. As Rowell complained in 1870, "One of the great ends of an editorial convention, it seems, is the abuse of advertising agencies."[27] Although an agent might bring in out-of-town advertising a publisher could not otherwise obtain, the newspapermen paid a high price for this revenue. They complained that agents like Rowell "insidiously attacked the rates of publishers—in most cases, if not all, fairly reasonable—and induced the masses of publishers to accept a very large discount aside from the 25 percent commission." Meanwhile, unscrupulous men entered the agency business: "The evolution has produced not advertising agents but 'scalpers.' "[28] Agents also rankled publishers with their excessive curiosity about newspaper and magazine circulations; agents who had once clearly been representatives of newspapers, soliciting advertising, were now publishers' adversaries when they questioned circulation figures too intensely. Agencies that published newspaper directories, from the publishers' point of view, merely combined this unseemly inquisitiveness with the implicit blackmail of pressure to buy ads in the directories.

Although nineteenth-century agencies had fallen away from their initial position as sales agents for newspapers, they had not clearly established another loyalty. In 1866, when the manager of the *Chicago Tribune* posed George Rowell the simple, if ungrammatical, question, "Who does the agent represent?" Rowell could only reply that the agent represented himself. At a meeting of advertising agents in 1873, it was resolved that "the agent must work for the advertiser quite as much as for the publisher whom he represents," but this hardly resolved the issue.[29] In fact, the ambiguities of agency status vexed relations among advertisers, agents, and publishers for the next several decades.

In the Gilded Age, only N. W. Ayer & Son managed clearly to resolve to serve the advertiser, not the publisher. When Francis Wayland Ayer founded the agency in 1869, with his father as its nominal head, his only discernible motive was "to get business, place it, and get money for it." After several years of space brokerage, Ayer found himself in a conversation with an older associate who chastised him as "nothing but a drummer." Ayer resolved "not to be an order taker any longer." This led, in 1876, to the first Ayer "open contract." The agency agreed to handle all the advertising of Dingee and Conard, rose growers, for a 12.5 percent commission, which the advertiser would pay on the volume of advertising Ayer placed. Ayer's conversion to the open contract was not instantaneous. In fact, in 1877, the agency's house organ claimed, "Our profits are not derived from the advertisers, but from the newspaper publishers, to whom we become responsible for all orders sent, and by whom we are credited a commission on each." Still, by 1884, nearly three-quarters of Ayer's advertising billings were on an open contract basis.[30] By the 1890s, Ayer was the largest agency in America, so its switch to direct payment by advertisers was no minor oddity. However, other important agencies did not follow and continued to sell space to advertisers for whatever profit they could obtain.

Dissatisfaction with the services agencies offered provided a motive for change in the agency system in the late nineteenth century; new developments in the market for advertising space offered an opportunity. Initially, advertising agents existed because of the disorganization of the market for advertising space, but their own work and the efforts of others had begun to rationalize that market. By the end of the century, these trends seemed to threaten the profitability and even the survival of the independent advertising agency.

Publishing a newspaper directory with circulation data and advertising space prices apparently gave agencies a certain competitive advantage in the hunt for advertisers and their dollars. At the same time, however, the directories made available to advertisers and rival agencies a great deal of information. Before 1869, agencies jealously guarded their knowledge of newspapers' charges and even of what newspapers were published in a locality. Armed with a newspaper directory, an advertiser could consider the strategy of corresponding directly with the newspapers that seemed attractive to him.

Those who had done well in advertising faced another problem in the market for advertising space. They were unable to control entry into their own trade. The number of agents soared. A New York City business directory listed forty-two advertising agencies in the city in 1869–70. That number at least doubled each decade through 1899, when there were over four hundred agents listed.[31] Given that many of these were individuals who solicited advertisements for newspapers that employed them or who passed on personal notices and classified ads for individuals and small local businesses, the figures overstate the growth of competition; but the trend is unmistakable. More and more agents wanted to buy advertising space for resale, and the number of extraordinary bargains an agent could secure was therefore reduced. The list system that George Rowell had found so profitable immediately after the Civil War faded in importance by the 1890s. Rival agencies offered their own packages of newspapers to prospective advertisers and drove down the prices these lists could obtain. By the turn of the century, financial crises beset several of the older advertising agencies. Most shocking was the collapse of S. M. Pettengill and Co. of New York in 1903; nearly a million dollars of unpaid debts to publishers were outstanding. After calling the roll of defunct ad agencies in his 1905 memoirs, George Rowell mused, "I realize that I am very much behind the times."[32]

During the 1880s and 1890s, a new class of advertising middlemen partially pre-empted the work of the general advertising agency. Newspapers appointed so-called special agents (also called newspaper representatives) who worked explicitly for them as space sellers. Located in New York, special agents found that they could take on space-selling responsibilities for several noncompeting newspapers at once. An advertiser who wanted to use those media that had special agents could go directly to a representative's office or correspond with him, by-passing the regular agent. By 1893, New York was said to host over fifty special agents, averaging about five newspapers each. Two years earlier, a special agent had astutely explained the reason for the rise of his trade: "If the original purpose and methods of general advertising agencies had been perpetuated there would be small need of the special agents. . . . The first general agents were the direct and authorized representatives of papers. . . . Gradually, naturally and necessarily they became the ministers of advertisers."[33] While this commentator exaggerated the loyalty of space dealers to advertisers, he correctly gauged the trend.

Special agents were a feasible alternative to the advertising agent only for large urban papers. Smaller publications could not afford the cost of hiring one to represent them in New York. Moreover, even for the larger dailies, controlling the special agent was difficult. They expanded the lists of papers they represented, demanded the right to set their own prices for the space they sold, and began purchasing (openly or covertly) space on their own accounts. Thus they began to follow some of the same paths that their space broker colleagues had trod. By 1900, general agents and specials had achieved a *modus vivendi*. *Printers' Ink* reported that the specials "do not appear to be playing as great a part in the world of advertising as they did some years ago." Many publishers apparently were willing to pay two commissions for advertising, one to the general agents representing advertisers and a second to special agents representing the media.[34] Nevertheless, special agencies must have looked like an ominous development to agents who profited as middlemen in the space market.

These competitive forces put pressure on the size of agent commissions. As early as 1870, publishers were restive about paying a full 25 percent discount to advertising agencies. Agents that year complained of publishers' intentions to set up a cooperative "Press Advertising Agency," which would then grant a puny 10 percent commission to the regular agents who submitted ads to the coop. Although this scheme did not materialize, a convention of agents held in New York in 1873 complained formally about newspapers that cut commission rates. In those early years, when the space brokers were almost indispensable for getting out-of-town advertising, Rowell and his cohorts could persuade many publishers that "a small something" of advertising revenue was better than "a big nothing at all." That argument weakened in later years; popular media became more conscious of the value of their advertising space for businessmen and were less prone to offer great price concessions to agencies. In 1887, for example, E. C. Allen lowered the commission on advertising placed in his mail-order magazines from 25 percent to 15 percent. At about the same time, Allen also seems to have eliminated special concessions he had offered certain agencies. Because his magazines achieved imposing circulations, he continued to fill their advertising columns, even with high rates and lowered commissions.[35]

Some leading publishers of the 1880s offered agents a commission of only 10 percent. In 1889, the American Newspaper Publishers Association recommended a 15 percent maximum and lowered this to 10 percent five years later. Although *Printers' Ink* in 1893 claimed that 20 percent was a common rate, most of the time agents in the 1890s were complaining that commissions were too low. One, for example, wrote proposing that his colleagues set up a "'blacklist' headquarters somewhere" to boycott media that were squeezing their commission rates. Yet by the first decade of the twentieth century a pattern of 10 percent commissions from magazines and major urban newspapers and 15 percent from other newspapers had emerged. Agents continued to grumble.[36]

The weakening of the advertising agent as space broker reflected not only change in the market for advertising space but also new sources of supply and demand for advertising. As manufacturers began to market branded products in national markets and as department stores handled comparably large volumes of goods (though usually *not* advertised brands), they needed advertising services far different from the ones space brokers provided. On the supply side, new media—the popular newspapers in big cities and, even more importantly, the mass-circulation magazines—were organizations certain enough of the value of their advertising space to maintain their stated rates and visible enough to attract advertiser attention without the agent's intermediary work.

As we have seen in earlier chapters, until about the 1880s, national advertising was very much the province of marginal businesses. With the exception of a few successful patent medicine manufacturers, advertising budgets were generally small and the advertisements themselves prepared almost as afterthoughts. For local retailers, some mention of what goods were on hand and perhaps a boastful phrase usually sufficed. Thus, in the mid-nineteenth century, advertising was likely to be simply declamatory or "bald presentations of facts."[37]

Commentators in that era had maintained that every businessman could be his own best advertising copywriter. "Advertisers should generally write their own advertisements," proclaimed Rowell's magazine in 1872. "The man who cannot do this is not fit to advertise."[38] From the start, agents were willing to prepare the copy for advertisements but this was at most a secondary aspect of their job. S. M. Pettengill, for instance, was writing advertising doggerel in Boston newspapers as early as the 1850s, but this was merely a side-line—one that almost proved costly when a careless printer took his pseudonym, "Shortfellow," and set it in type as "Longfellow," to the great displeasure of the poet, who threatened to sue. Agencies in the decades before the 1890s had no workers who specialized in writing ads.

The first important advertisers who needed skilled assistance in preparing their advertisements were large department stores. As they expanded the range of goods they carried and as new urban streetcar lines widened their marketing territories, downtown retailers needed to let customers know what was on hand and to induce them to shop at their stores. John Wanamaker had opened his huge store in a depot built by the Pennsylvania Railroad to handle the traffic coming to Philadelphia for the Centennial Exposition of 1876. In 1880, Wanamaker, committed to a policy of intensive advertising, hired John E. Powers, an American who had initially attracted Wanamaker's attention with his advertisements for Wilcox & Gibbs sewing machines in England. Powers' plain-spoken publicity featured descriptions of merchandise that were unprecedented for their detail and accuracy. His ads also reflected the cost advantages of Wanamaker and other mass retailers by clearly stating the products' prices and promoting the one-price-for-all, no-haggling policy Wanamaker had set. Powers was probably the first man to make a living from writing advertisements. (It was a good living; in the late 1880s, after he had left Wanamaker's, his income was estimated at $10,000 a year. Selling was apparently Powers' favorite pursuit; he spent his summer vacations from Wanamaker's store selling insurance in New York!) "Powers-style" copy proved attractive to many other mass merchants; Wanamaker management estimated in 1890 that more than fifty stores across the country were imitating Powers ads.[39]

Although department stores needed copywriting services (and, as merchandise changed, needed fresh advertisements almost every day), they could usually dispense with the space-buying functions advertising agencies performed. Since the stores bought large amounts of space in newspapers of only one metropolis, they were actually better able to negotiate with the media than an agent could. Beyond this, retail copywriters needed to have continual contact with the merchandise and sales conditions in the stores; an agent would have less opportunity to keep in touch with the sales activities. For these reasons, the advertising agents were ill-equipped to handle the massive advertising budgets of the great urban emporiums of the late nineteenth century. The sums involved were large: in 1899, according to an estimate by Manly Gillam who had succeeded Powers at Wanamaker's, the twenty largest stores in New York and Chicago spent about $1,775,000 on advertising. The biggest, Wanamaker and Siegel-Cooper in New York, were said to spend over $300,000 each, which would put them among the very first ranks of American advertisers.[40]

The other urgent new demand for skilled advertising preparation appeared slightly later than the department stores but affected the development of advertising agencies more profoundly. Manufacturers who made branded consumer goods frequently turned to intensive advertising. As these firms invested in the distribution of their products, persuasive advertising became a pressing need. These companies needed much more than low prices for small ads in country weeklies or stodgy religious magazines. They could not afford to leave their publicity to the ministrations of the space brokers. Copy, layout, and artwork had to be carefully considered; advertisements had to fit a broader marketing strategy. The appropriations of some of the very largest advertisers of the late nineteenth century were high enough to give them strong bargaining power in negotiating the purchase of advertising space. These and other large national advertisers were the ones whose needs reshaped the advertising agency business. As we shall see, the changes agencies underwent left them best prepared to serve the requirements of national advertisers.

As new advertisers came to the fore, so did new media, and the space brokers' room for maneuver was further reduced. Newspaper publishers recognized the value of their advertising space and began to adapt their formats and even their coverage to this growing source of revenue. New technologies reduced costs and speeded printing, allowing circulations to surpass urban population growth. Stereotyping equipment, which allowed printers to attach a full page of material to a cylindrical press without the use of cumbersome type forms, was first introduced in the 1850s; the machinery was expensive, and only forty-five sets of stereotyping equipment were in use by 1880. However, these papers were able to remove the thin vertical column rules and print advertisements of more than one column's width. Electrotyping methods of preparing printing plates were introduced in the 1880s, reducing the cost and improving the quality of illustrations. Photoengraved line illustrations were soon followed by half-tone processes for reproducing photographs; by the turn of the century, most large dailies printed photos regularly.[41] Meanwhile, circulations grew far more rapidly than population, prices fell, and newsboy sales on streetcorners supplanted subscriptions. Aggressive publishers of the "penny press" era recognized that they could sell their readership to advertisers just as they could sell their newspapers to readers. Fifty-six percent of newspaper and periodical revenues came from subscriptions and sale in 1879; the figure fell steadily. By 1919, only about 34 percent came from these sources; nearly two-thirds was generated by advertising.[42]

The advent of mass-circulation national magazines further altered the nature of the advertising market and the tasks of the advertising agency. In the 1870s and 1880s, mail-order magazines were in their heyday. These publications served a rural clientele and carried advertising that the next generation of advertising men would consider distinctly retrograde. But the mail-order publications, typified by E. C. Allen's magazines, were a real innovation in periodicals. Publications had become media—channels for the transmission of advertising messages. In the 1890s, a new generation of mass-circulation magazines appeared whose styles ranged from the careful proprieties of Cyrus Curtis's *Ladies' Home Journal* to the impassioned reformism of *McClure's* and the demagogy of Frank Munsey's publications. What united these magazines was their appeal to a middle-class readership and their reliance on advertising. Indeed, Curtis's drive to boost the circulation of the *Journal* depended crucially on the $200,000 advertising credit Francis Wayland Ayer advanced him in 1889. The varying formulas that brought success to these magazines all depended on the existence of an audience ready to buy consumer goods advertised in the correct surroundings and proper fashion.

All these developments threatened the advertising agent as space broker. For a generation, the agents' raison d'être had been their ability to guide unwary advertisers through the labyrinth of space buying. The best argument for the agency system had been the chaos of the market for advertising space. As that market became more orderly, with buyers and sellers alike gaining in size and knowledge, agents had to make drastic changes. Their success was by no means assured. "Will the great increase in the knowledge of advertising . . . eventually result in the entire extinction of the advertising agent?" This was the question *Printers' Ink* posed in 1899.[43]

By the 1890s, the question asked of Rowell a generation earlier was being answered. The agent owed his allegiance to the advertiser, not the publisher, and serving the advertiser was the agent's justification for existence. Advertising men began to understand that they needed to prepare advertisements for manufacturers and others who sold branded goods in broad markets. For one thing, businessmen no longer had the time or the ability to prepare their own ads. "Although I have some faculty for writing good advertisements," commented one executive, "I have employed advertising experts . . . " for best results. *Printers' Ink* was more emphatic: "Generally neither the merchant nor the solicitor [for a newspaper] is able to make a good advertisement." Imitating the advice of established professions, advertising men claimed, "The man who acts as his own advertising agent sometimes has a fool for a client."[44]

Despite these recommendations, preparing advertisements remained a sideline for advertising agencies of the 1890s. In 1891, a Boston firm distinguished between the agency's work for established clients and its responsibilities to newer, "weaker" advertisers. For the former, "The agent simply follows definite instructions. He does not originate schemes, does not write advertisements, but simply does as he is told." For less experienced clients, "It will require an experienced and high-priced brain to write the advertisements." N. W. Ayer, more committed than most agencies to client service, nevertheless told an inquirer in 1893, "The writing of advertisements is not our business. It is only a small part of it, and is done by us only for regular customers." As late as 1901, even *Printers' Ink* published a claim that professional advertising writers were not necessarily superior to the honest businessman who knew his own products and could describe them clearly.[45]

The agencies that were to thrive in the new century were already adapting to new advertiser demands. N. W. Ayer hired his first full-time copywriter in 1892. By 1900, preparation of copy was a standard part of the agency's service. Procter & Collier, a Cincinnati agency closely tied to Procter & Gamble, implied in 1896 that it employed specialists in copywriting and maintained that an agency's value resulted from its ability to divide labor and assign different tasks to specialists. When Albert D. Lasker started work at the Chicago agency Lord & Thomas in 1898, the firm employed one part-time copywriter and a commercial artist. Lasker soon expanded this staff by hiring some of the best known (and most highly-paid) free-lance advertising writers he could find. The process was similar at other important agencies.[46]

Early in the twentieth century, the task of preparing advertisements had become a central responsibility of advertising agencies. For example, an organization chart for a typical advertising agency in about 1910 shows the copy and art department in the middle, directly below the executive level. Textbooks and advice manuals for advertising men concentrated on the writing and illustration of advertisements and relegated the question of relations with media to a brief discussion. Among the nearly one hundred employees at the George Batten agency in 1910 more than ten "think and write; most of the latter have been trained in journalism."[47]

As copywriting moved from haphazard sloganeering to a firmer basis, skilled illustration and layout became necessary to achieve continuity and strengthen selling appeals. At first in England, and, by the 1890s in the United States, well-known artists and illustrators sold their pictures to leading advertisers. In 1886, Pears' Soap spent £2,300 for a painting by Sir John Millais and used it as an advertisement. Despite some qualms about commercial ethics and esthetics, few artists could long resist the money advertisers were willing to offer for their work. At the same time, color rotogravure printing and half-tone processes enabled illustrators to go beyond simple black and white line drawings. By 1899, an observer remarked, hyperbolically to be sure, "Advertisements were never so artistic, so perfect as they are today." In the first decade of the twentieth century, large American advertising agencies began to organize their own art departments to meet their clients' needs for illustrations and design work. Agencies seldom employed commercial artists to the same degree that they hired copywriters; they continued to obtain artwork from outside sources and free-lancers, but the Batten agency boasted an art department of about ten people in 1919.[48]

Successfully assuming the job of preparing advertisements for national advertisers was in itself a big step toward assuring the survival and well-being of advertising agencies. However, major manufacturers of branded products soon became aware that they needed more than clever copy and illustrations to sell their goods. The free-lance advertising writers of the 1890s had specialized in ingenious slogans, but by the turn of the century some advertising agents were criticizing these as insufficient, even trivial, responses to marketing needs. "The success of all advertising hinges upon its plan— the theory on which it is based," commented *Printers' Ink* in 1900. No matter how catchy a phrase might be, it did not amount to adequate advertising. Advertisements had to be made parts of planned campaigns, and the campaigns had to be integrated into a coherent and appropriate marketing strategy. Inspiration and intuition were not enough. National advertisers needed marketing services to sell their products.

As early as 1879, N. W. Ayer & Son found a prospective client demanding a rudimentary kind of market research. When Ayer's partner Henry McKinney visited the Nichols-Shepard Company, thresher manufacturers, he was told to devise a list of papers that would reach good buying prospects. Nichols-Shepard insisted that it was the agency's task to find out where threshers were sold. Since time was short, the agency wired telegrams to state officials and publishers around the nation and in three days put together a survey of the market. They offered it to the manufacturer in return for getting the account. According to Ayer's historian, the agency was performing similar analyses for advertisers sporadically, but not infrequently, by 1900. In 1900, Ayer assigned the planning of advertising campaigns to a separate Business-Getting Department, which was to devise the strategies for prospective advertisers based on their marketing needs.[49]

However elementary, Ayer's work appears more advanced than what other agencies offered at the time. Market research was slow in getting started. However, by about 1910 several large agencies were beginning to make preliminary market studies as adjuncts to advertising campaigns. The Curtis Publishing Company's model organization chart for an up-to-date advertising agency showed a "Trade Investigation" division within the copy and art department. According to one Chicago agency in 1917, a truly modern agency put "diagnosis of market and selling conditions" first on its list of client services, and its work for advertisers extended to such matters as pricing, packaging, general business forecasting, public relations, and sales promotion.[50] Invoking the prestige of established professions, the agency stated, "The Modern Advertising Agency, like the modern Surgeon or Attorney appreciates the necessity of first *understanding the situation.*"[51]

The J. Walter Thompson Company, despite its background as space concessionaire for religious magazines in the 1870s and 1880s, most clearly illustrates the transition from space dealing to advertiser service. J. Walter Thompson, who had purchased the agency for $500 in 1878, had become, by the early twentieth century, something of an anachronism. The agency billed nearly three million dollars by 1916, but Thompson, as he aged, withdrew from active management and the agency was saddled with many small, unprofitable accounts. Stanley B. Resor, who was originally hired to set up Thompson's Cincinnati branch office in 1908, entered the advertising business with a very different perspective from Thompson's. Resor was trained in history and economics at Yale and had been convinced by reading the English historian Thomas Buckle that human behavior in the aggregate could be described and predicted by observable statistical laws. Under Resor's influence, J. Walter Thompson published *Population and Its Distribution,* a compilation of demographic and economic data culled from the Bureau of the Census. The agency has published updated volumes ever since. In 1916, Resor and several associates purchased the agency from Thompson for half a million dollars. That year he established a market research department at Thompson. By 1919, the J. Walter Thompson organization chart boasted both a Planning Department and a Statistical Investigation Department.

Some leading advertising agents scoffed at research and used it only to propitiate a demanding client. Yet even where quantitative analysis was scorned, agencies realized that they had to offer their clients a range of marketing advice. Agency services to national advertisers, then, developed in two distinct, though overlapping, phases. In the 1890s and the early 1900s, the agencies that saw the need to take copy preparation and advertising design seriously stepped ahead of the space brokers. A 1905 textbook, for example, contrasted old-fashioned agencies with progressive ones, for whom "brokerage in space is merely incidental to the professional side of the campaign." Their skilled preparation of advertisements distinguished modern agencies from the "advertising agent who merely 'places' copy." But by the second decade of the new century, the most advanced advertising men were already branding copy preparation as insufficient. "In small advertising clubs," commented *Printers' Ink* in 1912, "advertising is usually looked on as mere copy-writing; the business-promotion idea is not grasped." N. W. Ayer & Son lumped copywriting and space buying together as "entirely subordinate to some of the fundamental principles" of advertising campaigns and warned against "the tendency toward copy exaltation." A Chicago agency in 1915 insisted that "our Service is *Merchandising,* which *includes* Advertising." It went on to explain that, "Merchandising embraces marketing processes involved in getting a commodity from the factory to the consumer."[52]

The evolution from space broker to advertisement creator to marketing advisor was quite swift. As we shall see, the American Association of Advertising Agencies, formed in 1917, forbade its members to engage in practices that were routine for agencies twenty years earlier. At the same time it defined the tasks for the advertising agency broadly and gave agencies wide scope in drawing the boundaries of their services. Agencies that took the Four A's standards to heart were inclined to make big claims. As early as 1915, one boasted, "The good advertising agency, instead of being merely a more or less loosely joined appendage to the business, is coming to be a very important factor in the conduct of the business itself." In what one leading agent called the "third stage" of agency development, "The agency today is the advertiser's partner. It offers him the refreshing viewpoint of the thoughtful, interested outsider, trained in technique and experienced in the fundamentals that underlie all the business."[53] These bold claims smacked of organizational imperialism; advertising agencies (and the individuals who ran them) would ascend to ever more important and honored positions in the corporate world. For the agencies, marketing expertise was no doubt more often advertised to prospective clients than practiced successfully. At the same time, many advertisers continued to treat their advertising agencies as mere appendages—expendable, vestigial ones at that. Yet, considering the impasse the space brokerage agencies of the late nineteenth century had reached, agency pride in the World War I era was justified. Agents had shown the ability to shed one cloak and don another. To switch metaphors and put it crudely, the national advertisers who paid the pipers were calling new tunes, and the agents managed to play them.

In their occasional attempts at self-analysis, advertising agencies maintained that only independent, service-oriented agencies could fulfill the marketing needs of American business. Expertise, specialization, and objectivity were the industry's watchwords. Since some 95 percent of national advertising was handled by agencies in 1917, advertisers seem to have accepted the agents' claims.[54] We shall not deny that the large advertising agencies that evolved during the Progressive Era and reached their heights by the 1920s were well-suited to the needs of big businesses. However, the explanation of agency survival and success is complex, not self-evident.

Consider first the alternatives to the full-service advertising agency. National advertisers could have internalized advertising activities entirely within the firm. Alternatively, they could have acquired services from several independent providers, separating, for example, the decision about who was best qualified to do market research from the choice of a company to purchase advertising space. Finally, corporations could have combined these approaches; advertisers might wish to perform some advertising tasks (for example, preparation of ads for wholesalers and retailers) internally and to contract with outsiders to do the rest. The problem of explaining why these options rarely were chosen and why the independent, full-service advertising agency became the locus of marketing services is further complicated when we put agency evolution in the context of other business trends. At the same time that businesses were extensively integrating forward into marketing, investing heavily in nonmanufacturing facilities to handle the flow of their products to customers, they were becoming more firmly committed to acquiring their advertising services from independent firms through market transactions. Businesses were building warehouses, creating service offices, offering consumer credit, and, especially in electrical and chemical firms, setting up corporate research and development laboratories. Meanwhile, advertising work stayed largely outside the scope of big businesses.

Efforts to construct a theory of the scope of the firm—what activities it performs internally and what it obtains through market transactions—usually are aimed at showing why markets have given way to administrative coordination. Oliver Williamson, building upon the theoretical contribution of Ronald Coase and the historical scholarship of Alfred Chandler, has proposed a theory based on transactions costs. When the transactions costs of enacting an agreement through a market mechanism are higher than the costs of arranging, executing, and monitoring the same tasks within an imperatively-coordinated organization, Williamson argues, a firm will internalize those tasks. Market transactions costs are likely to be high in the presence of complexity and uncertainty, where negotiating a contract that will be satisfactory for a variety of unpredictable future situations is most difficult. Market relations are also likely to be costly when one or the other party to the transaction can engage in "opportunistic" behavior, conveying false or incomplete information or making promises he does not intend to keep. Where it is expensive to find alternative buyers or sellers to replace an opportunistic market partner, the relationship is filled with booby traps. In these instances, Williamson argues, internal, administrative coordination offers advantages. Parties within the same organization can meet unforeseen contingencies through "adaptive, sequential decision processes" instead of costly contract renegotiations. In the same organization, suppliers and users are likely to share a common institutional "code" or jargon that facilitates communications and to partake in a shared organizational "culture." Similarly, administrative coordination can reduce opportunism, by reducing the incentives to guileful behavior in a transaction and by allowing more thorough monitoring of behavior.[55]

By these criteria, the work that advertising agencies did would seem to be a prime candidate for internalization by heavy users of advertising. Almost all the conditions for high market transactions costs were present; few, if any, of the compensating benefits of market arrangements obtained. First, the specifications for a major national advertising campaign were highly complex. The nuances of creating the "correct" copy and artwork were compounded by the problems of selecting media, specifying sizes and dates for ads to appear, and the technical details of preparing and mailing printing plates, checking to see that an advertisement appeared, and paying bills. To put it mildly, there were many chores to attend to and many opportunities to fail. At the same time, appraising results was difficult; uncertainty about what an advertising campaign can do was never fully banished. Advertisers had to approve a host of agency decisions, and the parties had to remain in continual contact in order to confer on tactical matters.

Equally, "opportunism" would seem to have threatened the harmony of the agency-advertiser relationship. In particular, the commission system of compensation gave agencies a strong incentive to persuade clients to increase their appropriations and to direct them to media where an agency commission was paid. Only the most statesmanlike agencies were likely to counsel restraint and to place ads where commissions were low. Thus, the commission system tinged the services ad agencies rendered with an almost unavoidable conflict of interest. Opportunism could, in principle, have been arrested by competition among agencies, and indeed advertisers often switched agencies when they distrusted or disliked the service they were receiving. However, agency rivalry did not entirely eliminate the problem. An advertiser-agency bond often meant close personal ties between the client's advertising manager and the agency's account representative; clients sometimes depended upon the abilities of a particular individual at an agency; advertising campaigns in general required continuing surveillance of competitor firms and the absence of long-term contracts. (Many agencies and advertisers had no more than oral agreements, cancellable at will.) The advertisers could not switch agencies without incurring costs.

In short, then, the very conditions Oliver Williamson identifies as leading to internalization and integration of functions—complexity, uncertainty, and opportunism—bedeviled advertisers. Yet between the 1890s and the 1920s, independent agencies became the suppliers of advertising services to virtually all important national advertisers. For example, all of the fifty-eight major advertisers we discussed in chapter 2 were placing their advertising through agencies by 1922.

Advertising agencies had in fact been challenged for their role as advertising counselors. Several large advertisers had strenuously resisted using an agency. Royal Baking Powder was perhaps the largest newspaper advertiser in the nation in the 1890s; it used about 14,000 publications and spent close to half a million dollars in 1893. Royal's advertising manager "has no use for the advertising expert . . . " and maintained his own advertising department with about thirty-five people.[56] Royal was not alone. Several prominent advertisers set up their own agencies, openly or covertly under their own control. For example, C. W. Post claimed that when independent agencies were handling his Postum advertising, they extracted cut rates for advertising space from publishers based on his large advertising volume and then applied the savings to other, smaller accounts. Post, who was spending $750,000 on advertising by 1908, set up an "in-house" agency headed by F. C. Grandin, and demanded that publishers allow Grandin the agency commission.[57] H. K. McCann worked as advertising manager for Standard Oil until 1911 when the Supreme Court ordered it dissolved. McCann then established an advertising business bearing his name; Standard of New Jersey was his most important account. Procter & Gamble, until after World War I, relied on an agency, Procter & Collier, where there was a family connection. Although Procter & Collier did handle advertising for other clients, its ties to the soapmaker were exceptionally close.

The house agencies were not the only alternatives to the independent agency. In the late nineteenth century, several new sources of advertising copy appeared. The 1890s saw the growth of "ready-made" copy services, especially designed for retailers. For example, the American Press Association sold sheets of twelve ads to storekeepers across the country. The user simply filled in his name and address at the bottom and sent it to the local papers. For larger advertisers, especially national advertisers, some publishers offered free advice on how to prepare copy. Edward Bok, the shrewd editor of the *Ladies' Home Journal,* often suggested advertising strategies and even contacted firms he thought should use the *Journal,* offering to plan advertising in it. Business and technical publications were particularly helpful to national advertisers in helping to prepare ads suitable to their specialized media. Most important for well-heeled advertisers, free-lance copywriters who followed the lead of John E. Powers were available for brief assignments or longer periods. Well-known advertising writers like Artemas Ward, Claude C. Hopkins, Manly Gillam, John E. Kennedy, and Charles Austin Bates worked for firms like Swift, Enoch Morgan's Sons (manufacturer of Sapolio cleanser), Schlitz Beer, and Bissell Carpet Sweepers. In the mid-1880s, "If a man announced himself an advertisement writer, he would have been regarded with comtempt by the literary element of the community"; by 1891, several of the free-lancers were said to be making as much as $3,000 to $5,000 a year. The most successful advertisement writers found that their craft could make them rich. John E. Kennedy, whose background included a stint in the Royal Canadian Mounted Police, was making $28,000 annually by 1904 preparing advertisements for a concoction known as Dr. Shoop's Restorative. Claude Hopkins, who had advertised the Bissell Carpet Sweeper and a shortening manufactured by Swift, joined a medicine manufacturer as well. After a time with Dr. Shoop's, he became a partner in the firm that made Liquozone. His share of the profits on this solution of one part acid in ninety-nine parts water amounted to nearly half a million dollars in his first full year there.[58]

During the 1890s, then, the locus of advertising work was uncertain. Agents and publishers vied to offer the services advertisers required, and more than a few of the manufacturers chose to establish their own advertising departments and dispense with agency services. The alternatives to the independent, full-service advertising agency were both theoretically attractive and historically possible.

Advertising agencies themselves had little trouble explaining how they had survived. "Organization and specialization . . . " and "experience and judgment" were the agencies' assets; "by serving a number of clients," they could "render service at a fraction of the cost that would be required to maintain an organization working on a single problem." This was the rationale the newly-formed American Association of Advertising Agencies presented in 1918.[59] Individual agencies offered comparable justifications and contended that the evolution of the service-oriented agency had demonstrated the fitness of its organizational form.

The arguments are not entirely compelling. Leading advertisers, spending a million dollars or more annually on advertising by the World War I era, might have reaped the benefits of specialization, experience, and judgment themselves by internalizing at least some of their advertising work. Companies like Campbell Soup, Eastman Kodak, Procter & Gamble, or National Biscuit were large enough to achieve the economies of scale that large agencies could obtain. Certainly these companies had operations large enough to support advertising departments with specialists in a variety of marketing activities. Since these advertisers had to maintain advertising departments to monitor the work of their agencies anyway, the in-house option might have allowed these departments to be more efficiently utilized. Even a very heavy advertiser might not be able to utilize certain advertising specialists on a full-time basis. A firm's demand for market research or artwork might be too seasonal to call for hiring specialists year-round. Yet these were activities agencies themselves often subcontracted, and there was apparently no intrinsic reason why advertisers could not have done likewise.

For smaller advertisers, the case for the advertising agency's services is somewhat stronger, but it is nevertheless possible than many advertisers might have gained from internalizing some activities and purchasing other services on a fee basis. The complaint was often raised that smaller accounts with "full-service" agencies received less service because the commission system made them relatively unprofitable. Yet agencies generally resisted the notion of providing their talents and resources "à la carte," so their clients could rarely choose what services they needed most.

Among the virtues asserted by advertising agencies, their ability to offer independent judgment stands out. The agency perspective was, agencies claimed, broader and more market-oriented than an in-house advertising manager was likely to achieve. "The advertising manager is the connecting link between his business, which pretty generally thinks in terms of cost and volume and profit, and the advertising agency, which should think in terms of markets and people and their wants."[60] The manager had a valid function as an executive in the firm, but he was too often prone, according to the agent, to interfere with the creative work of the agency. Beneath the self-serving claim that only an independent agent could provide objective service, the agency spokesman quoted above made a valid point. The production-oriented subculture of a large manufacturer might indeed stifle the development of a marketing orientation which these corporations increasingly needed. In that sense, the independent judgment and experience of the advertising agency might prove valuable. Yet that judgment was at least potentially polluted by the inherent complexities and ambiguities of evaluating advertising's effects and by the commission system, which based agency compensation on advertiser budgets, not the cost of services performed.

In sum, the case for the independent agency on transactions costs grounds remains unconvincing. Why did the system survive? The postulate of Williamson's approach, that market arrangements will be superseded when they are more costly than administrative coordination, may not hold in this case. Certainly, for some national advertisers, conventional agency relationships were amicable, smooth, and mutually profitable. Advertiser grumbling and account switching suggest that other national advertisers were not so well pleased. The almost constant refrain of the Association of National Advertisers, that the agency compensation system was too rigid, points out an important irony. The commission system, which created or exacerbated much of the structural conflict between agencies and advertisers, was in itself probably the most important reason for the triumph of the independent, full-service agency. If it had been eradicated, the industry might well have witnessed a partial internalization of agency activities among large advertisers. Routine but procedurally complex functions, where economies of scale might obtain at very high volumes, and highly specialized activities requiring very distinctive skills or equipment might have been handled independently. Advertisers then could have handled the design and execution of advertising campaigns internally while purchasing ancillary marketing services independently. The commission system as it evolved in the early twentieth century made such a fragmentation of advertising services almost impossible.

The Agencies of Persuasion

From the 1870s onward, most important advertising agents and many publishers had formed an alliance of convenience in support of the commission system. Advertisers, especially the bigger spenders, and some smaller agencies kept up a stream of criticism of the arrangement as they searched for ways to evade it. The survival of the commission indicates that the power of the national advertisers of branded products to control the advertising industry was limited. On the other hand, despite their inability to eliminate the system, national advertisers ultimately learned to live with it and adapt its workings to their interests.

Advertising agencies attempted to maintain the commission system through a mixture of exhortation and pressure. Their concerns were twofold. First, they wanted the commission granted only to genuine independent advertising agencies and to make all others pay the gross price of advertising space. Second, they hoped to raise the commission and persuade all media to pay it. Throughout the nineteenth century, when haggling in the market for advertising space was a fine art, agents constantly warned advertisers that they lacked the agents' expertise in bargaining for low prices and knowledge of circulation quantity and quality. Even if a national advertiser could persuade media to quote him "net" rates (stated gross rates less the agency commission), publishers could trick advertisers into paying exorbitant prices for inferior media. As we have seen, this argument failed to convince some of the era's largest national advertisers; companies like Royal Baking Powder, Singer Sewing Machines, Hood's Sarsaparilla, and many of the patent medicine firms relied upon the weight of their advertising appropriations to win favorable treatment from media without employing independent agencies. As agencies widened the scope of their services and turned away from space brokerage, they justified the commission as a payment for the work they did both for the advertiser and for the publisher. According to one Chicago agent, troublemakers who wanted to abolish the commission plan consisted of manufacturers' advertising managers who dreamed that this would increase their salaries and status, a few disgruntled special representatives of publishers who blamed their own failures on agencies, and some advertising trade publications who wanted to establish their own advertising service bureaus in place of independent agencies.[61]

Rather than rely entirely upon their advertising skills, advertising agencies chose to pressure and cooperate with publishers to maintain the commission system. They insisted that it was the publishers' duty to refuse the commission to all but established agencies. At the first convention of advertising agents ever held, in New York in 1873, they harshly criticized "certain publishers [who] have . . . been known to allow the Agent's commission to certain advertisers." Agents hoped that the formation of the American Newspaper Publishers Association in 1887 would strengthen the publishers' resolve to deal only with leading agencies. However, the ANPA's founding convention refused even to pass a resolution pledging to do business only with genuinely independent agents. In 1889, the publishers compiled a list of forty-one agents they deemed reputable, but a gathering of some of the leading advertising men declared that the ANPA standards were too lax; according to these advertising men, only sixteen of the agents the publishers named had shown ability to do "a business not only with the papers of a class, a city or a section, but with the papers of the whole country." Worse yet, the Association's recommendations were only advisory and were widely flouted. In 1894, *Printers' Ink* complained that only about a dozen newspapers would refuse the agency commission to advertisers who placed their copy directly, without an agency. Not until the end of the century did forces favoring strict recognition criteria manage to set up a committee within the ANPA to draw up an official list of recognized agencies. In 1905, George P. Rowell was still complaining that most publishers would accept a name on a letterhead as sufficient proof that an agent was legitimate.[62]

Although newspaper publishers moved only haltingly to tighten enforcement of agency recognition standards, the new mass-circulation magazines were generally friendlier to the agencies' interests. Most magazines were more dependent than newspapers on national advertisers who used agencies, more hopeful that agents would boost their advertising revenue, and less able to deny them advantageous space rates. Among the publishers of the low-priced popular magazines, only Frank Munsey tried to break down the commission system. Probably the most hard-bitten and materialistic of the new breed of magazine publishers, Munsey declared in the fall of 1898 that the agency commission was unethical. He was paying a corps of solicitors to find advertisers for his magazines and could see no valid reason to offer price concessions to a purchaser of advertising space simply because he called himself an agent. Besides, Munsey claimed, "A commission is paid for a purpose, and that purpose is nothing more or less, in very truth, than bribery . . . a bribe to influence the advertiser's trusted agent to place advertising with the publisher." After the end of the year, Munsey insisted, he would charge the same rates to all advertising buyers. The agents' response to Munsey's announcement was swift and vehement. They withdrew much of the advertising they controlled from his publications and castigated him in the advertising community. The publisher was unwilling to allow the circulation of *Munsey's Magazine* to be verified, and agents hinted that his reticence on this matter made it an untrustworthy advertising medium. Within a year, Munsey was forced to revoke his policy and reinstitute an agency commission.[63]

Munsey's dissatisfaction with agency service had led him to try to circumvent the intermediaries. Cyrus H. K. Curtis, publisher of the *Saturday Evening Post* and the *Ladies' Home Journal,* was also unhappy with agency practices but responded by trying to strengthen the agencies' independent role. In 1898, annoyed at finding out that an employee of the J. Walter Thompson agency had accepted a client's order for a *Journal* ad at a cut rate, Curtis refused to grant the commission to the agency. Another Thompson worker proposed to one of Curtis's advertising sales managers that they draw up a contract that would forbid future price cutting. In May, 1901, Curtis introduced a model advertising contract: Agents agreed "not to quote any price for advertising . . . at less than your full card rates," under penalty of being stricken from the list of acceptable agencies for a second offense. They also agreed not to pass along any of the publisher's 10 percent commission to advertisers. Curtis, in return, pledged not to grant the agency commission to other agencies nor to "under any condition or circumstance, allow the agent's commission to any advertiser."[64] In effect, if agents would desist from pushing down Curtis's rates for advertising space, the publisher in turn would make them the gatekeepers of his advertising pages. Price competition for both the medium and the agencies' work would be averted.

Because of the *Ladies' Home Journal*'s soaring circulation, Curtis's influence was powerful. By 1905, other general interest and women's magazines, including *Century, Delineator, McClure's, Munsey's,* and *Scribner's,* also refused the commission to advertisers or to agencies that split their commission with advertisers. Meanwhile, advertising managers of most national magazines of importance banded together in a trade association, the Quoin Club. From 1902 through 1904, its members deliberated over standards and evaluated candidates for agency recognition. The Quoin Club changed its name to the Periodical Publishers' Association in 1917 and continued to be a leading advocate of the commission system. Meanwhile, newspaper publishers also took steps to eliminate marginal or bogus agencies and to disallow the commission to advertisers who placed directly. By 1913, the American Newspaper Publishers Association accepted only 280 out of 718 advertising agencies as bona fide, financially responsible, independent firms.[65]

Other media had less interest in fostering the agency system. For example, publishers of business and technical magazines claimed that agents were of little use because they provided their own assistance to advertisers. The publishers asserted that agencies lacked the technical knowledge needed for advertising in their specialized media. In 1902, the American Trade Press Association unanimously resolved to refuse commissions to all advertising agencies. Companies that specialized in handling outdoor signs and mass transit advertising were also generally hostile to the idea of paying commissions to advertising agencies, but in 1916 a group of agencies created a National Outdoor Advertising Bureau which accepted agency orders for advertising. By the 1930s, the Bureau controlled about three-quarters of the outdoor national advertising in America.[66]

The most enthusiastic advocates of the commission system were the large advertising agencies that established the Association of New York Agents in 1911 and dominated the movement leading to the creation of the American Association of Advertising Agencies in 1917. This organization, known as the Four A's, was the first effective agency trade association. It aimed to persuade media to grant commissions only to established service agencies, to increase the commission rate and standardize it at 15 percent of the gross space rate, and to prevent agencies from rebating commissions to clients. The Four A's noted that it was open to agencies of all sizes, but only about 110 of the approximately 1,400 firms that called themselves advertising agencies in 1917 were members, and these were usually industry leaders.

The Four A's was remarkably successful in solidifying the agency compensation system its members preferred. Its drive to raise the magazine commission from 13 to 15 percent, where it would equal the figure allowed by most newspapers, quickly bore fruit. In September 1918, *Printers' Ink* reported that over forty publications had increased the commission within a six-week period and that others were expected to follow suit shortly.[67] The agencies' success depended on good timing. During the First World War's inflation, publishers had rapidly increased their gross advertising rates and could more easily afford to grant a larger agency discount. At the same time, the excess profit tax induced many manufacturers to invest in "good will" advertising, polishing corporate images with dollars which otherwise would go to the tax collectors. Under these boom conditions, it was not difficult for agencies to assert their demand for increased compensation.

For the same reasons that many publishers and most prominent advertising agencies supported the commission system, national advertisers tended to oppose it. They stood to gain the most if direct placement of advertising was made the norm. The Association of American Advertisers, founded in 1899, and a successor, the Association of National Advertisers (formed initially in 1911 as the Association of National Advertising Managers) were the organizations leading the advertisers' fight. If the commission system could not be replaced fully by a fee-for-service system, advertisers contended that any advertiser should be able to split commissions with its agency. If commission splitting were widely practiced, then the size of agency compensation would become in fact, though not in principle, an issue between agency and advertiser, not agency and publisher. Despite the fact that some of the nation's largest advertisers were active in the ANA, its anticommission activities were usually effective only in stirring up animosity between manufacturers and ad agencies. Realizing this, the ANA feared that "radical reform" of the system might cause "destructive chaos." Although it was on record as favoring a fee plan, the ANA dropped the topic from its agenda between 1916 and 1921, when it again resolved to agitate for change. This provoked, in turn, an angry and adamant response from the Four A's and little substantive change. However, advertisers' hopes for reform never faded entirely and were most likely to be voiced when economic downturns made them look for ways to cut costs.[68]

Although advertising agencies managed to preserve, standardize, and even raise their commissions, it is harder to tell whether they managed to prevent their income from draining away to their larger and more aggressive clients who demanded a share of their commissions. Agencies and some publishers called this rebating, and the standard contract the Four A's devised prohibited it; advertisers, on the other hand, contended that since agencies were legally and ethically the servants of advertisers, commission sharing was not a rebate at all. According to the clients, rebates were payments from parties at adverse interest, but agencies and advertisers were presumably both on the same side of the market. Scattered evidence suggests that rebating (to use the common but pejorative term for the practice) was not infrequent. For example, in 1910, of the twenty-five agencies that placed the most advertising with the Curtis Publishing Company, ten were "suspected of rate cutting" despite the dire consequences spelled out in the Curtis contract. A decade later, four of the ten agencies were still doing business with Curtis. Presumably, rebating of commissions from media less punctilious about the fate of the discount must have been at least as common. There were also some agencies, Ayer being the most important, that rejected the commission system outright and insisted that the price of agency services must be "a matter of mutual agreement between our clients and ourselves." In 1934, when Depression conditions must have forced agencies to cut prices by whatever means were necessary to get and keep accounts, a study by the ANA found that about four-fifths of all advertisers still used the straight commission to pay for newspaper, magazine, radio, and outdoor advertising—the principal media offering discounts to agencies.[69]

The legal status of agency compensation further befogged the situation; court rulings provided little indication of where the advertising agency's allegiance lay. If the advertising agency was, as it originally in fact had been, the agent of publishers, the commission system would be natural and correct. To rebate without the medium's approval would be improper under such circumstances. If, as had also once been the case, the agent was an independent broker, commission splitting was of uncertain legality. A rebate to an advertiser might illegally compromise the broker's independence. Finally, however, if advertising agencies were legally true agents of advertisers, obliged to behave "with an eye single" to client interests, then the price of agency services was properly a matter for agency and advertiser to decide.[70]

Judges found it hard to decide among these possibilities. Beginning in 1876, a series of decisions had labeled the advertising agent an independent broker. In 1902, for example, the Ben Hampton Agency of New York, sued a Mr. Schlesinger, a client who had cancelled his advertising contract before it had run its course. The media billed Hampton at the rates for short-term contracts, disallowing the discounts granted on the assumption that the ads would run for a longer period. Hampton, in turn, sued Schlesinger to recover the additional expense. In 1906, a New York court ruled in the defendant's favor; the discount arrangement bound only the agency and the medium. Schlesinger had no obligations under it. In short, Hampton was an independent contractor, not an agent in any legal sense.[71]

On the other hand, as early as 1884, the courts had held that an advertising agent was indeed a legal agent of the advertiser and owed him "an honest and fair fulfillment of their agreement." In 1913, the ruling in *Kastor* v. *Elders* further advanced the agencies' legal responsibility to their clients. The court noted and apparently accepted the practice of commission rebating; "It appears that the agent sometimes gives his advertising patrons the benefit of part of the agent's commission, but this is a matter of contract in each instance, and is determined by the nature of the account." In *Clarke* v. *Watts,* decided in the same year, the ruling was that an agency that had signed a contract to buy space from a medium was nevertheless not liable for payment for the purchase. The fact that the advertising agency had signed itself "Advertising Agency" was "indisputable proof" that it was really acting on behalf of an advertiser. The client, not the agency, was responsible; the agency was judged to be an agent working under the control of the advertiser.[72]

In 1924, the Federal Trade Commission filed a complaint against the American Association of Advertising Agencies, along with certain publishers' groups. The Trade Commission charged that the organizations were conspiring in restraint of trade to compel "national advertisers to employ respondent agencies or other advertising agencies in the placing of national advertising, . . . to prevent said advertisers from advertising . . . at net rates and to compel said advertisers to pay for direct advertising at gross rates."[73] Although the FTC action created a good deal of apprehension among members of the Four A's, the case was eventually dismissed in 1930. Legally, neither judicial decisions nor administrative actions were enough to dislodge the commission system.

The survival of the commission system was an anomaly in the evolution of the advertising industry. As national advertisers grew in size and number, agencies directed their talents and energies to fulfilling the needs of these clients. On the other hand, even powerful national advertisers could not put an end to a compensation system for agencies although it penalized them financially and perpetuated possible conflicts of interest with their agencies. Without the commission system, a more diverse and fragmented advertising industry would have likely been the outcome of the ferment at the turn of the century. What prevented the system's downfall?

First, media as well as agencies and advertisers had a stake in the outcome of the agency compensation question. Mass circulation magazines and big city daily newspapers believed that the commission system helped them get and keep national advertising. In the words of the Periodical Publishers' Association, "the publisher looks on the agency as a combination salesman and technical service engineer, who shall create and develop advertising by enhancing its value to the advertiser. For this service the publisher pays a commission to the agent."[74] Agents chimed in with warnings to advertisers that if the commission were to be eliminated, publishers would have to raise their rates to cover their increased costs. In the publishing world there were powerful voices raised against the discount; for example, *Editor and Publisher* magazine proclaimed its opposition in 1921. However, as long as leading publishers were able to carry out their policies of recognizing active, financially-responsible agencies and rewarding them with a substantial discount, they were an almost impenetrable barrier to major change in the industry structure.

Second, and more important, the seeming conflict between the commission system and the interests of large-scale national advertisers of branded merchandise was muted in practice by limitations on agency independence. Agencies knew full well that advertisers were the ultimate, though not the proximate, source of their income. Industry norms and practices which developed between the turn of the century and the 1920s reduced the perils of agency opportunism that had made many advertisers suspicious of advertising men.

At the heart of the matter was the fact that advertisers could, and often did, cancel accounts and switch agencies. Although this could be costly it was still an all-too-real threat to agents. By the early years of the century, advertising men were trying to establish a taboo against luring rival accounts by aggressive solicitation and were urging clients not to switch agencies for trivial causes. However persuasive these entreaties may have been, agents were rarely so safe that they could afford to neglect their responsibilities to their clients. In the years 1925 through 1933 (the first for which we have adequate data), more than 10 percent of national advertisers using agencies changed agencies each year.[75] Agencies did not dare exploit their opportunities for gain if it made their accounts join this unending game of musical chairs.

Several standards of agency conduct also strengthened the allegiance of advertising men to their clients. For example, by around World War I, it was generally established that agencies would not handle competing accounts. An agency could hardly offer unqualified loyalty to a client if it had another customer who vied for the same market as the first.

Nineteenth-century advertising men apparently had no qualms about competing accounts. Since their purpose was, above all, the sale of advertising space, not the creation of selling campaigns, space brokers had no more reason to refuse to handle rival accounts than a railroad would have cause to reject the traffic of rival shippers. For Ayer the problem first arose around 1899, when it asked its largest client, the National Biscuit Company, whether it could take on the advertising of a competing baker. When National Biscuit objected, Ayer began to accept the notion that it should not acquire a competitor's business "if we felt it jeopardized their [the original client's] interest."[76] Despite this, Ayer was guilty twice before 1930 of taking on competing accounts without informing the clients involved. The development of the prohibition on rival accounts is hard to trace, but by 1912 an advertiser could mention in passing that "when an agent has one account he is ordinarily forestalled from having another account of the same kind."[77]

Advertisers could easily agree that agencies should shun competitive accounts, but how should agencies try to win new customers? Both advertisers and agencies were uncertain. Aggressive solicitation of new clients, especially advertisers who were already using rival agencies, might constitute a nuisance to businesses and demean the image of advertising agencies, but it was hard to prevent. In the 1910s, when many agencies issued promotional brochures explaining their services and proclaiming their high standards, almost all renounced high-pressure soliciting practices. Formerly, the man who successfully recruited a client had great power and became "ex officio, its manager. He inwardly regarded the account as *his personal* property." One advertising man recalled that when he had entered the business in 1904, it was common for a solicitor to pocket one-half of the agency commission on his clients' expenditures. Even at J. Walter

Thompson around 1907, "Each of the solicitors . . . owned his advertising accounts; he merely cleared them through the agency." The rise of copywriting, research, and planning weakened the solicitors' stranglehold, but even today complaints on Madison Avenue are heard about ad men who have accounts "in their pockets" and can take clients along when they switch agencies to advance their own careers. Even the agencies that abjured aggressive account solicitation did establish new business departments. The men who handled relations with clients were now known as "account executives," "account representatives," or "contact men." These were more dignified titles than "advertising solicitor," but of course solicitation itself survived.[78]

Was it proper for such soliciting to include preparation of advertising plans, rough drafts, or even finished advertisements for businesses that were merely prospective clients? In their oratory, service agencies denounced these so-called speculative presentations. First, the agencies held, it was impossible to create good advertising without careful study and detailed investigation of a company's marketing needs; any work done "on spec" was likely to be worthless. Second, the agencies maintained that their personnel were fully committed to their existing clients, the time spent preparing advertisements for a prospective advertiser could only come at the expense of current ones. Finally, agencies simply resented the uncompensated expense of speculative solicitations; it was far easier to put together a portfolio of past work than to create new advertising for a firm that had no commitment to pay for the work. In a 1920 brochure, the American Association of Advertising Agencies surveyed agencies, found them hostile to speculative presentations, and suggested ways to avoid the iniquitous practice. Agents seemed agreed that advertisers were becoming less insistent on these advance plans and that the problem was fading.

In 1934, however, when the Association of National Advertisers studied the compensation issue, nearly three-fifths of the advertisers polled stated that speculative presentations of advertising copy were more frequent or as common as they had previously been. Some large agencies, like Ayer and Thompson, have consistently refused to engage in speculative presentations, but cynics on Madison Avenue (and the street is full of them) contend that almost all agencies succumb at least occasionally to the temptation when a lucrative account seems within reach. In 1967, according to agency head Jerry Della Femina, agencies spent over a million dollars to win the Trans World Airlines account. Ironically, TWA considered the alternative presentations and then awarded the account to Foote, Cone & Belding, the agency that had held it all along.[79] Unlike the prohibition against conflicting accounts, the ban on speculative presentations did not always appeal to the national advertisers who footed the agencies' bills.

Like other small businesses, especially those facing powerful and cost-sensitive buyers, advertising agencies groped for ways to avoid price competition. The continuation of rebating, however, indicated that at least some advertising men felt that they could not compete solely on the basis of the quality or amount of their service. Price competition made its way into the advertising business in other ways as well. The growth of ancillary services, such as handling sales promotions, product design work, and sales-force training, sometimes was a form of concession to a powerful client. These peripheral tasks generated no immediate additional advertising billings, and agencies often performed them at cost or without compensation. Larger advertisers, according to Haase's 1934 study, were more likely than smaller ones to get their agencies to do market research for them at no charge. Sometimes, in their eagerness to attract and hold lucrative clients, agencies went too far. Their lagniappes might look like wasteful excesses to advertisers: "We believe the average agency has over expanded its functions and is attempting to perform services today which it should not perform" commented a spokesman for a large national advertiser in the early 1930s. "We think most agency services are superfluous," noted another, smaller advertiser. A different, less acceptable form of agency competition for accounts was to promise to put an agency worker at the disposal of the client or to pay part or all of the salaries of the client's advertising department. To the Four A's and its members, this smacked too much of the dreaded rebate, but it was apparently far from unknown in the 1910s and 1920s.[80]

Thus, in several ways, advertisers were able to maintain their agencies' loyalty and to curb inclinations to opportunism inherent in the compensation system. The joint work of national advertisers and advertising agents to eliminate the "circulation liar" indicates that, despite the undercurrent of conflict, advertising men and national advertisers shared common interests which transcended their differences. At the same time, the culmination of efforts to provide accurate, independently-verified circulation figures for media removed a key incentive for agencies to act as independent entrepreneurs and helped tie them more closely to client service.

In the generally uncertain market for advertising of the late nineteenth century, no aspect was more mysterious than the circulations of the publications that sold advertising space. Agencies avidly scouted out information, but were usually in the dark about how many copies publishers printed and, even more so, about how many they actually sold. Agents could offer manufacturers a shaky combination of guesswork, inside tips, and the incomplete information found in the published newspaper directories of the era. George

Rowell's *American Newspaper Directory* estimated circulations for most newspapers, and he even offered $100 to anyone who could disprove the claims of those publishers who gave him sworn statements of their circulations. Other directory publishers did not even try to compile circulation figures. S. M. Pettengill, for example, claimed that publishers who told the truth would suffer by having their estimates alongside the "exaggerated statements of unfair rivals." Another agency refused to include circulation data because of their "basis in fantasy."[81]

Thus, until well into the new century, agents and advertisers bought literally billions of dollars of advertising space—worrying all the while—without a reliable idea of how many copies of the publications they were using actually were printed or reached customers. They condemned both the publications that refused to issue circulation figures and the "circulation liars" who issued inflated readership claims, but the truth was elusive.

For many years, simply defining circulation proved difficult. In 1896, *Printers' Ink* stated that "the circulation of a newspaper is expressed by number of complete copies printed," but upon reflection this seemed inadequate. There were too many tales of bundles of newspapers left sitting in the back of printing plants, shipped off to distant postmasters with requests that they be distributed, or given to newsdealers without checking on actual sales. Even the American Advertisers Association, which conducted circulation audits from 1899 through 1913, never satisfactorily defined what it wanted to count. More stringent standards, such as the number of copies actually purchased, presented their own complications. Was a subscription sold well below cost as a trial offer to count? Should publishers be allowed to continue to send copies to readers whose subscriptions had expired and count them? How should the circulation of special editions and other unusual issues be weighed? What about magazines sold in bulk to clubs and associations?[82]

Meanwhile, publisher resistance and an absence of organizational backing stymied efforts to find out circulations. A few nineteenth-century newspapers had taken the lead in announcing their circulations and permitting advertisers and agents to verify them. In 1876, the *Chicago Daily News* began to print its circulation each day, and a few other major dailies like the *Washington Evening Star* and the *Indianapolis News* followed suit; these were exceptions. Agents and advertisers remain skeptical. To them, most newspapermen were like the apocryphal one described in 1885:

> The editor was dying, but when the doctor placed his ear to the patient's heart and muttered sadly, "Poor fellow—circulation almost gone!" he raised himself up and gasped, "'Tis false! We have the largest circulation in the country!" Then he sank back on his pillow and died, consistent to the end—lying about his circulation.[83]

In 1891, leading advertisers, polled on the idea of forming an association to audit circulations, endorsed the concept but doubted its practicality. In the same year, an advertising trade publication objected to the plan of a magazine publisher to form a group of periodicals with guaranteed circulation claims. This policy, the magazine warned, would push high-quality publications into a forced rivalry with "a class of publications whose circulation would be largely 'unnatural,' and whose literary or class reputation were a way below par, to put it mildly." (This theme—that circulation was to be judged by quality of readership more than by numbers alone—was a familiar refrain of low-circulation newspapers and magazines. These publishers, however, seem to have been just as reluctant to disclose hard information about quality as about numbers.) In 1898, it was conceded that advertisers were "prone to regard the circulation liar as a necessary evil." George Rowell appealed to the American Newspaper Publishers Association to hold a conference on honest circulation, but he was rebuffed. About half of the ANPA's members around the turn of the century did offer sworn statements to the *American Newspaper Directory;* the rest, as well as most of the smaller papers that were not members, were equally content to keep mum. Rowell warned in 1900 that only one in four newspapers was "willing to tell what its circulation is, and of this one in four, there are only about a quarter that have the capacity for expressing what the circulation is, and they make all sorts of blunders in their efforts."[84]

The American Advertisers Association (AAA), formed in 1899, was the first organization to take on the task of independently auditing circulations. It dispatched inspectors across the country to investigate newspapers' claims and distributed their reports to its dues-paying members. However, at least three factors limited the group's effectiveness. Poor financial support from its members and the apathy of advertisers who would not join left it with money problems. One of its officers was later to complain bitterly that no more than one in a hundred advertisers "seems to care three whoops in the home of Mephistopheles whether the circulation figures laid before him are authentic or not." Second, the AAA was out to settle scores with agencies as well as with publishers; agents reacted by giving the group a cold shoulder even when their common interests were involved. Finally, patent medicine makers played a disproportionately large role in the AAA; this was an unseemly leadership group during the Progressive Era.[85]

Although other advertisers and agencies supplemented the AAA's work with their own attempts to ascertain circulations, chronic dissatisfaction remained. *Printers' Ink* reported in 1911 that circulation deception was waning, but, discouraged by the slow pace of AAA audits, a group of advertisers, mostly from the Midwest, incorporated the Association of National Advertising Managers (ANAM) in May 1912. Unlike the older organization, the ANAM made some allies among agents and sympathetic publishers, at least on the circulation issue. Also in 1912, Congress passed a rider to a postal bill requiring publications to print sworn circulation statements semi-annually. There were no means of verifying the statements nor explicit penalties provided for false ones; advertising men considered it "foolish," but it did indicate wider concern.[86]

In 1913, the logjam broke. That May, the ANAM convened advertisers, agents, and publishers in New York to discuss new audit procedures. The plan that emerged called for a Bureau of Verified Circulations. Publishers would finance circulation audits themselves and have influence in the Bureau's operations. Of the groups attending, only the AAA objected, insisting that advertisers, not publishers, must pay for the audits and manage them. With the financial backing of cereal manufacturers C. W. Post and Emery Mapes, the AAA reconstituted itself that fall as the Advertising Audit Association, admitting publishers and agents but keeping an advertiser majority. It proclaimed ambitious plans to expand auditing operations.

For several months, the Bureau of Verified Circulations and the Advertising Audit Association jockeyed for position while advertising agents in both secretly planned a merger. Principles of a common organization were achieved in January of 1914, but it was now the ANAM's turn to balk. It apparently feared that the midwestern advertisers in the AAA would dominate the new group. By May, however, most doubts were assuaged; an amalgamated convention met in Chicago with 595 delegates attending, four-fifths of whom represented media. Nevertheless, the Board of Directors reflected the national advertisers' authority. They held eleven of the twenty-one seats. The new organization adopted the title of Audit Bureau of Circulations (ABC) and set to work.[87]

After decades of frustration, the Audit Bureau was a sudden success. Publishers quickly saw the light—or felt the heat—and volunteered for audits faster than the Bureau could train examiners. The ABC standardized auditing procedures and tightened up definitions of paid circulation. Although it suffered financial problems in its early years and was torn by controversy over how publishers could use audit reports in their own advertising, the ABC managed to make the circulation of the vast majority of important periodicals a known quantity.

The Audit Bureau of Circulations signaled the growing influence of national advertisers of branded goods and the willingness of reputable advertising agencies to devote their efforts to serving these businesses. No longer willing to treat advertising as an incidental expense, companies needed to know what they were purchasing. At the same time, an independent source of circulation information meant that agencies lost one of the principal bases of entrepreneurial profit—their inside knowledge about media circulation. Once again, despite the paradox inherent in the agency compensation system, advertising agents were impelled to serve as counselors to advertisers, not space brokers.

Many of the largest agencies in the 1920s could trace their ancestry back well into the nineteenth century. N. W. Ayer & Son, J. Walter Thompson, and Lord & Thomas, three of the very biggest, all bore the names of the men who founded them two generations earlier, and, in some cases, agency executives' careers stretched back to the earlier era of space dealing. However, modern advertising agencies were very different institutions, both in what they did and in how they did it. As promotion of medical nostrums gave way to sustained advertising campaigns for a spectrum of branded consumer merchandise, agencies themselves changed apace. By the years around World War I, agents were pridefully asserting their professionalism and proclaiming their own importance in an economy of mass consumption and mass persuasion.

Changes in terminology reflected changes in advertising men's definitions of their roles. As early as the 1890s, they recognized that the title of "advertising agent" had become ambiguous at best, misleading at worst. Service agents were eager to disclaim what seemed like a shady past. "Everyone admits it is a far cry from the space selling of twenty years ago, to the varied service now rendered by efficient agents," stated the Curtis Publishing Company around 1910.[88] Could the label be changed along with the product itself?

Back in 1892, *Profitable Advertising,* a well-known trade publication, had settled on the practice of calling advertising agents "attorneys." "Hire an attorney to look out for your advertising business the same as you would hire an attorney to look out for your legal business," the editor announced. In 1899, *Printers' Ink* proposed that "advertiser's agent" would best define the agent's true role, and this suggestion was repeated from time to time thereafter. Despite these efforts, however, "advertising agent" remained, ambiguity notwithstanding. Advertising men had to look to other devices to clarify and exalt their status in the business world.[89]

Concern about advertising nomenclature was one way in which advertising agents tried to translate their new responsibilities into increased respect. They felt that occupational slang threatened to demean the status of the craft. In an article instructing readers not to call themselves "ad men," *Associated Advertising* inquired, "Aren't we past the nickname age?" The abbreviation was too familiar, an undignified name no more proper than "doc" for a physician. More than one writer suggested that advertising experts should call themselves business "engineers." (The growing authority of the new professions based in the physical sciences may account for the shift from "attorneys" a generation earlier.) Agency leaders like Stanley Resor of J. Walter Thompson balked at referring to advertising as a "game," and using "dope" as a synonym for advertising copy was also considered destructively flippant. Even the simple abbreviation, "ad," was suspect. During World War I, while advertising men were advocating the standardization of everything in sight, the Associated Advertising Clubs urged its member groups to adopt titles in the form "Advertising Club of [Community]," to eliminate "ad" from the names of local clubs.[90]

Advertising men of the early twentieth century frequently insisted that they were just as good as men in the traditional professions or other prestigious occupations. There was an undertone of defensiveness accompanying the boasts. In 1902, for example, *Printers' Ink* contended that "writing, even the writing of advertisements, is as much a profession as that of medicine or theology." E. E. Calkins, in his 1905 textbook, maintained that "the profession of an advertising man steadily rose until now it aspires to rank with that of the three 'black graces'—law, medicine and divinity. Some day the advertising man . . . expects to be recognized as a member in one of the professions." A decade later, when Calkins revised the book, he was ready to proclaim that his prediction had been realized: "Advertising is a profession just as much as law or architecture." Others sounded the same theme more exuberantly. In the words of an Atlanta advertising agent in 1911, "There is no higher calling, ministers not excepted, in America or any other country than ours."

According to *Associated Advertising* in 1914, "The last ten years have accomplished wonders for advertising. Men now say that they are in the advertising business with just as much pride as the man who says, 'I am a professor at Yale,' or 'I am President of the United States.'"[91]

Ultimately, advertising men based their claims to social status on the business accomplishments of the modern service agencies. Despite the elements of continuity, agencies had changed drastically. In the early years of the twentieth century, agency offices in New York City had begun a migration uptown, their detachment from the newspaper business symbolized by their physical separation from the Park Row publishing district. Leading firms like George Batten and J. Walter Thompson took offices around Madison Square, in Manhattan's East 20's. Shortly after World War I, another exodus took place; the agencies moved farther uptown, locating along Madison Avenue and parallel streets near Grand Central Station. Also in the first decade or so of the twentieth century, agencies began to open branch offices in major cities. Thompson, for example, began operations in Chicago, Detroit, and Cincinnati. Ayer, long the preeminent agency in Philadelphia, started a New York branch in 1903 and had expanded into Boston, Chicago, and Cleveland by 1911. Most agencies had only one office, but in 1918, the 111 members of the Four A's had thirty-eight branches outside their home cities.[92] Although branch offices were often set up merely to attract clients in another city or to handle a particularly large or demanding account, they tended to evolve into full-service branches in their own right, taking on all but the most specialized advertising functions.

As advertising agencies came to mirror (on a smaller scale) the structures of the big businesses they served, advertising men pointed with pride to the same attributes large corporations boasted of. Growing size was one indication of success.

The work force at Ayer numbered 163 in 1900 but had reached 298 a decade later and 496 by 1920. The Batten agency had fewer than 50 employees in 1905, 126 in 1916, and 272 in 1928 when it merged with Barton, Durstine and Osborn.[93] Billings (the amount of advertising an agency handled) grew even faster, at least where statistics are available. Ayer placed less than $1,500,000 of advertising in 1900 but over $11,000,000 in 1921. Figures for J. Walter Thompson indicate comparable growth, even though Stanley Resor dropped almost three-quarters of Thompson's clients when he bought the agency in 1916. Like some other large agencies, Resor's company was unwilling to take clients whose budgets were too small to yield a profit to the agency. Even more spectacular was the growth of Lord & Thomas under the leadership of Albert Lasker. When he arrived at the agency in 1898, it billed less than a million dollars annually (but nevertheless was probably the nation's third largest agency); in the 1920s, the firm reached yearly volumes of $40,000,000 or more.[94] Thus, the largest agencies of the post–World War I era were substantial enterprises in their own right. They wanted to be treated with the respect their magnitude merited.

In growing, advertising agencies took on some of the trappings of large-scale bureaucratic organizations. As we have seen, specialization was the rationale of the service agency, and the lengths to which it could be carried are evident in the agencies' profusion of job titles and categories. Brochures issued by agencies around World War I to explain their services and attract customers tended to stress the complexity of agency operations. These pamphlets used the catch-words of their corporate contemporaries—efficiency, organization, specialization, and planning. Some featured elaborate organizational charts, putting planning and analysis in a central position and relegating space buying and customer solicitation to the corners of the page. J. Walter Thompson under Resor, with its blueprint for a Department of Standardization, a Statistical and Investigation Department, and not one but two Planning Departments (one for men, one for women!), took these notions to their most extreme. For new employees being groomed for management positions, the agency prescribed a two-year training course to initiate them into all aspects of agency operations. Plans for the training program included assigning long lists of required readings and giving periodic examinations for the advertising acolytes. Resor's belief that advertising could be based scientifically in the study of group psychology found an analogue in the organization's own efforts at systematic, scientific management.[95]

By the 1920s, advertising agency spokesmen consistently portrayed their organizations as sophisticated and complex, ready to tackle the most complicated marketing problems. "Specialization spread by leaps and bounds. How far it has gone is hardly recognizable," proclaimed one agent in 1923, writing on "The Departmentized Business of the Advertising Agency." He found no fewer than twenty-five separate areas where expertise was required.[96] To direct this kind of agency, advertising "craftsmen" alone were insufficient. Agencies needed "marketing business captains," leaders "whose sense of business enables them to read a financial statement or a cost accountant's report as closely as any financier. The agency head, the man who is at the wheel, must be possessed of a keen profit sense."[97]

The men (there were very few women; over 97 percent of the respondents to a 1931 *Who's Who* volume were men) who worked in advertising agencies in the 1910s and 1920s were in all likelihood a more skillful, trustworthy, and educated group than agents a generation earlier. About half of the men associated with general advertising agencies and listed in a 1916 directory had attended college, and more than a quarter held a bachelor's degree or its equivalent. Two-thirds of them had at least attended high school. These were fairly young men; the median age was around forty and only about one in ten was over fifty. Approximately half of the respondents had been born in the Middle West, most of them in small towns. Three were English and two Canadian by birth, but none came from Eastern or Southern Europe. On the contrary, the typical advertising man of 1916 seems to have been the product of middle-class, small-town Middle America. This portrait is reinforced by two other studies. A statistical study of five hundred advertising men working in Detroit in 1928 concluded that most were young—average age was only 33.9 years—and that nearly three-fifths had attended college. Over a third had graduated. The University of Michigan was the alma mater of far more ad men than any other school. English was the most popular major, but courses in economics, business, journalism, and engineering were also popular. Similarly, a sample drawn from a 1931 version of *Who's Who in Advertising* indicates that over two-thirds had attended college, and nearly half held one or more degrees. By birthplace, the 1931 group was even more rooted in the small towns of the Midwest than their 1916 counterparts. The homogeneous background of the advertising men is striking. None of the 1931 sample came from any of the nations of the "New Immigration" which sent millions of peasants and workers to America after 1880.[98]

In the 1950s, Martin Mayer observed in *Madison Avenue U.S.A.* that a disproportionate share of leading advertising men were ministers' sons. The same seems to have held true half a century earlier. Among these ministers' sons were: George Batten and William Johns of the Batten Agency; Bruce Barton of Barton, Durstine and Osborn (which merged with Batten in 1928); Joseph Appel, advertising manager and vice president of Wanamaker's; and Henry N. Mc-

Kinney, Francis W. Ayer's long-time friend and partner. Others, like Ayer himself, Earnest Elmo Calkins, and Claude C. Hopkins, had exceptionally devout Protestant upbringings. Whatever else we can infer from this, it clearly imparted to the advertising business a certain moralistic fervor. Especially pronounced in the truth in advertising movement, which we shall discuss later, this religious strain also imbued the efforts of advertising agents to exalt their status with an element of righteousness, even self-righteousness. At the same time, however, the small-town, midwestern, Protestant origins of advertising leaders may have hampered their efforts to comprehend and reach the diverse worlds of American consumers. The industry was, of course, not totally homogeneous; Albert D. Lasker, a Texas-bred Jew, ran Lord & Thomas for forty years. However, a certain insularity is hard to deny. In 1931, for instance, the editors of *Who's Who in Advertising* could blithely report, "Adherents to the theory of Nordic supremacy might relish the fact that blue-eyed advertising men are in the majority."[99]

In organizations like the advertising agencies of the post–World War I years, there was little room for the adventurers and gamblers who enlivened the advertising business (and cast shame upon it) in its earlier decades. Nor were there good prospects for nonconformists. As one advertising man told a convention in 1911, "Gradually, the advertising world has been waking up to the fact that you can do business without having long hair, dirty fingernails and the ability to push a pen." Five years later, a speaker announced that "the old conception of the advertising man as a genius who got results by a flash of inspiration has pretty largely passed.... It has given way to a more substantial, though less romantic conception of the advertising man." A few regretted the change. Helen Rosen Woodward had spent the first two decades of the century in advertising and had become a high-paid copywriter despite the fact that she was a woman, Jewish, and a political radical. After leaving advertising, she remarked:

> Advertising has the solid mentality usual in a large established business with heavy investment. It no longer attracts the lovers of chance, but rather those who look for safety. It has a pontifical dignity which robs it of much of its earlier fire. If never occurred to any of the pioneers to think about the dignity of advertising. It was much too interesting for that.[100]

Perhaps this explains why so many of the novelists and poets who worked in advertising disliked it and left when they could. Sherwood Anderson, F. Scott Fitzgerald, Stephen Vincent Benét, and John P. Marquand, among others, served time as copywriters. Anderson wrote advertising from 1900 to 1906 for a well-known Chicago agency and returned to the firm (Long-Critchfield) intermittently for more than a decade thereafter to supplement his income. An old colleague recalled that Anderson was unusually good. "Anderson was both a producer (of everything from layouts to sales policies) *and* a salesman. . . . His hunches were worth a dozen surveys." Indeed, Anderson's articles for the agency's house organ reveal none of the criticism he later applied to advertising. In his memoirs, however, Anderson equated the advertising business with prostitution. He felt "a sharp sense of uncleanliness" from spending his days "dirtying words." He called a friend at work "Little Eva" and the friend called him "Mable" in "a kind of mutual recognition of our common whoredom." Finally, Anderson recounted the story of a woman advertising writer who told him of her attempt to be a streetwalker. " 'I'd been another kind so long and wanted to see what it would be like to go the whole hog' was what she said." After confiding this to Anderson, the young woman went to her hotel room and shot herself in the head.[101]

Others also seized on the metaphor of prostitution for their work in advertising. James Rorty, a poet who worked as an advertising man for over a decade, recalled that an agency head had told another aspiring author who applied for a job, "Get out of here, you damned little fool. Don't you know this is a whorehouse?" Rorty himself referred to the fleshpots of Madison Avenue; when the poet Hart Crane asked Rorty to recommend him for a job at the latter's agency, Rorty "told him to go to hell, any hell other than Batten Barton Durstine and Osborn's."[102]

For some, the advertising business was foolish rather than vicious. F. Scott Fitzgerald composed for an Iowa laundry the slogan, "We keep you clean in Muscatine," while working in 1919 for the Barron Collier Agency in New York. He later recalled with amusement that his boss told him that he had a fine future in advertising. Stephen Vincent Benét wrote copy for another agency in 1919. He lasted three months, "bored by its mechanical tricks and depressed by the eight-hour day." John P. Marquand put up with nine months at J. Walter Thompson. At a staff conference, another writer proposed a slogan for a soap advertisement: "Every day an oily coating lightly forms upon your skin." Marquand immediately interrupted, "It scans, it scans! Don't you hear it? It's trochaic tetrameter. Who says there isn't poetry in advertising?" Stanley Resor, less than amused, told Marquand, "I don't think you really have the business instinct."[103]

Success bred self-assurance. By the 1920s, the advertising agencies had resolved to their own satisfaction their role in American business and were articulating with increasing force a social purpose for advertising. Yet the nay-saying novelists and poets reveal some of the inner tensions of the advertising business. Agencies wanted national advertisers of branded products to see them as skilled, learned marketing counselors. The sober, businesslike visage was partially negated, however, by the fact that advertising was by no means the rational, closely-calculated investment advertising men claimed it was. The intuition, empathy, and verbal fluency agencies needed were uneasily yoked to the rhetoric and values of business service.

A second inner conflict resulted from the fact that agencies expounding the optimistic platitudes of New Era business had not entirely broken with the shadier entrepreneurial practices of a previous generation. Despite undeniable progress, agents knew that rebating to clients, account stealing, speculative presentations, and financial arrangements at less than arm's length had not been eradicated. In 1927, E. T. Gundlach, president of a successful Chicago agency, published a bitter satire on the advertising business, *Old Sox on Trumpeting*. Set in Athens in the fifth century B. C., the book tells of the efforts of the Tauros Trumpeting Agency to persuade an oil merchant to launch an advertising campaign. Gundlach displays the advertising business at its worst, full of self-serving cant and vacuous oratory, in order to propound a more sensible view of advertising. But the picture he paints of advertising standards and ethics is quite devastating.[104] Agency spokesmen paid little attention to *Old Sox on Trumpeting*, but its charges ring true.

Finally, advertising practitioners who conceived of advertising as an objective science with nearly universal applications were, in reality, constrained by their own class and cultural biases. Unknowingly, they suffused the advertising they devised with their presuppositions and prejudices and created an advertised world in their own image. Few were prepared to recognize and fewer to accept the nation's heterogeneity. "People Have Become 'Standardized' by Advertising," commented a headline of a 1920 article in *Printers' Ink*.[105]

Yet for all their limitations, advertising agents had accomplished much in the years from 1890 to 1920. They had, in effect, created a new product. Formerly, agents with access to space in newspapers and magazines had sold that space. Now they sold something else—their access to American consumers. To use a chilling but revealing phrase of modern marketing, advertising agencies dared to offer their corporate clients a share of the American mind.

5

The Ethics of
Persuasion

WHEN advertising men have reflected on the development of advertising ethics, they have told a story of steady movement towards openness and honesty, motivated by the enlightened self-interest of the industry's paragons. As they have seen it, honest advertising validated their claim to professional status at the same time it enhanced advertising's value by increasing its credibility. However, the truth in advertising movement of the Progressive Era was not as simple as this optimistic portrayal would have it. The same developments that engendered the organized movement for self-regulation also raised new ethical problems which advertising men still have not satisfactorily resolved. The advertising industry insisted that it needed no more and no less than "the white light of truth," but it failed to recognize that its understanding of truth had been shaped by the new economic functions of advertising.[1]

This is not to deny that substantial changes were wrought in advertising principles between the late nineteenth century and World War I. Simply put, in virtually all newspapers and most magazines of the Gilded Age, many advertisements were outright lies. Patent medicine ads promised to cure every disease known, and quite a few unknown, to medical science. Readers were informed that by becoming agents for this product or making that one in their spare time they could earn a secure and generous income with slight effort. We cannot accurately estimate the magnitude of the fraud perpetrated by dishonest advertising, either in money taken or in pain and suffering of the victimized, but we can be sure that the losses were enough to make nostalgia unjustifiable.[2]

Beyond any doubt, advertising had changed by World War I. By then, the majority of established magazines and many important newspapers had eliminated, or at least greatly reduced, patently dishonest advertising. Such ads could still be found in less scrupulous media, direct-mail advertising, or local publicity, and they occasionally slipped by the most rigorous censors, but they were no longer the mainstays of agencies or publishers. There is no reason to denigrate the importance of this change or to question the sincerity of the advertising men who crusaded for it.

Yet, if total cynicism is mistaken, so, too, is uncritical acceptance of the purposes and accomplishments of advertising's reformers. National advertising for branded products and continual advertising by large-scale retailers required new standards of propriety and fair play among those who created and distributed advertising. Ad men themselves emphasized that ethics and self-interest went hand in hand. Inevitably, the realities of an age of big business both compelled reform and drew the boundaries of that reform.

ETHICS AND ELIXIRS

In the advertising journals of the 1870s and 1880s, truth in advertising was a very minor topic. Since, composing advertisements was, at most, an occasional service of advertising men rather than their stock in trade, agents had less reason than their later counterparts to be actively interested in the contents of advertisements. When comments on advertising ethics did appear, they fitted the needs of that age. Since advertising was basically a matter of announcing the availability of goods to potential customers, truth in advertising was subsidiary to the intrinsic qualities of the products themselves. "It is a pretty well established fact that an article cannot have a permanent sale unless meritorious," noted Rowell in 1872, summing up the fundamental ethical precept of the era. He maintained the necessity of dealing in "something that people want" and of having it in better quality than one's rivals did.[3] The merit of the commodity determined the merit of the advertisement.

This, at least, was the implicit theory. However, the dominance among advertisers of patent medicines belied the assumption that advertising simply meant "making known." This competitive industry was already filled with those who saw more creative uses for advertising. One drug promoter happily proclaimed, "I can advertise *dish water* and sell it, just as well as an article of merit. It is all in the advertising."[4]

In principle, medicine makers aiming for repeat sales to

satisfied customers might have an incentive to tell the truth about their products. But, of course, nostrum peddlers were notoriously deceitful advertisers, for honesty would usually have compelled them to admit that their drugs lacked curative power. In matters as uncertain and emotion-laden as personal health, experience was (and is) a fallible guide to truth, so worthless products might be bought again and again. The alcohol and other addictive drugs in many leading patent medicines of the late nineteenth century provided another reason for repeat purchases. Those campaigning for honesty in advertising would have to confront the "toadstool millionaires."[5]

A few publishers and department store magnates were the first to take real action against fraudulent advertisements. Orange Judd, a leading publisher of agricultural magazines, told the readers of his *American Agriculturist* in 1860 that he would exclude deceptive advertisements. A Philadelphia magazine, which had begun as an advertising circular for John Wanamaker's department store, proclaimed in 1880 that it would "guarantee the reliability of the advertisers using its advertising columns." On the advertisers' side, some of the reform impulse can be traced to John E. Powers, probably the first man to make a career of writing advertising copy. At first for Willcox and Gibbs Sewing Machines in England and then, in the 1870s for Lord & Taylor's dry goods store in New York, Powers prepared ads that were distinctive enough for later imitations to be called "Powers-style" copy. Powers held that bombast and "fine writing" were "not only intellectual [sic]," but also "offensive," and that "the common-place is the proper level for writing in business." When John Wanamaker hired Powers for his Philadelphia department store, the style was combined with the Wanamaker adherence to a "one-price" (no bargaining) policy and the store's money-back guarantee. Though some questioned whether Powers actually had eliminated misstatements from Wanamaker copy, accuracy was the norm and the ideal. By 1890, more than fifty other dry goods retailers were copying Wanamaker advertising styles.[6]

It is no coincidence that department stores pioneered in proclaiming honesty in advertising. The department store, with a clientele limited by geography, was less able to do without repeat sales than an itinerant patent medicine salesman or a mail-order dealer. A store selling thousands of different items would suffer more from alienating a customer by dishonest advertising of one item than would a store carrying a restricted line of goods. Truth was not a simple derivative of self-interest, but, as an 1887 Wanamaker advertisement put it, "We have proved that truth-telling is not only right but politic."[7]

Not all advertising that publications rejected was banned on grounds of dishonesty. As early as the 1840s, Horace Greeley's *New York Tribune* turned down ads for abortionists and for venereal disease "cures." The *New York Herald* in 1865 removed "the most repellent" medical ads. Indeed, there was a strong link between opposition to sexual matters in print and efforts to eliminate certain patent medicine advertising. Such epithets as "indecent," "suggestive," and "unclean" indicate the extent to which some reformers were concerned with the sexual as well as the fraudulent aspects of medical advertising. Fittingly, antivice crusader Anthony Comstock wrote to *Printers' Ink* in 1893 responding to an editorial discussing "Where to Draw the Line" in excluding medical ads that were "outrageous in their intimations and offensive to every idea of decency." Comstock suggested the dual nature of the problem: moral and physical decay were intertwined. "[A]dulterations in food and medicines, and the misuse of functions . . ." were responsible for the dearth of "strong, manly men and robust, healthy women."[8]

The Ethics of Persuasion

A scrapbook of "Medical Advertisements Not Accepted" for publication between 1886 and 1891 shows the scope of one large publisher's concern with advertising ethics. E. C. Allen of Augusta, Maine, was, at the time, publisher of a series of "mail order magazines," so-called because the mail-order advertisements dominated the popular fiction they surrounded. Allen's magazines were probably the most widely circulated in the United States in the 1880s, reaching millions of readers each month, most of them rural and poorly educated. With few exceptions, the ads Allen excluded were those with sexual implications or purposes. The company rejected the ubiquitous "weak manhood" advertisements, cures for "private diseases," offers of "rubber goods," products for "Ladies in Trouble," ribald song books, and a bureau offering "a correspondent for fun, self improvement or matrimony." Others rejected included marked playing cards, lottery schemes, Confederate bills, and a "Passkey to open 900 different locks."[9]

Virtually all of the major advertising agencies of the era, including J. Walter Thompson, N. W. Ayer and Son, George Rowell, and Charles H. Fuller, submitted these ads to Allen. There is no evidence that the agencies were censoring any of the copy they sent out. When the publisher rejected them, his tone, in fact, was apologetic. Allen informed one advertiser that his copy was not being declined "on the ground that patients are not, or may not be benefited, but for reasons of general business policy." "Of course the photos of actresses which are sent out are mild enough," Allen conceded to an agent, "but the suggestiveness annoys thousands of our subscribers." He went on to say that forthcoming issues would contain some very profitable ads. "Had we kept 'Weak Men,' Abortion Pills . . . and shady pictures to the front, we could not have made this advance." Readers' values determined policy. Allen told another agent,

"Papa and Mamma don't like it [the kind of ad the agent had sent in] and so we have to submit. Papa and Mamma do not object to certain other lines of ads, which we, who have good taste, don't like any better, and so we keep them in." Decisions about advertising acceptability were not always clear cut. At least once, Allen suggested that advance payment for an ad might influence his judgment of its propriety.[10]

One agent took the rejection of an ad he had submitted with bad grace. An employee of J. Walter Thompson complained after Allen had turned down copy for a breast developer. "I would like to get you some good biz from this shop, but when I send you something myself . . . I wish you would take it in. I can't always send ads of religious tracts and fine tooth combs." The agent told Allen that he was the only one of twelve publishers to reject the ads.[11]

In the 1890s, the ethics of advertising copy began to receive more intensive attention from both buyers and sellers of advertising. More and more publishers censored their pages, most notably Cyrus Curtis of the *Ladies' Home Journal.* In 1892, Curtis proclaimed that the magazine would no longer accept any medical advertising; with its circulation well over half a million, this was bound to make an impact, and other magazines, such as Butterick's well-known *Delineator,* followed suit. Newspapers were generally slower, but when Adolph Ochs bought the *New York Times* and introduced the slogan, "All the News that's Fit to Print," the spirit of the motto spilled over into the advertising columns. An advertisement in *Printers' Ink* for the Catholic magazine, *Ave Maria,* suggests the scope of censorship in a publication that claimed to be "America's most Exclusive Medium." The *Ave Maria* printed no ads for patent medicines, liquor, face powders, dress reform, corsets, land companies, investment companies, or speculative propositions.[12]

At least some advertising agencies in the 1890s were scrutinizing their prospective clients' ethics. The George Batten agency (a forerunner of the famous Batten Barton Durstine & Osborn) turned down a $50,000 account during the firm's second year of operations, because, as Batten said, "It was a quality of business we didn't care to handle." Since the agency's billings the previous year had amounted to only $25,000, the rejection was no small gesture. Later in the decade, N. W. Ayer turned down several lucrative accounts on ethical grounds.[13]

While the attempts to clean up advertising in the 1890s were isolated and sporadic, advertising men of the decade first stated some of the themes and postulates that later animated a more organized truth in advertising movement. First, along with the continuing injunctions to sell an article of merit, advertising spokesmen showed increased concern for the truthfulness and accuracy of the advertisements themselves. Second, *Printers' Ink* and others endorsed a "rotten apple" theory. One false statement in an advertisement would weaken its effect; one false advertisement would injure a seller's credibility permanently; one discredited advertiser would harm the advertising of all others. This logic was later to justify the industry's efforts to regulate itself. Third, despite the peril from dishonest advertising, advertising men asserted that their craft was continually becoming better and purer. Finally, and most emphatically, they insisted that truth in advertising paid, that advertisers, media, and the public would all gain from eliminating dishonesty. The rare soul who dared claim that fraudulent advertising might be profitable, or that media that rejected dishonest advertising might suffer losses, was likely to be quickly rebutted.[14]

Homilies on the efficacy of truth may be located in almost all writings on advertising. Even when deceit might bring short-term gains, "It pays better to tell the truth and lose

temporarily than to state a falsehood and lose permanently."
The extent of misrepresentation did not matter: "Little lies
in your advertising will frighten some people as quickly as
'whoppers' will frighten others." The effects of a lie would
linger on: "A slight misrepresentation in a single advertisement may often cast a shadow of doubt over all the advertiser's subsequent efforts, even though these be thoroughly reliable." Undesirable advertisements tainted legitimate ones by
association: "If every newspaper advertisement was strictly
legitimate, the returns from advertising would show a
marked improvement." In short, "Truth is the prime essential in advertising."[15]

One way in which the advertising community in the
1890s differed from its counterpart two decades later was in
its opposition to governmental action to prohibit dishonest
advertising. Even though they did not claim that existing
legal remedies were effective, advertising spokesmen criticized virtually all proposals for legislation. Artemas Ward,
who vigorously advocated truthful advertising in the columns of his trade journal, *Fame,* nevertheless opposed a bill
to prevent sales of adulterated and illicit patent medicines
because "it would be a hardship to manufacturers and a constant irritation to dealers." *Printers' Ink* criticized proposals
to require patent medicine makers to print their formulas on
the label. Generally cynical about legislative intervention
("Freak legislation is the order of the day.... The result of
all this is to make capital wary and distrustful."), Rowell saw
no justification for passing laws to forbid false advertising:
"The greatest enemy to fraudulent advertising is the increasing intelligence of the people. This will accomplish more
than a score of laws." Legislation, in other words, was at
best futile, at worst dangerous.[16]

In any case, advertising men contended, regulation was

superfluous. According to *Printers' Ink* in 1897, "There is comparatively little fraudulent advertising done today." An 1895 article maintained, "Ten years ago, the majority of people looked on all advertising as dishonest. Now the majority of people look upon the majority of advertising as strictly honest business news. This is an advance."[17]

"Strictly honest business news" could mean, on the one hand, news of honest businesses or, on the other, honest news about business. The former represented the older primary concern in advertising ethics; the latter formulation would suggest the growing attention to copy accuracy. Put simply, an advertiser "should never represent [his goods] as having properties they do not possess." Truth was coming to be defined as the absence of falsehood. This concept was to become a basis for a vigorous movement of self-regulation. But established standards of truth and falsity were themselves becoming less and less applicable. Daniel Boorstin has pointed out that twentieth-century advertising is often neither true nor false. The omnipresent image no longer either mirrors or distorts an underlying, more tangible reality. The advertising image itself dominates and becomes the reality, cast adrift from the physical products it sells. Credibility becomes the central issue, and the older moral problems of truth and falsity are not so much resolved as bypassed.[18]

Patent medicines represented an implicit challenge to advertising men to put their principles into practice. Although the predominance of proprietary drugs among nationally advertised products was waning by 1900, few agents or media could afford to ignore them. Of the 2,853 national or regional advertisers in an 1898 survey, 425, or almost a sixth, were selling "medicines, remedies, and articles sold in drug stores." The large and respected agency of N. W. Ayer still received over 15 percent of its advertising billings from patent medicines. Of the products chosen in an 1898 *Printers' Ink* poll as best-advertised, close to half were patent medicines.[19]

Thus, it was hard for advertising men to condemn the gamut of worthless and even dangerous nostrums that flooded the market. (The value of patent medicine products increased by 128 percent between 1899 and 1904.) Instead, the prevailing opinion held that indecent and prurient appeals should be suppressed, but that most remedies were above reproach. One advertising agent in 1898 asked defensively why reformers proposed to tax patents but not physicians' prescriptions. In 1903, as the forces of reform were gathering support for pure food and drug legislation, *Printers' Ink* continued to approve the drugs:

> There may be proprietary medicines which possess little value; yet the majority of them have been thoroughly tested and proved before they were exploited in newspapers.... That so many of them have been in the market for years and are stand-bys in respectable families is highest proof of their merit.

In 1904, *Printers' Ink* continued its vigilance on behalf of patent medicine advertisers, opposing state legislation to require listing ingredients on medicine labels and calling a New York bill to ban the use of pictures of human beings in medicine ads "a 'fool' measure."[20]

As we have seen, leading advertising agents sometimes maintained direct interests in patent medicine firms. The well-known agencies of Pettengill, Rowell, and Lord & Thomas were among the firms that purchased drug companies, while N. W. Ayer acquired the assets of a manufacturer unable to pay his advertising bills. Claude C. Hopkins, probably the most successful copywriter of the era, shared the management and held a minority interest in Liquozone.

The Ethics of Persuasion

In 1905, the journalist, Samuel Hopkins Adams, revealed this purported germicide to be 99 percent water and 1 percent sulphuric and sulphurous acid, with no curative value whatsoever. Liquozone had, only a few months earlier, announced a $1.5 million appropriation for advertising, to be placed through the respected Paul E. Derrick Company of Chicago. This was "said to be the largest single appropriation ever placed with an advertising agency." A. Frank Richardson, a leading agent in the 1890s, became the proprietor of a blatantly fraudulent and perilous tuberculosis "cure." George W. Coleman, business manager of a religious magazine and later president of the Associated Advertising Clubs of America when it launched the truth in advertising movement, was accused by a subscriber of accepting deceitful patent medicine ads in the magazine. He replied, "To the best of our knowledge and belief, we are not publishing any fraudulent or unworthy medicine advertising." Samuel Hopkins Adams surveyed the magazine and found nineteen medical ads of "at best, dubious nature." Adams noted that the *Christian Endeavor World's* readers were treated to offers of "magic foot drafts" to cure all rheumatism and Dr. Bye's Oil Cure for cancer, among other unsavory advertisers.[21]

In the first decade of this century, however, some advertising commentators considered the medicines to be atavisms. In their 1905 text, *Modern Advertising,* Earnest Elmo Calkins and Ralph Holden concluded "that, today, the advertising of proprietary remedies does not stand on the same high plane as the advertising of commercial articles and, possibly, never will. The advertising of manufactured articles— the real bone and sinew of commerce—is today the great field in which the best energy and the best talents are being used." Considerably older and more tolerant of the patents, George Rowell nevertheless noted in his 1906 autobiography

that "money made in the patent medicine business is a practical barrier to social success."[22]

These qualms appeared at the same time that a movement for federal regulation of proprietary drugs was gathering force. The energy of Harvey W. Wiley, chief chemist of
the U. S. Department of Agriculture, had, by the late 1890s,
brought the issue of food adulteration to the public and to
Congress. Beginning in 1898, the National Pure Food and
Drug Congress provided a forum where socially-concerned
scientists and doctors, women's groups interested in individual and public health, and businessmen hoping to gain advantage over their rivals came together. For the next eight
years, delaying tactics and internal squabbles kept pure food
and drug legislation from enactment, but pressure was growing. In 1903, Wiley, who had previously been concerned
almost exclusively with food adulteration, proposed that patent medicines be included in the bill before Congress.
Muckraking attacks on the patents by Mark Sullivan in the
Ladies Home Journal and by Sullivan and Samuel H. Adams
in *Collier's* in 1905, publication of Upton Sinclair's *The Jungle* in early 1906, and Theodore Roosevelt's commitment to
securing significant legislation all contributed to the passage
of the Pure Food and Drug Act in June 1906.[23]

By the time of its passage, *Printers' Ink* viewed the Pure
Food and Drug Act without alarm, albeit with reservations.
The law was mild enough to win the acceptance of much of
the leadership of the patent medicine industry as well as the
advertising business. For signing the bill into law, *Printers'
Ink* called Roosevelt a "responsible statesman." Two
months later, expressing worry about the implementation of
the statute, the editors called the law "puzzling," but soon
reported approvingly that administrative regulations enabled
dealers to sell stock that had been on hand before passage of
the law. A report at the end of 1906 headed "Food Law

Benign," noted, "A canvass made of manufacturers affected has shown general satisfaction with the statute."[24]

Since the law's provisions failed to penalize false advertising and pertained only to ingredients and labels, consumers did not always find the law benign. In 1911, the Supreme Court ruled that the Act did not outlaw false curative claims. The Sherley Amendment of 1912 banned such assertions on packages and labels, but the need to prove intent to defraud weakened this proviso.

Printers' Ink's accommodation to the Pure Food and Drug Act followed a pattern of government-business rapprochement common in the Progressive Era. Businessmen realized that legislation and administrative regulation were often tolerable and sometimes desirable, and they increasingly sought to shape government intervention to fit their needs. Not surprisingly, in the case of the Pure Food and Drug Act, the legislation itself showed some of the same assumptions that advertising leaders made. The bill aimed at penalizing fraud and misstatement, not at the harmfulness of the products themselves. In James Harvey Young's words, "The law did not strike a blow against self-medication, but sought to make it safer."[25] This orientation matched the advertising industry's belief that the ethical issue involved misrepresentation rather than the intrinsic qualities of the products advertised.

In the years after the Pure Food and Drug Act, advertising men sometimes used patent medicine manufacturers as whipping boys. Sounding a note of alarm about the staying power of improper patent medicine advertising, a 1911 editorial observed: "The grave part of the matter is that there still remain so many concerns willing to ignore the ethics of public and private responsibility." The magazine of the Associated Advertising Clubs noted in 1915 that the Proprietary Association was appealing to publishers to relax standards of advertising acceptability. The journal predicted that the heightened ethical sensibilities of newspapers and magazines would render the drug manufacturers' entreaties futile. According to *Associated Advertising,* publications that wanted to readmit patent medicine advertising circulated primarily in small towns. In other words, the mainstream of advertising was more and more estranged from the patent medicine makers. The nostrums were not well suited to the kind of advertising required by other national advertisers in an urban, industrial society.[26]

Advertising industry figures for the early twentieth century suggest the extent of separation of patent medicines from the dominant trends in national advertising. None of the leading advertisers in the 1913–15 sample was a pharmaceutical firm (see chapter 2). In an era when more and more national advertisers were using advertising agencies, patent medicine makers were more and more likely to place their advertising directly. This was true of such mainstays of the turn-of-the-century advertising pages as Lydia Pinkham's tonic, Ripans Tabules, and Mellin's Food, all of which had employed agencies in 1901 but were dealing directly with publishers a decade later.[27]

It is not fully clear whether agencies rejected patent medicine accounts or medicine manufacturers simply found they could do without agency services. Some agencies did turn down undesirable clients. In 1901, the Mahin agency of Chicago announced it "declines all kinds of liquor and 'fake' patent medicines, and other objectionable advertising." N. W. Ayer refused all advertising for products containing alcohol after 1903, but, despite Ayer's disapproval of fraudulent patent medicines, the agency sent out advertising for a tuberculosis remedy as late as 1905. For Ayer, however, discarding the medical accounts was counterbalanced by acquiring important clients manufacturing branded products,

including Procter & Gamble, Burpee Seeds, and several subsidiaries of Standard Oil.[28]

Apparently, most agencies, if they exercised restraint at
all, had no blanket policy on patent medicines. Even in
1915, Mahin sounded almost apologetic explaining why
some national magazines rejected drug advertisements. Ex-
clusion was no reflection on the products themselves; it was
done to "keep their columns filled with announcements that
contribute to holding the interest of subscribers." Progressive
agencies like Albert Lasker's Lord & Thomas, which held
the Liquozone account in 1911, and J. Walter Thompson
still had important medical clients.[29]

While curbing the scope of patent medicine ads was probably the most important development in advertising ethics in
the first decade of the twentieth century, advertising professionals also began to perceive the moral questions pertaining
to other issues. Opposition to overt rivalry and price competition in advertising, for example, was elevated from practical
advice to a moral injunction. Many turn-of-the-century advertisements denigrated their competitors, often by comparisons that portrayed products as useless or injurious. Royal
Baking Powder (formulated with cream of tartar) and other
brands (with an alum base) fought each other ferociously in
their advertisements. C. W. Post attacked coffee as bad for
the nervous system when advertising Postum. Rivalry
among different kinds of chocolate often took the form of
warnings of adulteration. In a classic of the genre, the American Tobacco Company later advertised its machine-rolled
cigars by advising readers that rival brands, rolled by hand,
might have been sealed with the workers' saliva. Other firms
made invidious comparisons unrelated to health. Insurance
firms issued broadsides asserting that their competitors' financial structures were perilous and that their executives

were wastrels and rogues. Less striking than these cases, though hardly less significant, were the instances in which advertisers claimed superior merit or lower prices than their rivals. Retailers, especially department stores, were prone to claim they offered better values than their competitors.

Advertising men had consistently advised against attacks on rivals on practical grounds. "Mention the name of a competitor and you advertise him; slander him and you do yourself no end of harm," warned Rowell in 1894. "Let your rivals pay their own advertising bills."[30] More and more, attacking rivals and claiming lower prices was considered not merely unwise but also hazardous for advertising as a whole and even unethical. "Advertising is a constructive force," declaimed one writer in 1904, "and cannot be used effectively to tear down the other fellow's business." In 1907, an article on "Social Evolution and Advertising" asserted that "while advertising was first competitive, it is now noncompetitive in form.... The older advertising is pathological; the later advertising is sane." The advertising code of the Curtis Publications banned ads "'knocking' competitors," and other media followed suit. Such provisions were "necessary to protect advertisers against themselves." "Modern business means co-operation," preached the Lord & Thomas agency. "Secrets have become uncommon.... Attacks are in bad odor." Firm after firm insisted that its advertising was intended to increase demand for the entire industry, not to woo customers away from competitors. In an article on "Advertising that Helps Competitors as Well as Yourself," an executive of the Kewanee Boiler Company explained that "originally, all advertising was selfish.... Real generous advertising began to be prominent when it was realized that advertising ... was a very potent force in establishing a market or creating a demand for something heretofore unknown."[31]

Moral censure also fell increasingly upon those who advertised that they offered lower prices or better values than their competitors. According to Macy's advertising manager, "To attempt to create interest by prices alone is to walk in a circle, for the sensational effect is over in a day." It was the task of advertising to teach consumers that price should not be the "paramount issue." The refrain, "People are fast learning that 'cheap' goods are dear at any price" was constantly repeated. John Lee Mahin stressed the immorality of comparative price advertising. "Mere price competition logically ends in the debasement of those who practice it.... People who buy things because they are cheap or because they are so-called bargains are wasting their substance."[32]

What accounts for the vigorous condemnation of advertising that criticized or made direct comparisons with other firms or products? First, there is little doubt that many of the more virulently critical attacks were false or at best misleading. Reading rival baking powder advertisements might convince the credulous that the bakers of America were raising a nation of dyspeptics. Second, advertisers who denigrated their competitors were besmirching the honor of advertising in general and making it less credible in the public mind. Third, aversion to price competition and other forms of unrestrained business rivalry dictated a nonantagonistic approach in advertising. Support for the idea of competition remained, but it was defined as competition *through* advertising, not rivalry *in* advertisements or attempts to undersell. "Competition through price cutting is generally ruinous," stated a 1904 article. "Competition by means of advertising isn't.... Price cutting doesn't educate the public. Advertising does, and that means increased demand."[33] For these reasons, advertising ethics by the early twentieth century had become a two-sided matter. Winning public acceptance of advertising demanded that advertising men deal truthfully with potential customers. At the same time, the increasing importance of demand-creating national advertising and the ambivalent attitudes of national advertisers toward competition made proper treatment of competitors a matter of great concern. As we shall see, the truth in advertising movement was rarely able to distinguish responsibilities to consumers from obligations of fair competition.

THE TRUTH IN ADVERTISING MOVEMENT

Trends in advertising ethics in the decade from 1900 to 1910 paved the way for the organized truth in advertising movement of the next decade. A spirit of cooperation, acceptance of governmental action, and a definition of truthfulness as the central requisite of ethical advertising were all important components of the truth in advertising movement.

However, although ideals and principles had been stated, the record of accomplishments in the earlier years was spotty. Individual advertising agencies and media could forswear dishonest advertising, but plenty of willing hands remained available to prepare and publish it. There was no effective legislation prohibiting dishonest advertising in force. By 1913, *Printers' Ink* declared that "instances where an advertiser stoops to knocking . . . are almost as scarce as proverbial 'hen's teeth,'" but most large retailers continued to claim superior values and cheaper prices, and major advertisers like Royal Baking Powder still were preaching the perils of rival brands.[34] Before 1911, local advertising clubs were generally devoted to sharing business gossip and socializing and were ill-suited for effective campaigns against dishonest advertising. National advertising voluntary associations were still weak and poorly organized and financed.

At the August 1911 convention of the Associated Advertising Clubs of America (AACA), the truth in advertising "fires burst into brilliant flames," in the hyperbolic words of H. J. Kenner, leader and chronicler of the movement. Attendance at this Boston meeting tripled to 2,260 and the number of clubs represented more than doubled the 1910 figures. Enthusiasm ran high. *Advertising and Selling* called it "The Most Important, Largely Attended and Successful Gathering of Advertising Men Ever Held."[35]

Convention oratory in 1911 focused on the intertwined themes of truth and professional stature. One of the most acclaimed speeches of the convention, delivered by Joseph Appel, advertising manager of John Wanamaker's and president of the retail advertisers' division of the AACA, was on the "Ten Commandments of Advertising." Paralleling the text of the Decalogue, Appel condemned a multitude of advertising sins, concluding:

Thou shalt not covet, nor imitate, nor run down thy neighbor's business; thou shalt not covet, nor imitate, nor run down thy neighbor's name, nor fame, nor his wares, nor his trade-mark, nor anything that is thy neighbor's.

Bert Moses of the American Advertisers' Association reduced Appel's ten principles to one of his own: "A code of ethics for advertising that all could espouse and observe might consist of one simple word: Honesty."[36]

The accomplishments of the AACA's Boston gathering cannot be measured by the oratorical heights to which delegates soared. The important work remained to be done after adjournment. Two aspects of the convention's aftermath stand out. First, both nationally and locally, groups moved to implement the convention's insistence on a movement to clean up advertising. Second, this surge of self-regulation appears to have been fueled internally. New York ad man Richard Waldo warned that "the evidence . . . on every hand of unbelief in advertising . . . is so great that it must be a question for us to solve and solve soon."[37] Yet, in fact, consumer discontent with advertising at the time remained inchoate and impotent. There was no real threat of externally imposed regulation in those years.

If the enthusiasm of the 1911 convention was to be translated into results, legal sanctions against dishonest advertising needed strengthening. On the federal level, in 1872 the postmaster general had been granted the power to bar fraudulent schemes from the mail. Although this authority had been used to suppress many dishonest enterprises, it was limited in two crucial respects. It could only be used after the fraud had been committed, the transaction completed. Moreover, it could, of course, be applied only when the miscreant used the mails. In Massachusetts, where a law against false advertising had been in force since 1902, and in New York, where a comparable law had passed in 1904, there had been only a handful of prosecutions and only one conviction. Other states lacked even these ineffective statutes. Finally, there was a common-law basis for action in cases of fraudulent advertising. In practice, this was almost wholly useless, primarily because the plaintiff had to prove that the deception was intentional and that it had been a material element in causing him to purchase the advertised item. The common-law principle of *caveat emptor* still dominated jurisprudence.[38]

In the fall of 1911, *Printers' Ink* editor John I. Romer called upon H. D. Nims, a New York lawyer and author of a treatise on unfair competition. Romer asked Nims to draft a model statute banning dishonest advertising. First presented in a series of three articles in *Printers' Ink* at the end of the year, the proposal was a single, 153-word sentence:

> Any person, firm, corporation or association who, with intent to sell or in any wise dispose of merchandise, securities, service, or anything offered by such persons, firms, corporations or associations, directly or indirectly, to the public for sales or distribution, or with the intent to increase the consumption thereof, or to induce the public in any manner to enter into any obligation thereto, or to acquire title thereto, or an interest therein, makes, publishes, disseminates, circulates, or places before the public, or causes, directly or indirectly, to be made, published, disseminated, circulated or placed before the public, in the form of a book, notice, handbill, poster, bill circular, pamphlet, or letter, or in any other way, an advertisement of any sort regarding merchandise, securities, service, or anything so offered the public, which advertisement contains any assertion, representation or statement of fact which is untrue, deceptive or misleading, shall be guilty of a misdemeanor.

Those able to wade through the proposal would note that the prosecution was not required to prove intent to deceive, the nemesis of common-law action and previous statutes. Nims recommended state, not federal, action, on the grounds that state laws would complement Washington's enforcement of its mail fraud laws.[39]

In explaining to ad men how the model statute would operate, Romer suggested that active surveillance by local advertising clubs would be essential to its success. Clubs would monitor advertisements, receive complaints, investigate them, and attempt to resolve them. Sounding a continual theme of the truth in advertising movement, Romer minimized the likelihood of resort to the courts. "I think," he wrote, "there will be comparatively few prosecutions under this statute." After a few cases had been tried and publicized, errant advertisers would no doubt mend their ways.[40]

Within two weeks of introducing the model statute, *Printers' Ink* claimed "Keen Interest in Remedy for Dishonest Advertising," citing endorsements from AACA President George W. Coleman, Herbert S. Houston, who chaired the Educational Committee of the Associated Clubs, Dr. Harvey Wiley, the Minneapolis Ad Forum, and several prominent editors and publishers. By 1913, the model statute had been introduced in about fifteen states. Enactment came first in Ohio, where the bill was signed into law on February 26, 1913. The number of states enacting the proposal grew steadily for the next decade, reaching twenty-three by 1921.[41]

Opposition to the statute came primarily from certain publishers who feared its enactment would cut into their revenues or would subject them to prosecution for falsehoods in their advertising pages. Some states explicitly exempted publishers from legal responsibility under the statute, and advertising leaders tried to convince publishers that the act *"should be the best advertisement for advertising that ever happened"* in order to assuage their economic anxieties. Yet in several states, less stringent alternatives to the model statute were adopted. Most of these included phrases like "with intent to deceive" or "knowingly" and gutted the laws of any practical effect.[42]

Although state action on the truth in advertising statute was gratifying, advertising men sometimes expressed a desire for national legislation "which will give the national advertiser the same protection against bad company in Texas that he enjoys in Maine." The passage of the Federal Trade Commission Act in 1914, though not directly linked to advertising industry pressures, showed once again that progressive advertising men had accepted the desirability of governmental action to promote their cause. At first concerned that the Federal Trade Commission "follow a constructive policy, in contrast to the policy of attack and disintegration which has been pursued by the Department of Justice in the past few years," advertising men soon found that the Commission shared many of the industry's sentiments about "fair competition." The FTC's first chairman, Joseph E. Davies, spoke at the 1915 Associated Advertising Clubs convention in Chicago, calling for cooperation between government and advertising men. Later that year, the FTC granted the AACW permission to bring it interstate cases of advertising fraud which state statutes could not cover. Edward N. Hurley, the FTC's second chairman, spoke to the final session of the 1916 AACW convention in Philadelphia, carrying the same message that Davies had. "So long as the Federal Trade Commission continues to be made up of gentlemen who regard their mission as a constructive ... one, we believe this body will receive in increasing measure the appreciation and co-operation of the best elements in the industrial world," commented *Printers' Ink* in early 1917.[48]

In 1912, George Coleman named an eighteen-member National Vigilance Committee of the Associated Advertising Clubs. Headed by Harry D. Robbins, advertising manager of an investment banking firm, the NVC intended to tread a cautious path. It reported in 1912 that there had been "nothing spectacular in the committee's work ... and none was desired." Indianapolis ad man Merle Sidener replaced Robbins in 1914, but the NVC's tone remained unchanged: "'To be progressive in thought and conservative in action'—that is the policy of the National Vigilance Committee for 1914–1915." This statement outlined a program in which educational and public relations activities predominated. In June 1915, the NVC asked the Associated Clubs to appropriate $15,000 for a permanent staff and office for its vigilance work. H. J. Kenner, who had run the Minneapolis Vigilance Bureau, became the first full-time national secretary.[44]

The Boston AACA convention also provided a stimulus for local advertising clubs to begin "vigilance" work for truth in advertising. In December 1911, the Advertising Men's League of New York City established a committee for "practical" truth in advertising work. Its thirty-three members included several men already identified with the cause—John I. Romer and J. George Frederick of *Printers' Ink;* William Ingersoll, the League's president and a vociferous advocate of resale price maintenance; and attorneys Clowry Chapman and H. D. Nims. In 1912, Boston advertising men formed an Advertising Vigilance Bureau to carry out similar tasks. By mid-1914, about one hundred local committees had formed. At first, these were usually known as vigilance committees, but gradually the title of Better Business Bureau gained favor, although the National Better Business Bureau did not organize until 1925. Perhaps the best way to grasp the practical effect of the truth in advertising movement is to trace the activities of these local vigilance groups from the scattered records that survive.[45]

Under the leadership of Mac Martin, an indefatigable advertising booster and reformer, the Minneapolis Ad Forum was particularly active in truth in advertising work. The club's vigilance committee was publishing a bulletin, holding regular meetings, and corresponding with national advertising leaders by 1913. The club proposed and lobbied the *Printers' Ink* model statute through the state legislature that winter, making Minnesota a close second to Ohio in the race to enact the law. For its activities on the statute's behalf, letters of congratulations came from several large local and regional firms, including the Chicago, Burlington and Quincy Railroad and Northwest Consolidated Milling.[46]

In February 1914, the Minneapolis Ad Forum became the first club in the nation to hire a full-time employee for vigilance work, establishing the Minneapolis Vigilance Bureau. Fifty-three local businesses subscribed $3,145 to pay his salary and maintain an office. That October, H. J. Kenner, a former newspaper man and advertising manager, became the Bureau's secretary. Within less than two years, eight other advertising clubs had employed full-time truth in advertising staff. By 1921, a survey found twenty-nine cities whose Better Business Bureaus were headed by full-time workers.[47]

The activities of the Minneapolis Vigilance Bureau accorded well with its stated purpose of "beget[ting] *maximum public confidence* in advertising" In its first year, the Bureau investigated 192 complaints. Finding in 64 of these cases that the ad was not false or misleading, the Bureau computed a "burden of unjustified suspicion" of 33⅓ percent. The figure rose to 41⅓ percent the next year but fell to 28½ percent in 1916–17. The Bureau was quick to warn businessmen that honest and dishonest advertisers alike would bear this burden unless the Vigilance Bureau's activities received support.[48]

Apart from patent medicines, the majority of complaints concerned retail advertising of dry goods and other consumer durables. Department stores, clothing merchants, furniture dealers, jewelers, and piano dealers received the most attention. Complaints came from both the public and from aggrieved competitors. Few of the cases, however, required invoking the truth in advertising law. The number of prosecutions declined from five in 1914–15 to four and then two in following years.[49]

Much the same pattern characterized truth in advertising work in Portland, Oregon, and Cleveland, Ohio, two other cities where vigilance workers were active and left records of their organizations. Cleveland's paid secretary, S. A. Weissenburger, and C. W. English, who assumed leadership of the Portland Better Business Bureau in December 1916, both had backgrounds in advertising and public relations. By June 1917, after about a year of work, Weissenburger had conducted over one hundred investigations, with only two requiring a "visit to the Police Prosecutor's office." English reported the same month that 145 complaints had resulted in 111 satisfactory adjustments and only five prosecutions. Discussing the settlement of a complaint against a piano dealer, the Portland Bureau stated it,"believes this advertiser will not again violate the law, and [the bureau] has no desire to prosecute except as a last resort." As in Minneapolis, retailers were the cause of most problems. In Portland, nine department stores, seven piano stores, and seven jewelers topped the list of early investigations, while only four of the cases involved manufacturers' advertising.[50]

In 1917, Kenner, by then secretary of the National Vigilance Committee, praised the Cleveland Advertising Club as "noteworthy . . . in that it endeavors to strike at the fundamental causes of fraudulent advertising rather than to investigate cases unrelated and taken at random." Nevertheless, in all cities for which records have been located, case-by-case adjustment constituted the bulk of vigilance work. In typical instances, the Portland Bureau persuaded a dentist to fix a set of store teeth for a dissatisfied patient and convinced the Portland *Oregonian* to reject ads for a patent medicine, Nuxated Iron. When a circus came to town falsely advertising prizefighter Jess Willard and wrestler Frank Gotch as star attractions, the Portland Club took the circus to court and won a conviction and a fine of $25. There are indications that clubs in larger cities went after bigger game upon occasion. The Cleveland Bureau investigated phony stock offers and probed the case of a petroleum company that untruthfully claimed to be connected with Standard Oil. The Minneapolis Bureau, perhaps because Kenner had begun his work there before moving on to the national level, cooperated most closely with the National Vigilance Committee, especially in the major investigation of the Ford Tractor Company, a manufacturing firm in Minneapolis whose advertising insinuated a nonexistent connection with the Ford Motor Company. The Minneapolis Bureau and the National Vigilance Committee worked together again in pursuit of one Samuel C. Pandolfo, who traveled from town to town promising to make each the manufacturing headquarters of the Pan Motor Company—if he was entrusted with sufficient local capital.[51]

Although the National Vigilance Committee went after these and scores of others whose false advertising spread beyond local borders, it devoted a good deal of its time to exhorting and assisting local clubs. "Wake up! Local Committees!" began one of the NVC's more effusive bulletins. "Scrutinize your local advertising carefully, and when you feel sure you have nailed a falsehood . . . which needs to be investigated at some other point, write or telegraph." Publishers were invited to submit questionable advertising copy to the NVC for its judgment and for information on any complaints about it in other cities. Beyond this, the NVC offered local groups advice on fund-raising, suggested educational activities, and notified the clubs of what their counterparts in other communities were doing. In short, although the NVC did carry on its own activities, much of its effort went to support the work of local clubs. Figures on case load reflect this balance. While the NVC was investigating "scores" of cases in the year ending in May 1917, local clubs handled some 1,800 complaints.[52]

BOUNDARIES OF THE TRUTH IN ADVERTISING MOVEMENT

The truth in advertising movement could, and frequently did, point with pride to real accomplishments in its first decade. The number of local groups increased steadily, and they handled more and more cases. By the year ending in May 1921, Better Business Bureaus investigated 6,815 complaints. The NVC's budget had grown to $90,000 in that year.[53] Passage of the model statue and "Blue Sky" laws against fraudulent financial promotions gave the movement new weapons against false advertising. Exposure and prosecution of swindlers like Samuel Pandolfo showed the movement's determination and energy. Vigilance work gave some publishers the courage they needed to enforce higher standards of advertising acceptability. Some manufacturers' trade groups, even the notorious Proprietary Association, devised standards of honest advertising for their industries.

Quite successful on its own terms, the truth in advertising movement of the Progressive Era seems in retrospect to be fraught with ironies. Exuding a genuine and ardent moralism,[54] the movement was shaped by hardheaded self-interest. Though local businessmen led many of the battles, the truth in advertising crusade ultimately strengthened the hands of manufacturers of nationally distributed brand-named goods, chain stores, and other mass retailers. Finally, the achievements of the truth in advertising movement helped pave the way for more advanced techniques of persuasion and their disturbing social and ethical implications.

Advertising men always justified the vigilance campaign as a measure that would bolster public confidence in advertising. Thus, it was tempting to accentuate the positive. Exposure and enforcement might clash with image building, and it was hard to fend off those who wanted the truth movement to become a means of institutionalizing self-congratulations. For instance, a member of the National Vigilance Committee proposed at the 1912 AACA convention in Dallas that advertisers who had joined their local clubs deposit $100 with the NVC. In return, the firm would get electroplates of the Associated Clubs' "Truth" emblem for use in advertisements. This plan, which had the added benefit of raising much-needed funds for vigilance workers, was actually implemented on a trial basis in Fort Worth, Texas, in 1914 and 1915, but was discontinued after criticism from those who pointed out difficulties in monitoring the emblem's use. Other schemes to franchise truth, however, continued to pop up.[55]

On the local level, vigilance workers never stopped reminding their fellow businessmen of the cash value of honest advertising. Club newsletters urged members to patronize their fellow members' businesses as reliable firms. "It doesn't hurt a bit, fellers, to remember Ad Clubbers when placing your business," noted the Portland Ad Club's *Spotlight*. The Advertising Club of New York feared this could get out of hand and passed a resolution against members' "soliciting business in the club."[56]

Some of the truth in advertising advocates wanted to keep the movement in check. The Pittsburgh Publicity Association voted to focus its vigilance efforts on praise of honest advertising, not on "wordy warfare against evils that do not exist." By about 1916, some advertising men seemed disillusioned with the movement. "It is time," proclaimed the chairman of the National Advertising Commission, "that we take truth for granted and talk less about it." Bert Moses, who, five years earlier, had presented honesty as the watchword for the profession, rejoiced that service had replaced truth as the dominant theme of the 1916 AACW gathering. As the United States moved towards entering the World War, leaders found newer ways to demonstrate advertising's virtues, and the ardor of the vigilance movement cooled accordingly.[57]

Hesitation about taking legal measures also vitiated some of the truth in advertising movement's force. Sometimes reluctance to go to court was based on purely practical grounds. The advertising clubs of Iowa could afford a part-time secretary for their state-wide Better Business Bureau, but the Bureau's $3,000 annual revenue "carries us very well as long as we do not undertake prosecutions." Writing to his counterpart in Minneapolis, the Iowa BBB secretary concluded, "My observation is that these Bureaus are universally starved to death."[58]

Beyond this, however, aversion to legal action stemmed from a typically Progressive faith that knowing the facts of a case would have a sufficiently salutary impact. By education and by shining the "white light of truth" upon malefactors, those advertisers who had simply misunderstood their responsibilities would be enlightened while the persistent wrongdoers would be set apart and stigmatized.[59] In this view, to prosecute was virtually to admit the inapplicability of the movement's precepts. Both the local clubs and national truth in advertising workers prized conciliation above all and valued exposure above prosecution.

As we have seen, the truth in advertising movement, though national in scope, expended most of its energies handling local cases. This accorded well with the ways in which advertising men generally defined the ethical problems of their craft. False advertising was perceived as a problem created by those on the fringes of the business world, parasites feeding on the good will and public confidence honest advertisers had laboriously created. Half a century later, retired *Printers' Ink* publisher C. B. Larrabee recalled that at the height of the truth in advertising movement, respectable advertising men had tried to distinguish themselves from the "Swashbucklers." However, noted Larrabee, "too many of the Respectables couldn't forget that a lot of the Swashbucklers were nice guys, good golfers and possessed of charming wives."[60]

Though they may have succumbed to these thoughts, truth in advertising activists felt they knew who the swashbucklers were likely to be. According to Jesse H. Neal of the NVC, most dishonest advertising involved "worthless stock ... the land sharp ... medical frauds, the matrimonial bureaus, the detective agencies, fake banks, fake employment agencies, etc." Richard Waldo of the *New York Tribune* told fellow newspaper men that, were it not for patent medicines, the problem of dishonest advertising would not be large. A 1912 judicial decision indicated that legal sanctions were applied against "'schemes' which ... have all smacked of the confidence game, of getting something for nothing." In the 1920s, a legal scholar analyzed mail fraud cases during an unspecified four-year period. Of the seventy-four charges of violations, only two related to "misrepresentations of articles offered for sale." The remainder fell into the confidence game category.[61]

Established businesses selling brand-named products through conventional marketing channels were treated circumspectly. In March 1914, the National Vigilance Committee sent out a confidential bulletin claiming that a chemist in Newark, New Jersey, had found refuse in a box of Wrigley's Spearmint Pepsin Gum, contradicting the advertiser's statement that the gum was "clean, pure and healthful." Five days later, Harry D. Robbins, NVC chairman, wrote personally to local vigilance groups, asking them to "treat the bulletin as strictly confidential, withhold all action and suspend judgment pending further advices [sic]," because Wrigley had denied the charge and promised full cooperation with an investigation. In May, the Newark Advertising Men's Club withdrew its complaint, and the NVC rescinded its initial bulletin with fulsome praise for "the most commendable attitude of cooperation on the part of Mr. Wrigley and his representatives."[62]

We find similarly deferential language in cases involving the Reuben H. Donnelly printing company and Hart, Schaffner and Marx clothing manufacturers. When the Minneapolis Vigilance Bureau wrote to inquire about a possibly deceptive "free" offer from the Donnelly firm, the NVC's secretary replied, "Of course you know that Mr. Donnelly is a big man in the publishing world and vitally interested in the Associated Clubs and is a man of fine character and standing." Five days later, the Minneapolis secretary echoed the endorsement, calling Donnelly "perfectly responsible in any undertaking." After the case was resolved, Herbert S. Houston, AACW president and a publishing company executive himself, chided Minneapolis: " . . . [F]rankly, I hardly see how such a complaint . . . should have been considered worthy of any particular attention. Just how do you draw the line in such cases?" In the Hart, Schaffner and Marx matter, Minneapolis Vigilance Bureau secretary J. Chester Armstrong, pursuing a reader's complaint about an ad appearing in that city, wrote to the manufacturer: "I believe it is only necessary to call this to your attention and I am sure you will give us some definite statement that we can return in answer to the criticism."[63]

Vigilance workers were sensitive to charges that they shied away from confrontations with big business. Replying to Herbert Houston's query in the Donnelly case, Armstrong wrote, "The truth is that we do not draw the line."[64] All cases were to be handled in the same fashion. No doubt that was the intention of the vigilance workers, but the record suggests that they tended to approach well-established firms with circumspection. Beyond this, the case by case approach could send investigators off in hunt of squirrels while the big game roamed the business jungle. Taking and acting upon complaints as they came in would not result in giving first priority to the most important case.

For truth in advertising activists, careful treatment of big business was a matter of self-interest as well as tact. Advertising clubs spoke for merchants who had advertised their own stores actively and for local agents, printers, commercial artists, and the like. These businessmen in the early twentieth century faced several challenges. Mass retailers with enough "countervailing power" to resist name-brand manufacturers threatened local merchants by price cutting and by emphasizing private brands. Itinerants, mail-order firms, and others without community ties might also compete with established businessmen. The truth in advertising movement tended to define false advertising as an aspect of unfair competition and to focus its gaze upon these troublesome competitors.

Thus, the Minneapolis Vigilance Bureau, for example, worked to enforce the city's Transient Merchant Act against street vendors. It approved of the *Minneapolis Journal*'s policy of banning ads of itinerant merchants. This, the paper noted, "protects the man who pays rent and taxes and insurance and wages in the community against the 'fly-by-night' unreliable, non-tax-paying itinerant." A Fort Worth paper praised the city's Ad Men's Club for protecting the local merchant from unfair competition by itinerants. Samuel Hopkins Adams noted that used typewriter and second-hand car dealers who misrepresented their goods hurt not only their honest competitors but also the manufacturers who "have spent years of time and millions of money in building up their good repute." Indeed, Adams asserted that the manufacturers suffered the most, for they had no effective recourse against dishonest second-hand dealers.[65]

Under the banner of truth in advertising, vigilance workers attacked comparative price advertising and the substitution of private-label store brands and generic products for nationally advertised items. Such activity was, in Kenner's words, "an open attack on the integrity of advertising." To deal with the substitution problem, the Portland Ad Club proposed a bill that would make it illegal for a retailer "to represent . . . that [goods] are the products of any other dealer, manufacturer or producer than the one from whom they actually came." Clubs also considered comparative price advertising an ethical issue. The Minneapolis Vigilance Bureau undertook a major investigation of its dangers. The Portland BBB urged stores to stop comparing their prices to their rivals, as did vigilance workers in Cleveland and New York. Most of the major stores of New York agreed to eliminate such advertising; by 1916, a Bloomingdale's executive could report that "practically all retail New York has . . . pinned its faith on the Square Deal." Cleveland stores agreed in 1919 to limit comparisons to their Friday ads, and the Bureau "saw to it that the lid was held down tightly even on that day."[66]

The line between upholding truth and limiting potentially destructive price competition was blurred. Comparative prices in advertisements might be an invitation to deceit, but they might also help consumers shop for the best bargains. Substitution could entail dishonesty, but it also could mean the efforts of salespeople to persuade buyers that there were cheaper equivalents for advertised products. By defining their commercial goals as ethical ideals, the advocates of truth in advertising channeled the self-regulation movement into areas where action was not only likely to be "safe" but also profitable.

For legitimate advertisers, agents, and media, it was easy enough to see the harm wrought by the most blatant liars, the "tramps and beggars and gypsies of the publishing world," as one activist called them. Truth, defined as the absence of factual misstatements, turned into the obsession of the vigilance movement. However, this concept of truth was less stringent than it sounded. Advertising men frequently contrasted deception with rhetorical exaggeration. "'Puffing' is one thing; lying another," as *Printers' Ink* put it in 1916. *Editor and Publisher* felt the same way. It approved of the view of country editor E. W. Howe, who said: *"If an exaggerated statement is a lie, there is no truth."* When, in 1916, the New York Stock Exchange banned the use of catch-phrases in its members' financial advertising, AACW President Herbert Houston demurred, calling them legitimate persuasive devices. *Printers' Ink* complained, "Surely the *intention* and the *performance* behind the advertising is of much more importance than its *form.*[67]

In practice, the concept of puffery could cover a multitude of misdemeanors. Even the *Printers' Ink* model statute, as its supporters often noted, outlawed only misstatements of fact, not expressions of opinion. A 1917 decision in the State of Washington acquitted a defendant who had advertised a price reduction on pianos. In fact, he had never sold the pianos at the higher price. The court ruled, however, that his advertisement had not explicitly stated that *he* had sold the pianos at the higher price; another dealer, perhaps, might have actually charged it. Other decisions under the model statute offered fewer loopholes, but even the most stringent law gave shrewd defense attorneys room for maneuver. Truth in advertising workers knew that the cases they brought were likely to be hard to win. Civil actions and prosecutions under the Federal Mail Fraud statutes were even more difficult. As late as 1923, the fact that a purchaser found a nail in a loaf of bread was held not to violate the baker's advertised promise of "100 Percent Pure" bread. In the 1912 case of *Harrison* v. *United States,* an appellate court reversed the mail fraud conviction of a vacuum cleaner advertiser who had claimed his machine had "terrific suction," would "abolish house cleaning," and could be run by a weak woman or child. The court held:

> If we except extreme phrases like "terrific suction" and "abolish house cleaning," the utterance of which cannot be seriously thought to be criminal, we find that every statement of fact is literally true, or, more accurately, might, under favorable conditions, be literally true.[68]

Thus, the truth could sometimes be stretched, if not broken. Major advertisers and advertising men of the Progressive Era found they could not live with the charlatans who degraded all publicity; at the same time, they found they could not live without the persuasive appeals and techniques advertising men were creating. So, in the course of the truth in advertising campaigns, the industry's leaders exalted the same kind of advertising later observers have found so problematical. A generation after the surge of self-regulation, when a new wave of critics challenged the ethical and social legitimacy of advertising, the industry was generally unprepared to muster convincing replies. In the long run, nothing failed like success.[69]

The Ethics of Persuasion

The combination of zeal for eradicating dishonesty and indecency and insensitivity to newer ethical issues can be seen throughout the Progressive Era. For example, the publications of Cyrus Curtis refused all patent medicine advertising and censored copy strictly. They were also the media for the introduction of appeals to the anxieties and aspirations of middle-class America. In 1911, Woodbury Soap began to offer *Journal* readers "The Skin You Love to Touch," selling sex appeal instead of cleansing power. As vigilance workers pursued phony automobile promoters, Cadillac in 1915 told readers of the *Saturday Evening Post* of "The Penalty of Leadership." Without any false statements, the McManus Agency of Detroit managed to compare the car with the art of Whistler, the music of Wagner, and the inventive genius of Robert Fulton. Claude Hopkins, the premier copywriter of his era, mastered what we might term the irrelevant truth. He informed millions that Schlitz beer bottles were cleaned with steam. They were; so were all other breweries' bottles. He glamorized a mundane manufacturing process by advertising that Puffed Wheat and Puffed Rice were "Shot from Guns." Hopkins also took pride in his copy for Pepsodent Toothpaste, which made an attractive smile, not decay prevention, the main appeal.[70]

Life insurance advertising illustrates well how Progressive Era reforms ameliorated some of the problems of advertising while accentuating others. From the 1870s through about 1905, life insurance advertising consistently emphasized the value of insurance as an investment. So-called deferred dividend policies, in which the insurer retained dividends for a specified waiting period, were the main "product" of the largest companies. At the end of the deferral period, dividends that had been earned on premiums paid by those who had died or let their policies lapse during the interval were credited to those whose policies were still in force. Because these "Tontine" policies rewarded those who lived longer and were able to pay their premiums consistently at the expense of those who died earlier or who were poorer, one expert called them "life insurance cannibalism." With a product like this, insurers competed by emphasizing the large dividends their customers might receive. Touted as investments, Tontine policies were given titles like "Guaranteed Compound Interest Gold Bond Policies."[71] Dividend estimates were often exaggerated and unfair attacks on rivals abounded.

In 1905, a full-scale investigation of life insurance, conducted by a Joint Committee of the New York State Legislature, rocked the industry. Known as the Armstrong Committee, the investigators found widespread financial and managerial abuses, especially among the Big Three firms—Equitable, New York Life, and Mutual of New York. Coupled with some muckraking journalism, the findings forced a series of reforms on the industry.[72] Their net effect on marketing was to establish family protection rather than a return on investment as the major selling appeal of life insurance.

A 1906 New York law prohibited false advertising by insurance companies. In 1913, Minnesota was the first of several states to ban mail-order coupons in life insurance ads. Beyond these and other legal restrictions, the rapid decline of deferred dividend and similar investment-oriented policies meant an end to the often deceptive offers of high returns. Life insurance advertising moved away from proclaiming the size and financial strength of the firms towards "buyer-oriented" appeals and "need selling."[73] Equitable Life in 1890 had asserted: "The man who assures his life *simply* for the *protection of his family* does wisely, but he who secures a policy, which, if his family cease to need protection, will revert to him, exercises greater discrimination." Two decades later, such rationalistic appeals were gone; Equitable pulled out the emotional stops in playing on the affections and fears of the bourgeois pater familias. In "A Private Talk with Men Only," Equitable asked, "Did you ever See a Tired SHOP-GIRL? Or a Worn Out ERRAND Boy?". A Mutual Benefit Life ad, featuring a maudlin poem, "To My Daughter," informed readers that a policy "will always KEEP THE FATHER'S MEMORY GREEN AT YULETIDE."[74]

In that the newer emotive appeals were not factually misleading, they were a major improvement over the deceitful predictions and attacks on rivals' integrity that characterized insurance advertising of the Tontine era. Nor were postreform life insurance advertisements especially manipulative. They constitute merely one example of a more general trend. The reforms that rid life insurance publicity of its more egregious falsehoods also led to advertising based on fear, shame, and anxiety. The truth in advertising movement, as it proudly routed out fraud and misstatement, rarely if ever stopped to consider what the proper scope and means of mass persuasion might be. Advertising men never transcended their own collective self-interest and self-image.

Maybe this critique is too demanding. Perhaps it is too harsh to suggest that advertising men judge their own business by the standards of latter-day moralists. However, men who insisted that they were responsible professionals and sought the rewards of professional status must be judged by their deeds. The privilege of self-regulation and the monopoly of specialized knowledge claimed by professions require, in return, that professional ethics be more than a mirror of long-term self-interest.[75] They imply that professionals should anticipate the social consequences of their work and restrain not only the "swashbucklers" but those who navigate the main channels of the occupation. Judged by this standard, advertising men failed to make good on their claim to professional status because they restricted their ethical concerns so sharply.

Despite this, it may still be utopian to expect advertising ethics to transcend the profit motives that propelled the industry's growth. Advertising men have long insisted that persuasion is both a legitimate and a necessary part of distribution in twentieth-century business. In the words of Marion Harper, former president of the enormous Interpublic Group of advertising firms, the "evaluation from an economy of scarcity to one of abundance logically has altered the function of advertising from its original objective of pure announcement to that of persuasion." Given this, business economist Neil Borden was right when he stated: "In attacking advertising and aggressive selling, critics are not attacking advertising as such, but the capitalist system." Three decades before Borden's statement, *Printers' Ink* responded to a manufacturer who had called advertising wasteful. "What is it that he would have us do about it? Shall we revert to the condition of primitive man or shall we forthwith introduce some form of socialism?"[76]

Some critics of advertising have accepted the defenders' logic even as they attack their values. They have agreed that purging advertising of its persuasive elements is a utopian delusion. In John Kenneth Galbraith's view, managing the demand for a product "requires well-considered mendacity.... Flat lies ... are generally impermissible. But a surrogate for the truth, in which minor or even imaginary qualities confer great benefits, is essential." Giancarlo Buzzi, Italian essayist and a former advertising man himself, derides naive liberals who, he says:

> preach honesty and truth in advertising; advertising that only furnishes the basis for rational choice ... advertising that behaves as if the environment were not what it is—oligopolis-

tic, forcing unreasonable consumption through an irrationality and a lack of aims in the political and economic structure.[77]

Marxists have agreed that persuasive advertising is essential in buttressing monopoly capitalism. For them, significant reform is impossible. Thus, Paul Baran and Paul Sweezy write, "Clearly, to condemn so-called subliminal advertising as particularly obnoxious is hardly justified; all advertising is in essence subliminal." James Rorty, in 1934, combined the intellectual influences of Marx and Thorstein Veblen with nearly two decades of copywriting experience. For Rorty, "Ethical value judgments are inapplicable" to advertising. Though ad men were decent individuals and "would doubtless like to be ... truthful and just in the conduct of their business, ... this, in the nature of the case, is impossible." Self-regulation, as exemplified by the Better Business Bureaus, was designed only to keep "the methods and the practices of the advertising profession within the tolerance limit of an essentially exploitative society."[78]

These radical analyses of advertising appear weakest when they suggest that changes in advertising standards are hypocritical shadow plays. Indeed, the role of advertising in a capitalist society may define the boundaries of acceptable advertising practices, but within those limits it is surely possible to distinguish, as the vigilance movement did, between outright fraud and more subtle distortions of reality. The claim that advertising is now persuasive rather than informative is largely correct, but persuasion can be an assault on our intelligence and personal dignity, or it can act with a degree of restraint and a sense of proportion. Radicals who fail to observe differences and who insist that advertising *must* degrade and deceive weaken their case by overstatement.

Nevertheless, the limitations of the truth in advertising movement indicate that radical critics of advertising understand its place in the political economy better than those who castigate advertising men for failing to purify their business. In the early years of this century, changes in advertising ethics reflected changes in the business context of advertising. Suppressing overt lies became more rewarding and more feasible. Those who discouraged lying were often those who hoped to perfect the more sophisticated means of persuasion. In the final analysis, the impact of these newer practices, when backed by multi-million dollar advertising budgets, may be just as damaging as the potions modern advertising men came to revile.

6

The Messages of Persuasion

A portrait of Dr. John H. Woodbury stared out at newspaper and magazine readers in the 1890s. The picture, which showed Woodbury's head but not his neck, created an effect "so startling as to be almost grewsome [sic]," according to the advertising writer Charles Austin Bates. Bates mused over this peculiar illustration but concluded that the advertising must be successful since it was so widespread. Woodbury was selling his "complexion soap" and other cures for skin and scalp problems. His ads offered samples by mail and promoted a book on "how Facial Irregularities are corrected." Appropriations for advertising were estimated to be as high as $150,000 in 1893, which made Woodbury's Soap one of the nation's most heavily advertised brands.[1]

By 1915, Woodbury's Soap, which had become a product of the Andrew Jergens Company of Cincinnati, struck a very different advertising note. A full-color, full-page advertisement in the *Ladies' Home Journal* displayed the headline, "The Skin You Love to Touch." Gone was Woodbury's peculiar portrait (although it still adorned the soap wrapper). In its place was a painting of a handsome gentleman embracing a stylish, attractive woman. The text of the ad went on to offer not only cleanliness but radiance and charm. Magazine advertising alone for Woodbury's in 1915 cost about $144,000. Five years later, the company was spending over half a million dollars on magazine publicity.[2]

Cigarette advertising underwent an equally striking transformation in the same time period. Promotional activity in the 1880s and 1890s was vigorous and costly, but most of it took the form of premiums and other special offers. In the 1880s, James Buchanan Duke began to place cards with pictures of actresses, athletes, and other subjects in his cigarette boxes. Soon, other more elaborate premiums gained popularity. But little was actually done to promote the alleged pleasures of cigarette smoking or to preach the superiority of particular brands. Indeed, it appears that the Tobacco Trust's advertising appropriations went primarily to pay for prizes and premiums. Even after the American Tobacco Company was dissolved in 1911, the successor companies could not at first break away from this kind of promotional policy. However, by about 1915, a new brand, Camels, made by the upstart R. J. Reynolds Tobacco Company, had found a new strategy. "Don't look for premiums or coupons, as the cost of the tobaccos blended in Camel Cigarettes prohibits the use of them," read a message on the package. Camel advertising employed print media and emphasized the intrinsic rewards of the brand. Soon, the other leading cigarette manufacturers were running elaborate print campaigns for Lucky Strikes and Chesterfields. The three brands, each intensively advertised, dominated the American cigarette market until after World War II.

Life insurance advertising was also drastically transformed. As we have seen, through the end of the nineteenth century, advertisements stressed the financial aspects of insurance. Headlines like "The Wonders of Compound Interest" and "Guaranteed Compound Interest Gold Bond Policies" were the rule. As late a 1901, a circular sent to agents of the Equitable Life Assurance Society stated, "Get the idea out of your own head, and keep it out of the investor's head, that you are simply *assuring his life*. . . . You are selling a block of Bonds—that is the first idea."[3] Life insurance advertising was characterized by "a string of meaningless sentences and useless figures." Long lists of company directors and officers shared space with accounting statements. One advertising trade journal remarked that life insurance advertising "cannot be worse than it is."[4]

Equitable had changed its tune by 1910. "We preach the Doctrine of PROTECTION—In Life Insurance—not investment—not savings—not profit—all good in their way—but subordinate—minor—relatively unimportant in comparison with the one big—important—*essential feature of life insurance for the benefit of women and little children*." Another ad warned, "Home—BREAD and BUTTER—CLOTHES and SHOES—SOMETIMES the DOCTOR—and the Chance to go to SCHOOL. All these your *widow* or your *orphans* must have." The shift from a pecuniary argument to an emotional appeal was characteristic of the leading life insurance firms of the era.

Advertising men of the World War I era were very much aware that they had come a long way in a generation or less.

Advertising was "more scientific and certain," and quality had greatly improved, despite more intensive competition for consumers' attention.[5] Beyond these self-aggrandizing judgments, however, how had advertising changed? And what marketing forces had brought about the newer styles of advertising?

One approach to describing the changing styles of advertising is content analysis. Yet there are pitfalls in quantitative content analysis conducted retrospectively. In the past, for example, several studies have tabulated advertising themes over time and contended that changing themes are indices of changing American values. These authors fail, however, to distinguish between changed appeals in advertisements for the same products and shifting appeals resulting from variations in the kinds of items advertised. For instance, advertisements appealing to desires for intimacy are more likely to be found in ads for perfumes than for sewing machines. If perfume advertising volume has risen as sewing machine advertising has diminished, this might account for the alleged change in "values."[6]

We may avoid some of the dangers of imposing our own categories on past advertisements if we tabulate only certain formal aspects of advertisement design, such as size, types of illustration, or type faces. There can be no quarrel with this method of recording changes in formats, but the results are difficult to interpret. Do they indicate changing values, new media capabilities, or shifting marketing strategies? The data may be hard, but they lie on quicksand.

Finally, content analysis tends to overlook the active role of the audience for advertisements. The meaning of an advertisement does not inhere in the source alone; the meaning is created by readers, listeners, and viewers as they perceive and misperceive advertising messages. Content analysis may suggest a mechanistic view of consumers passively receiving messages with predetermined meanings.

Therefore, for the purpose of understanding how national advertising's new roles shaped advertising copy and design, it may be better to concentrate on stated intentions rather than on our own interpretations of results. Advertising men of the late nineteenth and early twentieth centuries set forth theories of advertising and consumer behavior and designed their ads accordingly. The theories were sometimes as crude as the advertisements themselves, but they reflected, however imperfectly, the marketing tasks national advertising was called upon to perform.

"Advertisements were never so handsomely arranged, or set up in such clear, varied and attractive styles as at present . . ." wrote George P. Rowell in 1871. Still, he warned, "The secret of advertising is not yet discovered by all who advertise. A good deal of money and space is wasted in clumsy announcements, which nobody reads."[7] Fortunately for fledgling advertisers, Rowell was willing to divulge the secret. "The mystery of writing advertisements," he explained "consists mainly in saying in a few plain words exactly what it is desired to say, precisely as it would be written in a letter or told to an acquaintance."[8] The house organ of the S. M. Pettengill agency also contended that good advertising was a matter of plain spokenness and good manners: "There is a quiet courtesy and modest unobtrusiveness about a [good] advertisement that creates a certain responsive feeling of sympathy in the reader."[9] Similarly, the Cincinnati publisher Murat Halstead recommended that advertisers avoid "excessive solicitation." Classifying advertisements according to their subject matter would be a better way to allow readers to find a notice.[10] Few later commentators would place such faith in readers' initiative.

Beyond such homilies, there was little advice on advertising design in the 1870s and 1880s. There were, after all, no specialists who wrote advertisements for national manufacturers and only a bare handful who composed department store copy. Advertising agencies, as we have seen, placed advertisements and brokered newspaper and magazine space; they only sporadically assisted advertisers in preparing advertisements. There was, in other words, almost nobody with enough expertise to offer advice.

The paucity of theorizing also reflects the marketing situation of most of those who advertised. Retail advertisers informed their customers of the goods they had on hand. Increasingly, as the one-price system replaced haggling, department stores featured prices in their advertisements. The few manufacturers who advertised were themselves usually small businessmen. Some of these sold by mail, which meant that there were no middlemen in the channel from producer to consumer. Thus, the need for brand identification and recognition was minimal. Most manufacturers advertising in the 1870s and 1880s were medicine makers. Here, whatever art and science there was in advertising could operate. Indeed, medical advertising of the era was the proving ground for persuasive techniques like testimonials, story-form ads, and vivid illustrations. The intense competition among medicine manufacturers impelled them to be energetic, sometimes inventive, advertisers. However, patent medicines were a special category. There were few other branded staple products of large-scale manufacturers available for advertising to sell in that era. Manufacturing and marketing conditions in general did not demand complex theories of persuasion.

Early advertising doctrines fit these realities. The injunction to treat advertisements as personal communications made sense when enterprises were small and buyers and sellers were likely to be on comparable, if not equal, footings. Buying an advertised product frequently required a considered decision. Purchasing might entail writing a letter of inquiry to a manufacturer and following it up with an order. Even retail buying of dry goods and hard goods was likely to entail some advance planning; a trip to town or to a downtown store was a major event in people's lives. With low discretionary incomes, there was little room for impulse buying in most family budgets.

This is not to say that Gilded Age advertising was either honest or truly informative. On the contrary, as we have seen, all manner of false panaceas, get-rich-quick schemes, and insubstantial trash cluttered advertising columns. Advertising rhetoric was often bombastic and pretentious, sometimes vulgar and illiterate, and too often obscure and incomprehensible. A good deal of advertising was presented as editorial matter; "articles" in newspapers might, in fact, be paid publicity notices masquerading as news stories. Nevertheless, many ads had a straightforward, plain-spoken character that expressed the rough parity between buyer and seller which then existed. Consumers were expected to be familiar with standards and specifications of dry goods, hardware, and food staples, for example. Advertisers generally assumed that they were talking to people who were already in the market for their products.

By the 1890s, advertising specialists, often associated with service-oriented advertising agencies, noted the contrast between their work and that of their predecessors. In the 1870s, commented *Printer's Ink,* newspapers directed attention to their advertisers with an editorial reminder. However, "The idea now is to make the advertisement so attractive that readers will see it." An 1890 survey of "Changes in Advertising" found increased care in typography, more use of good illustrations and decorative borders, and more imaginative and flexible layouts.[11] Artemas Ward, advertising manager for the much publicized Sapolio soap, saw the approach of the advertisers' millenium: "How advertisements themselves will change [in the future] is difficult to speculate about. It seems hardly possible that they could be improved."[12]

Whereas "announcement" had served as a synonym for "advertisement" in the 1870s and 1880s, by the 1890s experts recognized that announcing was inadequate. Increased advertising volume meant that each individual advertisement was engaged in an escalating struggle for the reader's attention. To be successful, advertisements had to win the battle for prominence. Not only were advertisers competing with each other for attention, they were fighting against a host of other stimuli and concerns for the consumer's eye and mind. Readers rarely sought out advertisements; manufacturers had to seek out potential consumers. Ideas of demand creation began to be heard. "The modern advertisement is not intended for the man who wants the things already," stated a 1904 article. "It's for the one who don't [*sic*] in order to make him."[13]

Until after the turn of the century, advice on attracting attention was generally vague and equivocal. "A *good* ADVERTISEMENT must be bold enough to attract attention, and yet so neat in appearance that it will not offend good taste," suggested the George Batten agency.[14] There was general agreement that advertisements that were too small would fail to gain attention. "Make your own space so large that every reader may see the ad without searching," noted an 1890 editorial. "People have so much to think about nowadays," another observed, that large ads pay "proportionately better" than small ones.[15] When Nathaniel Fowler polled advertisers in 1897 for their opinions, he found that most agreed that, "A general advertisement of two inches is worth more than two advertisements of an inch each."[16]

Illustrations were also recommended as means of attracting attention. *Printers' Ink* pointed out, "The busy American is loath to read. His eye must be attracted, coaxed, cajoled." Those who studied the psychology of advertising in that era were quick to assert that illustrations were "particularly essential where goods are sold to women." Harry Hollingworth, an instructor at Columbia University, noted that "as the race has progressed," it has moved "beyond the pictorial stage"; men were, he asserted, "most active in this process" of advancement.[17]

Later investigations showed that advertising practice generally followed this sort of advice on ways to attract attention. For example, advertisements grew larger. In 1892, 18 percent of the advertisements in *The Century* were full-page; in 1908, they amounted to 43 percent. Between 1870 and 1910, headlines in magazine advertisements almost doubled in height.[18] Illustrations became more widespread as well. As late as 1894, only about 30 percent of advertisements in *Collier's, Literary Digest,* and two Indiana newspapers contained any pictures. The proportion increased steadily; by 1919, close to 90 percent of all ads were illustrated.[19]

The focus on attracting attention in the 1890s produced some vivid advertisements but also led to stunts and schemes that earned the scorn of later advertising practitioners. Advertisers were liberated from some technical confines by developments in printing that allowed better reproduction of illustrations, larger type faces, and display ads across the width of newspapers. However, most lacked marketing strategies to give direction to their new resources. This was the era of the slogan; some, like Eastman Kodak's "You press the button. We do the rest," memorably expressed the camera's unique features. Others, such as the endlessly repeated, "Good morning! Have you used Pears' Soap?" or DeLong Hooks and Eyes' "See that Hump" were merely inane. The nineties and the early years of the new century were also the era of doggerel verse. A few of these schemes were vivid and successful. One series introduced Phoebe Snow, a young woman dressed in white who rode in comfort and cleanliness on the Lackawanna Railroad, "The Road of Anthracite." Sapolio's advertising manager, Artemas Ward, introduced the characters of "Spotless Town," all, not surprisingly, dedicated users of the soap brand. Earnest E. Calkins had a series of verses about "Jim Dumps" who was transformed into "Sunny Jim" by eating Force breakfast cereal. Nevertheless, Calkins saw the failing of many of the era's rhyming ads. "It would seem," he wrote, "that the would-be author, after ignoring every rule of rhythm, rhyme, grammar, and construction, would certainly be able to make at least a straightforward statement about his goods, but he fails even to do that."[20]

In 1898, *Printers' Ink* polled its readers to find out who was doing the best advertising. The answers revealed how underdeveloped techniques and standards remained. Ripans Tabules, a patent medicine, which happened to be owned by *Printers' Ink* publisher George P. Rowell, won the most votes. The voters seemed to equate quality with quantity, since runners-up included Ivory Soap, Sapolio, Royal Baking Powder, and Pears' Soap, all massive advertisers by standards of the day. Comments accompanying the ballots indicate that ubiquity, not persuasive appeal, was the main criterion of good advertising. "Because you see it everywhere" and "You can't help but see it in a paper" were typical remarks. Few of the respondents found anything to mention about the contents of the ads they selected.[21]

Critics in the early twentieth century recognized that national advertising required more than gimmicks. "Large type and large space attract attention. Attracting attention, however, isn't equivalent to selling goods."[22] Walter Dill Scott, a psychologist at Northwestern University and one of the first to apply experimental techniques to advertising, reserved his sharpest criticisms for advertisements which bore no relationship to the items they promoted. Daniel Starch, another early advertising psychologist, complained that "advertising is replete with vague generalities. . . . Descriptions are often nothing more than a mass of dead verbiage that would apply to one commodity as well, or as poorly, as to any other."[23] In sum, theorists of the pre–World War I years noted that advertising must appeal as well as attract. Advertising that did not evoke a desire to buy was simply not doing its job.

The need to appeal—to create interest and desire—reflected the growing importance of national advertising of branded products. Recognition of the need to stimulate interest and desire produced two seemingly disparate theories in the first decades of the twentieth century. The first, "reason-why" advertising, aimed to present the consumer with convincing arguments to purchase the advertised brand. Its many proponents claimed that "reason-why" advertising was almost always applicable. The manufacturer of a branded product had to attract customers not only to the type of product but to his own brand. Advertisements had the task of pointing out the distinctive characteristics of a brand and explaining its superiority. In this sense, "reason-why" advertising was the appropriate method of implementing a strategy of product differentiation. As oligopolistic industries producing differentiated consumer goods came to the fore in the early twentieth century, "reason-why" found more and more adherents.

It is hard to date the appearance of the doctrine of "reason-why," but there was one early moment that later assumed almost mythic stature in the advertising industry. In

1904, Albert D. Lasker was a twenty-four-year-old Texan who had recently become a partner in Chicago's largest agency, Lord & Thomas. Although he was earning the startling salary of $52,000 a year, Lasker still felt he lacked an understanding of how advertising worked. This was vouchsafed to him one spring afternoon when a clerk handed him a message. "I am in the saloon downstairs, and I can tell you what advertising is. I know that you don't know. . . . If you wish to know what advertising is, send the word 'Yes' down by messenger." The signature belonged to John E. Kennedy. On a whim, Lasker agreed to meet Kennedy, who turned out to be a free-lance copywriter with a checkered past that included a stint as a Royal Canadian Mounted Policeman. Kennedy told Lasker that the essence of advertising could be summed up in three words, "Salesmanship in Print."[24] Vacuous as this formula may now appear, it taught Lasker the fundamental lesson that advertising had to sell goods, not just announce their availability. Lasker many years later described the impact almost lyrically. "Kennedy's definition released previously unconceived forces of advertising, gave the industry wings, because for the first time advertisers had a *concept* by which to judge true advertising *copy* for itself."[25] The copywriters who worked at Lord & Thomas in the first decades of the century were to find out that "Salesmanship in Print" was a guiding theory, not merely a slogan.

Kennedy expounded his theories in a 1910 pamphlet, "Intensive Advertising," which earned him a $25,000 fee from a group of business publishers. He scorned mere "publicity" and "display." Ads had to engage the reader's interest; "Keeping the Name before the People" was a formula for failure. At a time when the N. W. Ayer agency, probably the nation's largest, displayed the motto, "Keeping everlastingly at it brings success," Kennedy's insistence on selling was a challenge to the established order. His advice to stress the distinctive qualities of the advertiser's brand in a way that made them newsworthy and desirable prefigures the advice of hard-sell advertising man Rosser Reeves half a century later. Reeves's recipe for success was the "Unique Selling Proposition." Kennedy also insisted that an advertisement must do a "complete selling canvass," written "as if this was the *only* ad we ever meant to use." Advertisements were not adjuncts to a personal selling pitch or a storekeeper's display. Advertising was "salesmanship intensified."[26] Kennedy's emphasis on telling customers why they should purchase a client's brand was the essence of "reason-why."

Two other influences also shaped "reason-why" advertising. One was the example of department store advertising which used the blunt, unadorned "Powers style." John E. Powers, who gained his fame as advertising manager for John Wanamaker's stores, described merchandise in simple, unexaggerated prose without the fustian generalities of his competitors. Powers-style specifics made more sense than flowery irrelevancies. Yet such a style was almost too modest for "reason-why" advocates. Its aim was to describe the merchandise to already motivated shoppers, not to stimulate desire. Consequently, it lacked the dynamic appeals that "reason-why" supporters urged.

A second force was the work of early advertising psychologists. Walter Dill Scott, the first to study advertising systematically, had worked at Leipzig under Professor Wilhelm Wundt; like his mentor, Scott usually saw behavior as resulting from mental activity. Instincts played a large role in accounting for what people do, but the will and voluntary action were often decisive. Voluntary action entailed comparing two or more different ends, forming an idea of the means necessary to attain each, choosing the most valuable end, and acting in order to accomplish it. The role of voluntary action made it "necessary to proceed logically and to appeal to the reason in advertising."[27]

Whatever its sources, "reason-why" advertising became highly popular in the first decade of the new century. It seemed to provide a practical and workable prescription for copywriters. By 1906, *Printers' Ink* claimed, with some exaggeration, that "the assailants of 'reason-why' copy are those who can't produce it."[28] For advertising men who had not abandoned the nineteenth-century view of the buyer as rationally self-interested and deliberative, "reason-why" was an attractive doctrine. It preserved the rationalistic model of consumer behavior, but it justified putting sales appeal into advertisements.[29]

"Reason-why" advertising did come under some attack. William A. Shryer, a Detroit publishers and mail-order merchant, put it most bluntly: "It is a favorite superstition that because reason is peculiar to the human being it is his prevailing guide to action. Nothing could be much farther from the truth. Man ... actually ... is a creature of habits."[30] Consumers did not calculate costs and benefits, they responded to suggestions and stimuli. Reasons, facts, and information did not in themselves cause action. Thus, Shryer contended, it made no sense to trust reason to motivate purchasing.

Advertising psychologists propounded this new, nonrationalist view of human behavior. Even Scott stressed the role of suggestion. Suggestion came from an external source and evoked behavior "with less than the normal amount of deliberation."[31] Scott tried to show that direct commands were a useful form of suggestion in advertisements; pictures that indicated what the user could do with the product were also suggestive; return coupons constituted another valuable method of suggestion. So much did Scott believe in the power of suggestion that he wrote, "Man has been called the reasoning animal but he could with greater truthfulness be called the creature of suggestion."[32]

Other advertising psychologists, notably Harry Hollingworth and E. K. Strong at Columbia University, inclined to somewhat different models of behavior. Hollingworth, in his 1913 text written for the New York Advertising Men's League, employed a stimulus-response terminology. Advertising messages were stimuli designed to cause a chain of responses. They should gain attention, become "dominant in consciousness," arouse "central associations," and result in "motor response."[33] This progression, from attention to action, has remained a staple concept of the literature on the psychology of advertising. Hollingworth and Strong also contended that people had a set of fairly stable, predictable "instincts." These motives were present throughout the population, and advertisers could appeal to customers by tapping the stronger human motives.

Although these nonrationalist theories of behavior appeared at first to contradict the "reason-why" approach, it soon became clear that the distinction was really slight. Early advocates of "reason-why" may have seen it as a doctrine about human behavior; soon, however, it changed from a theory to a tool, a method of persuasion that was appropriate in certain marketing situations. "Reason-why," according to later experts, did not require logical argumentation. It was designed to persuade and offer rationales for buying the advertised brand. "Not all copy classified as reason-why appeals solely to the reason," advised one text. In fact, "reason-why" could offer consumers after-the-fact justifications for their purchases. It was hard to classify advertisements, in any case. "The distinction between reason-why and human-interest is often one of convenience only," wrote the authors of a popular textbook.[34]

Therefore, the debate over copywriting methods cooled

down. Practitioners recognized that the marketing context determined copy strategies. "Reason-why" styles were appropriate for "impersonal, utilitarian, instrumental" products and for "articles which are intended not so much to fill present needs only, but also to create new needs or desires—such articles as books, plows, buttons, hammers, trucks, etc." Human interest advertising was more suitable for products with strong emotional connotations for buyers—jewelry, toys, medicines, and food products.[35] Advertisements had to fit the selling situation, not the psychological doctrines of those who composed them.

While advertising men of the early twentieth century agreed that successful ads had to be persuasive, there was much discussion about various techniques of appealing to readers. One constant theme was that advertisements should make simple appeals and be grounded in common experience. Scott, in the mentalist tradition, which emphasized conscious ideas, stressed the value of apperception, a psychological process of relating present perceptions to past learning. "It is very difficult," he explained, "to get the public to think along a new line, because they cannot connect the new fact with their previous experience, i.e. they cannot apperceive it."[36]

Thus, advertising should be linked to the familiar. Scott also warned that the faculty of apperception was limited to a small number of things at a time. Unity and simplicity were therefore necessary. Advertisers should carefully avoid a "superfluity of details." Plain-spoken copy also required advertising writers to shun ornate prose or snob appeals. "An ad writer should emulate Lincoln's liking for the plain words of the plain people," advised a 1903 editorial.[37] Flowery prose earned scorn consistently, and "literary" was a harsh epithet in the advertising business. In persuading the mass market, there was no room for artistic pretension. As one textbook bluntly advised, "The writer of advertising copy should forget style, forget self, think of those readers that he wants to reach, find the ideas that will appeal to them, the emotions that can be aroused in them, the language that they can understand, and the action they can be forced to take." In short, "... the advertising writer must adjust to the mass."[38] Such warnings often hit the mark. In too many ads, ornate prose was a bad perfume to mask the odor of falsity; in others, writing affectations smothered the message and made it incomprehensible. On the other hand, this stress on simplicity and appeals to everyday experience coincided with the need to sell standardized products to mass markets.

Another tenet of persuasion in the early years of the century was the desirability of positive appeals. Both common-sense practitioners and psychological theorists inclined to this conclusion. As early as the 1890s, commentators praised advertisers who subordinated fear appeals and highlighted the "agreeable" results of using their products.[39] A generation later, an editorial drew an analogy between the obsolescence of scare advertising and the alleged unpopularity of ministers who preached "hell and damnation."[40] Psychologists made the same point. Scott stated that advertisements should promote pleasant feelings. "In pleasure our minds expand. We become extremely suggestible and are likely to see everything in a favorable light," he maintained. Indeed, by 1915, another text stated that negative appeals were in such poor repute that it was necessary to say a word in defense of their use when necessary, as in advertisements for fire protection equipment.[41] Copywriters followed the advice to accentuate the positive. One study of advertisements in *Harper's Weekly*, the *Literary Digest*, and *Collier's* at five-year intervals between 1900 and 1920 classified 17.6 percent of the 1900 ads as negative; the proportion of negative suggestion in 1920 was down to 3.4 percent.[42]

The proliferation of advertisements had, by the 1890s, made advertising experts aware of the need to attract attention. Soon afterwards, copywriters and artists recognized the importance of employing persuasive appeals. Gradually, too, in the early twentieth century, national advertisers accepted the principle that advertising was a form of investment in building a consumer franchise and inspiring brand loyalty. This was to alter the style of advertisements. Individual advertisements became elements in more comprehensive plans for promoting branded products. By the second decade of the twentieth century, the military and political concept of a campaign had found its way into advertising terminology. The foot soldiers who prepared advertisements were in the front line, but they marched to the orders of campaign strategists.

Of course, advertising agents had always urged businesses to advertise steadily and not to lose hope if early ads failed to rouse business. Ayer's injunction to keep everlastingly at it was a sentiment all advertising firms could endorse. Self-interest dictated that agencies advise their clients to keep advertising in good times and bad, through seasonal and cyclical slumps. Typical is one jingle ridiculing the quitters:

> *To advertise when trade is dull*
> *Is useless, don't you see?*
> *I advertise each day, and trade*
> *Is never dull with me.*[43]

Advertising men were slower to grasp the fact that advertising could yield a stream of repeat sales. As early as 1892, however, Artemas Ward noted that Pears' Soap was willing to spend four or five times the price of a bar of soap on advertising that would win a new customer.[44] As more and more manufacturers of low-priced perishable products branded and packaged their goods and undertook national advertising, the value of a loyal customer became more and more widely appreciated.

Advertising, then, had a cumulative, long-lasting impact. Again, psychological theories supported common-sense opinions. Walter Dill Scott set forth a law that the "attention value of an object depends on the number of times it comes before us, or on repetition."[45] Daniel Starch expressed the thought less rigorously: "Oft-repeated advertisements ... almost become friends which many readers like to see."[46] Although Starch admitted that it was virtually impossible to demonstrate statistically the cumulative effect of repetition, it was "quite abundantly demonstrated by modern advertising."[47] Successful businesses that valued their advertising-promoted trademarks as worth millions in goodwill were proof enough of the impact of repeated advertisements. A 1923 survey pointed out that the brand names most strongly identified with their product categories had almost all been heavy advertisers for many years.[48] Keeping everlastingly at it did seem to bring success.

One direct challenge to the theory of cumulative effect came from William A. Shryer. He called the notion "absolutely erroneous." "The law of diminishing returns ... is the real law of advertising."[49] Cumulative effect, he argued, was predicated on gradually convincing a consumer until a buying threshold was crossed. However, he pointed out, conviction was based on reasoning, and it was "unprofitable for the advertisers to center his appeals around ... the exercise of a function so slightly developed ... as that of reason."[50] Like John E. Kennedy, Shryer felt that each advertisement had to stand on its own.

Debates about cumulative effects and increasing returns to advertising continue to this day. However, it was marketing, not psychology, that made advertising campaigns crucial. National advertising of branded products had a variety of marketing objectives. With new products, it had to introduce them to potential consumers and spark enough interest to get shoppers to examine them. When a brand was beset by price competition from store brands or generic products, it had to claim superior quality or service. A few very well established brands could rely primarily on "reminder" ads. When faced with stable or declining sales, advertising might be a way to encourage new uses for the product, to get loyal customers to buy more often, or to shift to new markets. In all of these situations and others, advertisements had to be viewed as part of a "marketing mix," along with such elements as personal selling, product changes, and price strategies. Individual advertisements could not carry the burden alone. They had to be integrated into campaigns which in turn had to implement marketing strategies.

Daniel Starch pointed out that Shryer was basing his argument against cumulative effects on mail-order selling, where the tasks of advertising were quite different. The problems of manufacturers selling branded products through conventional distribution channels were not those of the merchant who sought direct orders by mail. The historical trend, Starch maintained, was towards advertising campaigns with continuity. Of the national advertisers he studied, nearly 60 percent employed a consistent appeal, a repeated trademark or other symbol, or a common design in their ads.[51]

Although Shryer was in a lonely minority who doubted the cumulative impact of advertising campaigns, his distrust of appeals to reason put him squarely in the mainstream of Progressive Era advertising men. As later observers have pointed out, psychologists and practitioners in the early years of the century shared a low opinion of the intellectual and logical capabilities of consumers. Despite occasional verbal bows to the innate wisdom of the masses, the image of human nature in the literature of advertising was not exalted.

Men and women "are but grown-up children," went one homily. One lecture on "Traits of Primitive Man" recommended that marketers might study the savage mind to understand their audiences.[52] The French psychologist Gustave LeBon, who saw crowd behavior as a threatening outbreak of mass irrationality, was cited as a source of potential advertising wisdom. Hypnotic suggestion, as we have seen, was Scott's model for recommendations on suggestion in advertisements.

Advice that flowed from this image of humanity made it clear that advertisers had to recognize their customers' limitations. Copywriter Herbert Casson summed up the situation: "Above all else, in planning an advertisement that will catch the public, AIM LOW."[53] Readers' vocabularies were limited; therefore, long and abstract words were wasted. A perusal of letters from customers would reveal, one advertising man warned, that most copywriters overestimated popular capabilities; there was a "vital . . . need for using plain words."[54] Complex ideas also created misunderstanding "The novice at advertising frequently gives the public credit for too much intelligence."[55]

Advertising experts recognized and sometimes celebrated the special role of women as consumers. "Woman is the buyer of everything," asserted Nathaniel Fowler, although others pointed out that men might still be important in influencing many purchasing decisions.[56] If humanity in general was rather weak and fallible, women in particular were, in the stereotypes of advertising men, irrational and subject to others' control. Women "don't want too much reasoning in an advertisement." They would not pay attention to detailed selling points or technical specifications. Women were more likely than men to follow direct commands in advertisements. In general, they were thought to be more suggestible than men. It was "far easier" to reach them by an appeal to the emotions than to the intellect.[57] As we have seen, illustrations were especially useful in advertising for women. Ill-informed, emotional, and suggestible, women took special interest in advertisements. "The woman who will not read advertisements is not a woman," claimed Fowler.[58]

New psychological doctrines and findings clearly influenced the advertising industry's consensus on mass irrationality and persuasion. However, it was the marketing situation of national advertisers that impelled practitioners and theorists to abandon the older rationalistic models of human behavior. At the same time, paradoxically, the need to sell to mass markets limited the influence of this apparent disdain for consumers. Contempt was accompanied by identification and even respect. Cynicism about popular abilities did not degenerate into a justification of naked manipulation and deceit.

The rise of mass production and mass distribution in the late nineteenth century damaged, perhaps beyond repair, the approximate parity of buyers and sellers in American life. In a society of freeholding farmers and small-scale entrepreneurs, a customer one day might be selling his wares the next. Buyers were likely to be familiar with merchandise that was produced in their own communities by men and women not very different from themselves. Granted, mid-nineteenth century America was no arcadia of egalitarian producers. Nevertheless, a model that posited rational self-interest as the motive and equal power as the condition of commercial transactions was not in the least absurd at the time. Advice about advertising rested upon this implicit image. Already, medical advertising belied those assumptions. Testimonials from satisfied users, as well as reading notices (advertisements disguised as editorial matter) that often took the form of a personal statement to the reader, were contrived and dishonest. Behind the facade of candid discussion were threats, extravagant promises, and irrational appeals to hopes and fears.

Manufacturers of the branded, packaged products sold in mass markets found neither the blandishments of the patent medicine makers nor the "modest unobtrusiveness" recommended in the Gilded Age sufficient. Medical advertising had the force and flamboyance, but its deceits were not the stuff of which brand loyalties could be built. Its unsavory reputation began to make other national advertisers reluctant to be seen in such bad company. Yet quiet statements of objective facts about products were equally inadequate. By the 1890s, buyers were not so much purchasing agents, acquiring utilitarian goods for instrumental purposes and making careful calculations of value, as they were seekers of satisfactions and comforts. Purchasers were becoming consumers. Marketing mass-produced consumer goods demanded a revised model of buyer behavior. Manufacturers had to catch the consumer's attention, arouse desires, and transform desires into purchases. Moreover, they had to perform these tasks wholesale, as it were, for hundreds of thousands or even millions of customers. To do this, advertisers and agents had to become as familiar as possible with the behavior of consumers and with the means of persuading them.

Familiarity bred a mixture of contempt and respect. If buyers were ignorant, emotional, and immature, they were, nevertheless, the ultimate judges of advertisers' fates. They could not be totally manipulated, and their wishes had to be taken into account. Advertisers had to cater to preferences because they could not alter them at will. The ambivalence is perhaps best illustrated by Claude C. Hopkins, probably the most influential copywriter of his era. *My Life in Advertising* (1927) combines deep-seated cynicism with sincere affection. "People are like sheep," he wrote. "They cannot

judge values, nor can you and I. . . . We go with the crowd.
. . . We rarely decide for ourselves because we don't know
the facts." In urging copywriters to be simple, Hopkins noted, "The great majority of men and women cannot appreci-
ate literary style. If they do, they fear it." "Simple people,"
as Hopkins referred to them, were "dilatory. They defer action, then forget." They lack foresight: "People will do little
to prevent troubles." Working people were careless about
their spending: "Suggest a thing to them because it is economical and you arouse opposition." In advertising to wom-
en, mechanical details should be omitted: "I have used very
little logic" with them.[59]

On the other hand, Hopkins insisted that it was empathy
with the common people that had given him success. He
would not be able to advertise luxury goods successfully. "I
do not know the reactions of the rich. But I do know the
common people. . . . Give me something which they want
and I will strike the responsive chord." He continually maintained that, despite the wealth he had earned, he preferred
the habits and styles of the common people. "Money means
nothing to me," he contended. The closing sentence of his
book sums up his feelings: "So I conclude that this vocation,
depending as it does on love and knowledge of the masses,
offers many rewards beyond money."[60]

Claude Hopkins's ambivalence indicates some of the continuing tensions in national advertising. Advertising men saw
the public as impulsive and irrational, but preached that consumer choices (suitably influenced by national advertising)
should dictate economic activity. Advertising experts promoted the products that enlarged the consumer's domain of
freedom in daily life, but the ad men also helped to extend
the domain of corporate power from the workplace to the
marketplace. They claimed to persuade rather than to com-

pel the public, and they were themselves sure that persuasion was the democratic alternative to authoritarianism. Yet they put their persuasive skills and techniques at the disposal of impersonal, hierarchical business enterprises. Modern advertising made the consumer both an imperious sovereign and a humble subject in democratic capitalist America.

7

Advertising Today: The Era of Market Segmentation

ON the evening of Friday, February 5, 1982, Americans witnessed the birth of an advertising campaign. After months of planning, Coca-Cola unveiled its new television commercials, featuring the theme and slogan, "Coke Is It!" To reach as wide an audience as possible, the company bought time simultaneously on all three commercial networks at 9:15 that evening. In the trade, this is known as "roadblocking." By the next morning, four out of ten Americans had viewed the ads.

Advertising Today: The Era of Market Segmentation

The "Coke Is It!" campaign followed a period of anxiety at the company that produces what may be the world's best-known brand. Its archrival, Pepsi-Cola, had passed Coke in food store sales in 1977, and in many parts of the country, Pepsi was running hard-hitting comparison ads. These showed tasters choosing Pepsi over Coke in blind tests. For months, too, price cutting and special promotional deals had been keeping soft drink profit margins low, and the price rivalry was showing no signs of abating.

Corporate officials fondly remembered the "Real Thing" Coke campaign of the early 1970s; the theme was considered one of the very best of the company's long line of successful slogans. The current campaign, "Have a Coke and a Smile," was not so highly regarded. "Coke Is It!" was designed to refocus consumer attention on the drink itself and to reassert Coke's leadership role. "We're not an ipsy-pipsy product that you sip at tea time," insisted John Bergin, president of McCann-Erickson U.S.A. and head of the Coca-Cola advertising account around the world.[1]

An advertising man of 1920 would be staggered by the sheer size of the "Coke Is It!" drive. Executives refused to divulge advertising appropriations, but industry sources placed the sum at about forty million dollars, roughly the same as Coke's 1981 spending for national advertising.[2] The precursor of the modern ad agent would also be unprepared for the advance planning of the campaign, Coke's "most extensive ever," involving elaborate tests of the theme, pictures, and music and comparisons with four other potential campaigns.[3] Most startling to the advertising man of 1920 would probably be the campaign's execution. Limited to the printed word, he could hardly conceive of the persuasive potential of the electronic media. Sound and motion have added vast new powers to the printed text and static images of older print advertising.

Yet one suspects that talented veterans, transported to the modern advertising scene, would soon become acclimated. Having lived through a generation of change between the 1880s and the World War I years, they would probably be able to adjust to the demands of the industry which has brought forth "Coke Is It!" A surprising number of features of American advertising remain largely the same. The same uneasy triad of advertiser, agency, and medium is still at the heart of advertising, although ancillary organizations have burgeoned. National advertisers purchase the services of agencies who create advertising and place it in media that offer access to potential buyers. Even the 15-percent commission, that tarnished and battered standard of agency professionalism, remains the most commonly employed compensation method. The idea of factual truth in advertising has shown itself to be too shallow and simple a goal, but the industry still strives to regulate itself and eliminate its excesses. There is little, if any, consensus on what ethical criteria should supplant or supplement truth in advertising. Finally, even though the advertisements of the Progressive Era now seem quaint, advertising people still extol the maxims of earlier copywriters. The advice of old-time copywriters like Claude C. Hopkins, John E. Kennedy, and John Caples is honored by reprints of their books.

If advertising's past continues to shape its present, this is primarily because important aspects of American business organization and corporate strategy have also endured since the early twentieth century. As we have maintained, the needs of American businesses determine the destiny of the advertising industry; insofar as those needs remain unaltered, advertising will retain many of its familiar contours.

Needless to say, in many respects the last sixty or so years have been ones of rapid change for American business. The enormous increase in size of the largest businesses has created new kinds of organizational complexity. Vertical integration was the main route of business growth in the Gilded Age and Progressive years, but diversification has proven more important since 1920. In that year, DuPont was virtually the only company experimenting with a decentralized, multidivisional organization. Most big businesses were working out the requirements of a centralized structure with functional departments. Since World War II, however, the multidivisional form has become the norm in big business. Sets of tasks that corporations performed informally or not at all in the World War I era have assumed great importance in many firms; public relations, personnel, and research and development departments are among the structures that have evolved.[4]

Naturally, broader economic and social trends have affected the marketing needs of the modern corporation. The transition from a goods-producing to a service economy has been one of these crucial changes. It has accompanied a striking rise in living standards and material comfort for most citizens. It is also worth noting that the 1920 census was the first to find that less than half the United States population was rural; since then, and especially since World War II, central city growth has slowed or reversed itself and the suburbs have become dominant. Thus, companies are selling to buyers who differ greatly from their counterparts of the twenties. Better educated, working in new kinds of jobs, living in newer communities, consumers buy a different mix of goods and services and receive them through altered marketing channels.

Nevertheless, many aspects of American business structure have endured since the early twentieth century. Just as it did sixty years ago, national advertising must respond to the needs of large, oligopolistic manufacturers of branded consumer products. The two largest auto producers in the

United States in 1920 were Ford and General Motors; today they are General Motors and Ford. The major tire manufacturers—Goodyear, Firestone, B. F. Goodrich, and Uniroyal (U.S. Rubber)—were all among the top producers of the World War I era, and all ranked on our list of leading magazine advertisers of those years. More than a third of our sample of leading advertisers of 1913–15 were among the hundred leading national advertisers of 1979. Lists of large corporations in the late Progressive Era show striking similarities to the *Fortune* 500 today, once allowance for mergers and name changes has been made.

Furthermore, large-scale enterprises have continued to be located in a rather distinct core of industries where technology and market conditions have dictated extensive investment by manufacturers in marketing, research, and central office activities. There were fourteen food producers among the top fifty-eight national advertisers of 1913–15 and twenty-six today in the largest one hundred. Nine firms made consumer chemicals (mostly soap and cosmetics) in those years, as do seventeen on the modern list.[5] These companies, along with beverage makers, tobacco firms, and manufacturers of personal-care products like toothpaste and deodorant have consistently maintained high advertising-to-sales ratios. In other industries, manufacturer brand identification is weaker; there are, for example, few heavily-promoted national apparel, jewelry, or furniture brands. Retailer advertising and other selling methods dominate the marketing mix in such industries. The differences among industries are not new; nor have they changed drastically in many decades.

Marketing channels constitute another area of continuity between the early and late twentieth-century advertising environment. Patterns of vertical integration in manufacturing industries were set early. As we have seen, few industrialists found it possible to sell their own products at retail. In some industries, manufacturer expansion into wholesaling has continued, but the often-predicted demise of the independent wholesaler has been greatly exaggerated. Manufacturers' sales branches and offices accounted for 28.1 percent of wholesale volume in 1948 and 35.1 percent in 1972, but the share of independent merchant wholesalers grew from 42.4 to 48.6 percent during those years.[6] Where goods require special handling, a technically-trained salesperson, help with financing, or extensive after-sales service, manufacturers are likely to make the investments necessary to handle such marketing needs. In other industries, independent wholesalers and retailers continue to perform marketing functions.

Admittedly, this continuity coexists with some striking changes in the marketing system. Chain stores accounted for approximately 22 percent of retail sales in 1929; by 1963 they had reached 36.6 percent. Retail sales are increasingly concentrated. In 1967, the largest 3 percent of retail establishments gained 44.4 percent of total sales volume, but nearly half of all stores (those selling less than $50,000) accounted for only 5.2 percent of all sales.[7] In fact, the largest mass marketers, such as Sears, K-mart, and J. C. Penney became giant national advertisers themselves. In 1979, Sears spent $379.3 million on national advertising and ranked third, behind only Procter & Gamble and General Foods; K-mart, with outlays of $287.1 million, was the sixth largest national advertiser. Since World War II, suburbanization, the growth of franchising and shopping centers, and the mixture of stability and change that has characterized the marketing environment for national manufacturers have required advertisers to adapt their selling strategies. Advertising leaders of the Progressive Era anticipated that progress and persuasion would create a more homogeneous national market for standardized, branded products. Growing prosperity was to give the working class the means to enjoy these goods; skillful advertising was to teach workers how to consume effectively. At the same time, advertising could be employed directly for ethnic acculturation and "Americanization" of immigrants. Even Albert Lasker, president of Lord & Thomas and one of the few Jews to reach the top in the advertising business, told his staff in the 1920s, that "we are making a homogeneous" people out of a nation of immigrants.[8] Meanwhile, national media carrying ads for nationally-distributed brands were said to weaken regional distinctions and peculiarities. These themes were expounded with varying intensity. During World War I, for example, "Americanization" through advertising was a favorite topic of advertising writers. During the Red Scare of 1919–20, advertising as a means of soothing worker discontent and breeding consumer consciousness was stressed. Throughout, the hope was for unity and for mass consumption of advertised, branded merchandise.

Paradoxically, however, growth has often implied diversity in consumption patterns. Experts who anticipated that advancing prosperity would mean a homogeneous society of loyal steady buyers of a small number of heavily-advertised brands have generally been disappointed. Consumption patterns mirror the demographic and social fissures in American life. Leading brands do not conquer entire national markets; they share the market with other brands that appeal to different target groups. For example, Budweiser, the most popular American beer brand, accounts for only 19.4 percent of beer sales. Marlboro leads the cigarette pack with only 17.2 percent of the total sales.[9] Declining market shares for leading brands are accompanied by a rapid growth in the total number of brands. The average supermarket now stocks about ten thousand different products and brands. Meanwhile, packaged brands are likely to come in a wide array of sizes, containers, and formulations. Profusion, not standardization, has been the dominant trend.

We should note that brand proliferation does not necessarily imply heightened competition or declining industrial concentration. Each leading firm in a consumer goods industry is likely to make several brands; Procter & Gamble, for example, manufactures a dozen different detergents. The array of different packages and labels on the supermarket shelf hides an impressive degree of oligopolistic stability in corporate structure.

Marketing theorist Wendell R. Smith, in an influential 1956 article, defined the corporate response to demand diversity as "market segmentation," and the phrase has become a staple in the profession's literature. Segmentation, Smith stated, "consists of viewing a heterogeneous market (one characterized by divergent demand) as a number of smaller homogeneous markets in response to differing product preferences among important market segments."[10] Smith contrasted segmentation strategies in marketing with attempts at product differentiation. In the latter case, a seller would claim to have something extra or better which made his brand preferable for all buyers. Too often, however, an appeal to everyone turned out to be an appeal to nobody in particular, or even to nobody at all. Better, therefore, to divide up the broader market and design a campaign that could reach and attract a specific target audience with distinctive needs or desires. One review of the concept called segmentation the most influential marketing concept of the twentieth century.[11]

Changing production processes, as well as new market conditions, gave an impetus to market segmentation. From the Civil War era through World War I, industrial growth was usually marked by the adoption of capital-intensive production methods that offered significant economies of scale or speed. Dramatic improvements in productivity arose where goods could be assembled or processed in large batches or by using continuous-flow techniques. The cost advantages of mass production could yield great savings to companies only if they were not dissipated in an expensive distribution system. This, as Alfred Chandler explains, was a key reason why manufacturers invested in marketing their products. The flow of goods to customers had to be maintained, inventories had to be handled efficiently, and production had to be paced to avoid costly shutdowns of expensive machinery. Since production technology dictated a standardized, homogeneous output, appeals to a mass market seemed justified.[12]

The technology and organization of physical distribution in the late nineteenth and early twentieth centuries also suggested standardization. Small-scale retailers could stock only a limited range of items and were not hospitable to many new products. The cost of getting a product variation onto a storekeeper's shelf could be high and even prohibitive unless the new item appealed to a wide range of shoppers.

After about 1920, several of the conditions that promoted product standardization began to fade. Manufacturing growth came less from providing each worker with more capital and more from setting up new work stations, assembly lines, or branch plants. This permitted more diverse output. Later, the cost advantages of long production runs began to shrink in some industries. Techniques of altering the mix of raw materials became more widespread, as did means of packaging and labeling different product sizes and assortments. Automatic control machinery could rapidly change the mix of products a plant turned out without greatly increasing marginal costs. New organizational methods of inventory control and traffic management also allowed firms to diversify their output.

In the automobile industry, it was Alfred P. Sloan who recognized the profit potential in marketing product variations and features that could be added onto the basic vehicle. When Sloan and Pierre S. DuPont assumed leadership of General Motors in late 1920, the company suffered both from financial and administrative chaos and from the lack of a marketing strategy. Sloan soon decided that General Motors "should produce a line of cars in each price area . . . ; second, that the price steps should not be such as to leave wide gaps in the line . . . ; and third, that there should be no duplication by the corporation in the price fields or steps." Not only would the automobile market be segmented; Sloan also stressed the necessity of placing GM's cars at the top of each price segment and emphasized that they were to offer extra value and features in return. In particular, GM's Chevrolet was to provide something more than the stripped-down basic transportation of Henry Ford's Model T. "The strategy we devised was to take a bite from the top of his position, conceived as a price class, and in this way build up Chevrolet's volume on a profitable basis. In later years, as the consumer upgraded his preference, the new General Motors policy was to become critically attuned to the course of American history." As Sloan stated, marketing requirements began to take precedence over engineering needs. "By the mid-twenties, the product engineer had begun to feel the influence of the sales people. He then began to yield to market considerations."[13] General Motors soared in the 1920s while Henry Ford continued to insist that the customer could have a car in any color he wanted as long as it was black. Ford's dictum had lost its technological rationale. By the 1960s Detroit had created the assembly-line "custom" car, an oxymoron on wheels.

While these new methods of production and factory organization permitted market segmentation, changing demand patterns have often necessitated it. Advertisers' dreams that their products would be universally and permanently welcomed into consumers' lives encountered the rude reality of another phenomenon of modern marketing, the product life cycle. The concept was set forth by Joel Dean in 1951. Dean reminded businessmen that their products faced the likelihood of earning diminishing profits. Products "start as novelties, develop into distinctive and protected 'specialities,' and then degenerate into undifferentiated commodities."[14] Marketing experts noted that the product life cycle could be turned to good account. In planning new products, managers could look forward to ways to extend the growth phase of the cycle by getting customers to use their brands more intensively and in new ways and by searching for new groups of potential users.[15] However, the product life cycle concept can also be taken as a warning to segment markets. It implies that advertisers cannot hope to reach all of the people, all of the time. They must further recognize that even regular customers are unlikely to stay loyal to the same brand forever.

The rise of the service sector has been yet another reason for greater segmentation. In 1920, less than half of all workers in the private, nonfarm economy were service producers; today, more than two-thirds are.[16] Most of the nation's leading advertisers are goods producers, but companies ranging from United Airlines to American Express to CBS are primarily service marketers. Moreover, embedded within giant goods-manufacturing companies are some very large service activities. General Motors Acceptance Company finances auto purchases; Time, Inc. is a leading cable television operator; McDonald's sells service and convenience along with its meals.

For several reasons, service marketing is likely to entail targeting of distinct customer groups. In the first place, the individual units where services are offered tend to be relatively small—the neighborhood fast food outlet or movie theater, the auto dealer's office where car financing is arranged. Typically, each unit may reach only a narrowly-bounded demographic, socioeconomic, or geographic group. Second, service operations usually entail personal involvement of customers. Where personal relations affect not only the purchasing act but the service itself, promotion based on broad claims of overall superiority is likely to be insufficient. Third, by their very nature, services are "produced" only as they are consumed. Given this, certain kinds of economies of scale are unlikely in service industries. The manufacturer can schedule production to make optimal use of costly capital equipment; unless the service provider can get customers to alter their usage patterns, he must be ready to perform the service when the buyer requires it. Again, this points to the user-centered nature of service industries and the marketer's need to focus attention on consumers' characteristics and behavior.

Admittedly, the unique characteristics of service marketing in theory are often blurred in practice. Services can be, in Theodore Levitt's terminology, "industrialized" and subjected to the same kinds of division of labor and control systems as goods production; in the case of, for example, automated bank teller machines, "prepackaged" travel plans, or computerized truck routing, industrialization has meant cheaper, more efficient delivery of a more homogeneous and dependable service product.[17] In some of these cases, segmentation marketing strategies may be inappropriate. Regardless of the trend, however, the current reality is that service firms generally provide a heterogeneous mix of products in a setting laden with personal interactions.

Not all companies choose to respond to variations in consumer behavior, service marketing, and the product life cycle by following a market segmentation strategy. In an influential recent book, Michael Porter sets forth three "generic strategies" and argues that successful companies must adopt one of these approaches. A strategy of overall cost leadership means that a firm (or a company division operating as a distinct profit center) will compete relentlessly on price, cutting costs wherever possible and avoiding even the most tempting opportunities that might entail increasing expenses. A differentiation strategy means "creating something that is perceived industry-wide as being unique."[18] That feature, usually a product attribute, can also be a distinctive distribution channel, service policy, or even an advertising-created image. Finally, there is a focus strategy, in which a company sets its sights on a subgroup of buyers and devotes its energies to reaching that target with a lower-priced product or an item best suited to the desires of the segmented group.

Each of these generic strategies has implications for advertising policy. The cost leader is unlikely to advertise heavily. Often content to sell through strong retailers and to manufacture private labels or unbranded merchandise, cost leaders will probably concentrate on price appeals when they advertise. The differentiation strategy often entails heavy advertising in mass media, especially for widely-used consumer products. The exceptional feature has to be pushed into the public's mind, because that feature is the product's raison d'être. Firms that are differentiating their physical products, rather than their image, distribution, or service, are also likely to center their ads on the product and feature demonstrations of its distinctiveness. The third strategy, focus, is by definition a market segmentation strategy. To concentrate on one target group usually entails finding media that reach it efficiently and using advertising appeals that reinforce the segment's group identification.

As Porter points out, all three generic strategies are viable.

Firms following each may all be in the same industry simultaneously. But for the purpose of ascertaining the impact of business strategy on advertising policy, we may safely ignore the role of cost leaders. Looking at the growing recognition of heterogeneous markets suggests the hypothesis that focus strategies are on the rise relative to differentiation strategies. In fact, the advent and ascendency of market segmentation as a principle of national advertisers may well be the most far-reaching development in national advertising in recent decades. In the last generation it has affected the structure and conduct of the advertising agency business, the standards and principles of advertising professionals, and the form and contents of advertisements themselves.

The same trends in structure and strategy that we find in many consumer-goods industries that employ national advertising can be observed in the advertising business itself. Advertising, after all, is a service industry, and its clients are demanding buyers with wide-ranging needs. Output cannot be standardized. Indeed, it must be custom designed. We should not be surprised to find the heterogeneity and segmentation characteristic of service industries. On the one hand, large firms have maintained, and perhaps increased, their share of the advertising industry. On the other, specialization and differentiation have rendered the advertising business more diverse.

In the last sixty years, the growth of large advertising agencies has kept pace with and may have outstripped overall advertising volume. In 1921, N. W. Ayer, at that point probably the largest agency, handled approximately $11 million of advertising; thus its gross revenues were in the vicinity of $2 million. In 1980, Young and Rubicam, the largest American agency, billed well over $2 billion and had revenues of $340.8 million. J. Walter Thompson, the largest publicly-held agency, had 381 employees in 1924, when it was probably among the three largest agencies; today it has 7,000. Before World War II, data on market share are not reliable, but in 1935, Thompson claimed that it placed one-twelfth of all national advertising in the United States while the next nine largest firms handled an additional four-twelfths among them, suggesting a ten-firm market share of about 42 percent. According to *Advertising Age,* the ten largest firms in 1970 handled about 39.6 percent of the volume of the 615 agencies surveyed. In 1980, the top ten handled over $15 billion, for a market share of 47.5 percent among the 791 agencies reporting.[19]

By almost any measure, then, the leading advertising agencies today are big businesses. Nevertheless, agencies are still likely to be smaller than their major clients. Most major advertising agencies are careful not to put all their eggs in one client's basket, but it is not uncommon for a single account to provide several million dollars in commissions and fees. Since the advertiser can cancel the account almost at will, client power still looms ominously large on Madison Avenue.

With size has come diversification. Agencies of the World War I era, having just begun to offer clients ancillary marketing services along with creating and placing advertisements, would no doubt be impressed with the scope of agencies' work today. As early as the 1950s, Marion Harper, the young president of McCann-Erickson, noted the breadth of agency activities. "To service our clients, we at McCann have developed a marketing concept," he explained. "We deal with the whole chain of distribution from board chairman to retailer. We are not a marketing organization, because we do not have the responsibility. Are we an advertising agency? I don't know what you'd call it."[20] Agencies today carry on political lobbying, provide advice on office and showroom decor, train executives in public speaking, and prepare for clients' sales meetings. Young & Rubicam calls its array of marketing services "the Whole Egg," and uses this theme to sell its own work.[21]

In the 1970s and early 1980s, major agencies have acquired specialized subsidiaries in order to expand the range of marketing and communications services they can offer. Thus, for example, the JWT Group, a holding company for the J. Walter Thompson agency, also controls an agency that specializes in recruitment advertising, a medical advertising subsidiary, a market research firm, and two public relations companies, including Hill & Knowlton, the nation's largest. J. Walter Thompson U.S.A. has divisions that concentrate on direct marketing services, on entertainment advertising, and on the Hispanic market.

Agency specialization bespeaks a growing segmentation of the agency business. Either as independent firms or as subsidiaries or divisions of larger companies, agencies that are specialized by product, by medium, or by audience have successfully asserted a claim to expertise and efficiency. For example, in 1980, forty-one agencies in the health-care field handled nearly two-thirds of a billion dollars' worth of advertising. The largest, Sudler & Hennessey (a subsidiary of Young & Rubicam, the nation's largest agency), billed practically $62 million.[22] Other growing agencies specialize in advertising industrial products, in direct marketing, in financial advertising, or in advertising to minorities. The success of such enterprises suggests the prevalence of segmentation in American marketing today.

Despite merger waves in the late 1960s and again today, there are limits to agency growth and consolidation. One restraint that dates back to the World War I era is the taboo against handling competing accounts. As clients have diversified, the problem has become more pressing. Mergers between large agencies are often thwarted because each partner has a major account with one of two rival companies. The competing account problem is one reason why large national advertisers today rarely leave all their advertising in the hands of one agency. Manufacturers of consumer packaged goods, such as Procter & Gamble and General Foods, customarily divide their brands' accounts. A 1976 study found that large national advertisers used, on average, about four agencies; of the sixty-nine surveyed companies spending more than $10 million on advertising yearly, only eight gave all their work to one agency.[23]

Changes in the system of agency compensation would also appear to curb the advertising business's tendency to concentration. The full-service agency's dominance after World War I rested, as we have argued, in part on the standard 15-percent commission system. Manufacturers who wanted to internalize advertising found that it was not easy to get the same media space rates that "recognized" agencies could. Especially during the Depression, national advertisers attacked the commission system bitterly. In the 1950s, as television and a heightened marketing orientation caused advertising budgets to soar, national advertisers once again began to complain about the commission system. The Federal Trade Commission probed for antitrust violations and, in the spring of 1956, the American Association of Advertising Agencies and several publishers' groups signed consent decrees. They agreed not to maintain lists of recognized agents nor collectively to deny the 15-percent discount to nonmember agencies or advertisers placing directly.[24]

Yet, more than a quarter-century after the constent decrees, the commission system remains the most common way of compensating agencies. In 1976, the Association of National Advertisers found that over two-thirds of the advertisers it polled were using media commissions as their primary method of paying agencies. Most advertisers and agencies surveyed in 1981 agreed that the straight media commission system was in widespread use. Its simplicity apparently remains an attractive feature to many clients as well as to agencies.[25]

On the other hand, since the consent decree, full-service agencies have lost their near-monopoly on handling national advertising in those media that grant commissions. There is no evidence that full-service agencies any longer get preferential rates from media. An advertiser who wants to set up an in-house agency can be assured of paying the same amount for media space and time that the Madison Avenue agencies do. This means that advertisers now have a range of choices. They may continue to use the full-service agency; they may handle their own advertising through an in-house division or subsidiary; or they may purchase advertising services "a la carte," either from regular agencies or from firms that handle only some advertising tasks. Since the 1960s, independent "creative" companies have offered to plan and execute advertisements for clients who purchase research, media work, and other services elsewhere. Disparaged initially by their larger rivals as faddish "boutiques," the independent creative firms have survived, although few have thrived. Media-buying services specialize in handling a demanding and technical advertising function. The wide variety of advertising media today means that planning a schedule for an advertising campaign is highly complex. Even the task of purchasing time and space has its skilled practitioners, because a dizzying array of volume and frequency discounts, along with a willingness to deal and barter, means that a good media buyer can save an advertiser large sums.

Thus, the full-service agencies must adapt to new forms of competition and new kinds of competitors. Compensation practices are no longer standardized by trade association fiat, and agencies must show clients that they are superior to other available alternatives. Functional specialists like creative boutiques and media-buying services, as well as the house agencies of advertisers themselves, put a potential limit on the concentration of the advertising industry.

Even in the largest agencies, life in the advertising business continues to be fraught with uncertainties. Advertising, as one industry expert put it, "is a nobody-knows-for-sure business."[26] Uncertainty implies insecurity, and this is manifested in several ways.

In the first place, the seeming stability and order among the largest advertising agencies disguises a churning motion among clients, agency owners and managers, and personnel. Of the ninety-two largest agencies in 1966, forty-one no longer existed by 1979.[27] The mergers that caused many of these companies to disappear made some of their stockholders rich, but rumors of consolidation have produced anxiety, especially among personnel who feared getting lost in the shuffle. Although failure is rare among the larger advertising agencies today, it is frequent among smaller, newer firms. Advertising is labor intensive, like most services, and there are no licensing requirements. Agencies begun in the flush of enthusiasm or on the promise of a profitable account may fold quickly. Most new agencies are partnerships, but colleagues who were good friends as employees elsewhere often find the strains of a business partnership unbearable. Meanwhile, financial obligations mount. Although it takes very little money to create an advertising agency, it is costly to present the facade of opulent success that many young agencies deem necessary to impress potential clients. Sometimes the clients never come.

Client relations remain the perpetual source of advertising industry anxieties. In 1981, there were more than seventy significant account switches involving $850 million in billings. Madison Avenue spokespeople prefer to emphasize that the average account remains with an agency for about eight years, but in a recent survey, four-fifths of advertisers and agency respondents believed that account switching was on the rise.[28] Since most contracts can be canceled on ninety days' notice and some can be ended immediately, the process can be jarringly swift.

Because salaries constitute the major expense in advertising agencies, those losing major clients will often cut staff sharply. Conversely, however, agencies acquiring an account are tempted to stretch their current work force to handle the new business without increasing the number of employees. Just as it did in the World War I era, news that an advertiser is looking for a new agency will set off a frantic scramble. Wooing potential new business consumes agency time and energy. For example, in 1981, it was alleged that the Dallas agency of Bozell & Jacobs spent a million dollars to win the American Airlines account. Rumor had it that the agency even built a model of the American Airlines boardroom, so that agency personnel would feel at ease when they made their presentation to that company.[29]

The personal stress these organizational pressures create is not easy to measure. Novels about advertising have often featured the theme of the dedicated and talented advertising man beset by capricious clients and craven bosses. That Madison Avenue is sometimes known colloquially as "Ulcer Gulch" would reinforce that stereotype. Copywriters and art directors (the "creative" people) seem especially stress-prone, since there are no clear, generally accepted standards for evaluating their work. As one agency president who began in the creative field put it, "As a creative man I've been so goddamn up tight I didn't know what I was doing. But in this business you are always up tight. If you aren't built that way, you'll soon become that way."[30] Job turnover reflects opportunity as well as insecurity, but it is probably noteworthy that in one recent survey, advertising men and women had been with their current company for 3.93 years. The equivalent figures for a comparison group of business and professional people was 7.08 years.[31]

To summarize, the advertising business since the 1920s has had a paradoxical development. Advertising leaders after World War I projected an image of a stable, orderly business on the one hand and an area of rapid growth and great opportunity on the other. The marketing imperatives of American corporations in the last sixty or so years have made these images into realities for large portions of the advertising industry. Nevertheless, some of the less attractive features of advertising agencies, which the early image-makers preferred to ignore, remain today. No amount of research can guarantee successful advertising; testing remains a very imperfect means of measuring accomplishments. The uncertainty that inheres in the work itself is compounded by the agency-client relationship and its endemic insecurity. A diffuse and segmented advertising business serving a clientele of giant corporations means dependency and anxiety along with opportunity and excitement.

Consumer distrust of advertising compounds the industry's worries. This continuing disaffection would disappoint advertising leaders of the World War I era. They were an optimistic, self-confident lot. Advertising, they asserted, was rapidly becoming a reliable servant of economic progress; the advertising business itself was skilled, disciplined, and professional; and a responsible movement of self-regulation, cooperating with public officials, was eradicating fraud and improving the climate for honest businessmen. However, new demands on and concerns about advertising ethics have arisen. Advances in the techniques of persuasion have evoked new doubts about the legitimacy and morality of advertising.

Advertising Today: The Era of Market Segmentation

In the early decades of the century, advertising leaders could generally set their own terms for the debate over advertising ethics. They thought that honest advertising would create public confidence, but truth—at least truth as the industry once defined it—has proven inadequate. New constituencies—consumer organizations, professional groups, government regulators—have broader agendas.

In the Progressive Era, supporters of the truth in advertising movement placed their hopes in pressure from honest advertising men and, as a last resort, legal sanctions. Industry self-regulation showed its limitations, however. Local vigilance committees lacked the resources and the enforcement powers to settle all the cases of deceptive advertising they encountered. Enthusiasm waned when vigilance appeared to threaten, not reinforce, public trust. Moreover, the case-by-case approach made these early efforts reactive and incapable of preventing broad categories of deception before they were committed. The Progressives' legal solution, the *Printers' Ink* model statute, also proved to be a disappointment. Courts construed it narrowly, and some state legislatures watered it down by requiring proof of intent to deceive. The statute contained no mechanism to bring cases to prosecutors' attention. For these reasons, there were few cases successfully prosecuted under the model statute laws.

Nevertheless, the arsenal of legislation and regulation dealing with deceptive advertising is much expanded today. The Federal Trade Commission has become the most important agency in this area. Its mandate to stop "unfair methods of competition," Section 5 of the 1914 Federal Trade Commission Act, soon led to its issuing cease-and-desist orders against dishonest advertising. In 1931, a Supreme Court decision held that the FTC had jurisdiction only when the advertising directly affected competitors. However, in 1938, the Wheeler-Lea amendments to the

Federal Trade Commission Act expanded the Commission's authority to "unfair or deceptive methods, acts or practices," thus re-establishing the agency's ability to act against dishonest advertising.[32] In 1975, the Federal Trade Commission Improvements Act gave the agency clear power to set industry-wide rules and to take knowing violators to federal court to seek civil penalties. In the last decade, the Commission has contended in several cases that it is unfair to make an advertising claim unless the advertiser has a reasonable basis for believing the claim to be true. Under this doctrine, it has required advertisers to submit material substantiating their advertising even when the Commission has made no assertion that the ads are deceptive.

Other agencies, notably the Federal Communications Commission, the Food and Drug Administration, and state consumer protection agencies also now possess power to regulate some advertising. However, the primary responsibility resides with the FTC. This authority has been employed against advertising claims which even the most vigilant truth in advertising advocate of 1920 would have found acceptable. Regulators have come increasingly to recognize the principle that deception is in the eye of the beholder, and that advertisements must be judged by their potential effects, not merely by a formalistic analysis of the wording of the copy.

Many deceptive advertising cases recognize that judgments must examine the "decoding" as well as the "encoding" of advertising messages. As an appeals court decision in 1956 put it, "A statement may be deceptive even if the constituent words may be literally or technically construed so as not to constitute a misrepresentation. . . . The buying public does not weigh each word in an advertisement or a representation. It is important to ascertain the impression that is likely to be created upon the prospective purchaser."[33] Based on this reasoning, the Commission and the Courts have, for example, held that products made in the small Japanese town of Usa and labeled "Made in Usa" were deceptively labeled. In another set of cases, the authorities have ruled that incomplete truth can also be deceptive. Thus, the Commission successfully objected to advertisements for Geritol which claimed that the tonic was a remedy for "tired blood," the manufacturer's much publicized synonym for iron-deficiency anemia. The ads had failed to mention that most people who feel tired and run-down are not suffering from "tired blood." Sometimes, the potential for deception seems quite remote. Clairol was told to stop advertising that claimed it colored hair permanently because some consumers might actually believe that hair that grew after the coloring was applied would also be colored. Examples like this have led industry spokesmen and even one dissenting FTC commissioner to complain about the agency's "literal-minded legalism."[34]

A revived self-regulatory process complements legal controls on dishonest advertising. Media codes of advertising acceptability have been tightened although a recent antitrust decision has called into question the legality of efforts by the National Association of Broadcasters to restrict radio and television advertising. In 1971, the Association of National Advertisers, the American Association of Advertising Agencies, the American Advertising Federation, and the Council of Better Business Bureaus introduced a new system to review advertising for deception. The motive was clearly to stave off external pressures. The industry sought to "defend itself against the onslaught [of] consumerism and of legislative efforts that would severely limit its ability to function as part of a system in a competitive business environment."[35]

Structurally, the self-regulatory procedure is rather complex. A National Advertising Division (NAD) receives complaints, reviews ads, and initiates its own cases as well. It requests substantiation of ad claims, appraises the material submitted, and, if it considers the problem to be more than trivial, advises the advertiser to alter or withdraw the message in question. Either the advertiser of the NAD can appeal cases to a National Advertising Review Board (NARB) panel. These are composed of advertisers, agency representatives, and public members, with agencies controlling a majority of the seats. If the NARB rejects an advertising claim or the advertiser still refuses to change it, the panel may turn the case over to the Federal Trade Commission for possible legal action. Thus, although the NAD/NARB system is voluntary, its workings can lead to government action.

The record of the NAD/NARB indicates that advertising leaders have taken their work seriously and have not attempted to whitewash deceptive practices. Between 1971 and 1980, in handling 1,697 complaints and queries, the NAD exonerated 38 percent of the questioned advertisements, but in a larger number of cases it induced the advertiser to withdraw or revise the message. In twenty out of the thirty-five cases that reached the NARB panels on appeal, the NARB ruled that advertising claims were not properly substantiated. Although self-regulation has sometimes been portrayed as an opportunity for businesses to collude against unwanted rivals, consumers and consumer organizations filed more complaints than did competitors, and the largest single source of cases was the NAD monitoring staff itself.[36] In sum, the NAD/NARB is evidence of the advertising industry's sincere desire to combat deceptive advertising. Its effectiveness is harder to evaluate, but there are signs that it has been able to respond to the complaints of consumers as well as to the objections of business rivals.

The more assertive posture of the FTC and the honest efforts of advertising men and women to police their own

ranks have quite certainly reduced the proportion of advertising making deceptive product claims. Nevertheless, public
trust in advertising is low and industry representatives fear
that it is slipping further. Forty years ago Neil H. Borden
began his classic study, *The Economic Effects of Advertising* with the statement, "Advertising is under fire." The
same words could have introduced almost any advertising
industry study of public attitudes since that time.[37]

In fact, over nearly a half a century, a variety of surveys
reveal that approximately half of the public has found advertising to be dishonest. In 1939, 51 percent believed that advertising was truthful, "on the whole." In 1964, 47 percent
generally or partially agreed that "advertisements present a
true picture" of the product advertised. In 1977, 46 percent
of Harris Poll respondents said that "most or all" ads on television were "seriously misleading."[38] These surveys would
indicate a stable balance of opinion, but there are some indications of declining trust. Respondents to surveys from the
1930s through the 1960s expressed the belief that advertising's standards were improving; the 1977 study, on the other
hand, found that respondents felt that the gap between advertisers' claims and product performance was growing. A
more limited segment of the populace, the readers of consumer testing magazines, shows a pronounced rise in unfa-
vorable attitudes to advertising between 1970 and 1976.[39] Finally, a 1981 public opinion poll ranked advertising men next
to the bottom among occupations (above only used car salesmen) for ethical standards.[40]

Why have the efforts of advertising men and the con-
straints imposed by regulators failed to win public support
and trust? There are several reasons, not the least of which is
the growing popular cynicism about institutions in general;
advertising is not immune to the erosion of public confidence. But it is also true that changes in the nature of adver-

tising have compounded the problems American advertising has in legitimating itself in consumers' eyes. Honesty may be the best policy (although there are still many advertisers who stretch truth to the breaking point), but it is not enough.

Truth itself has proven to be a more problematical concept than early vigilance workers cared to recognize. One recent study of consumer opinions about truth in advertising begins with the claim that "complaints about truth, whether made in 1970 or in 1900, seem remarkably similar," and suggests that the problem is "unchanging." But this is so only in the narrowest sense.[41] As we have seen, early twentieth-century advertising men, unburdened by any epistemological subtleties, were generally content to define truth as the absence of demonstrable falsity. At most, some recognized the importance of implying untrue claims without directly stating them. Buffeted by experience and, in some cases, theoretical reflection, observers today are less sure. Peter Drucker, answering a query from American Management Association researchers, wrote, "I have not the foggiest notion what 'Truth in Advertising' might mean. I am practically convinced that it is a mindless and meaningless slogan."[42]

One reason for this uncertainty is that market segmentation advertising campaigns have made older criteria for judging deception outmoded. For example, consider the issue of consumer rationality. Nineteenth-century common law generally adopted the standpoint of the "reasonable man" in cases involving fraud and deceit, a standard that was perhaps appropriate given the assumption that transactions involved rationally self-interested entrepreneurial individuals. The Federal Trade Commission for several decades, however, pursued cases in which only the exceptionally credulous could be deceived. For example, a skin cream, "Rejuvenescence," was required to change its name because some buyers might actually believe that it would make them younger. More recently, however, criteria have been relaxed. According to a 1963 decision, "A representation does not become 'false and deceptive' merely because it will be unreasonably misunderstood by an insignificant and unrepresentative segment of the class of persons to whom the representation is addressed."[43] The advertising industry would be glad to see this position widely adopted. As David Ogilvy, the founder of the giant agency, Ogilvy & Mather, put it, "The consumer isn't a moron. She is your wife." Why not judge deceptive potential accordingly?[44]

Segmentation, however, suggests that neither the "credulous consumer" nor the "reasonable person" standard is appropriate. The characteristics of the targeted segment may themselves determine the deceptive potential of the advertising. On the one hand, when ad campaigns are aimed at experienced, well-informed, heavy users of the product, it would seem fitting to assume that these intended consumers would not be easily fooled. Sellers and buyers are presumably on a more equal footing than in other cases, and deception is less likely. On the other hand, segmentation campaigns may target especially vulnerable consumer groups. Even frequent purchasers and heavy users of products may be exhibiting a form of addiction; their purchases may be based on powerful nonrational buying motives.

This problem has arisen most frequently with ads designed for children. Children are the targets of some $400 million of television advertising annually, and young people's programming is a lucrative field for the networks.[45] Although the impact of television commericals on children is the subject of continuing controversy, there is little doubt that children react to advertisements differently than adults. One advertising executive put it pungently:

When you sell a woman on a product and she goes into the store and finds your brand isn't in stock, she'll probably forget about it. But when you sell a kid on your product, if he can't get it he will throw himself on the floor, stamp his feet and cry. You can't get a reaction like that out of an adult.[46]

In other areas, too, segmentation-based advertising campaigns raise doubts about the adequacy of older standards of truth and deception. Advertising to the elderly for health products and services may be strictly factual, avoid false implications, and yet evoke anxieties that prevent rational buying decisions. The same might be said of some advertising to adolescents, such as, campaigns for acne medicines. One study of advertisements in *Ebony,* directed towards black readers, found more deception than in ads for the same brands in *Life* and the *Ladies' Home Journal.* Among the problems with ads in *Ebony* were incomplete warranty disclosure, omission of technical product specifications, and deceptive layout.[47]

Contemporary advertising also raises vexatious ethical issues when it focuses on users rather than the physical product. Segmentation and the rise of service marketing have apparently increased the proportion of user-centered campaigns. An ethical evaluation that looks only at the veracity of product claims will miss much of the persuasive action of these advertisements. Where ads appeal to the consumer to enter a "consumption community," they stress the attractiveness of the community, not just the desirability of the product. It comes as no surprise that ads show products in pleasant surroundings and that models and actors are generally attractive. But when the context rather than the product becomes, in a sense, the object of the consumers' desires, judging an ad by its product claims is insufficient.

User-centered advertising is likely to raise issues of fairness and manipulation. Although the FTC has had the legal power to act against "unfair" advertising since 1938, the authority has seldom been employed. In one of these rare cases, the J. B. Williams Company advertised a caffeine-based stimulant, Vivarin. A woman spoke:

> One day it dawned on me that I was boring my husband to death. It was hard for me to admit it—but it was true. . . . I decided that I had to do something. . . . Last week . . . I took a Vivarin tablet. . . .
>
> All of a sudden Jim was coming home to a more exciting woman, me. . . . The other day—it wasn't even my birthday—Jim sent me flowers with a note. The note began: "To my new wife . . . "[48]

Certainly this is an extreme example of corporate efforts to profit from private anxieties, but it is far from unique. Advertisers have preyed upon intimate hopes and fears for many years; the long-running Listerine mouthwash series in which bad breath ruined a host of promising romantic and professional opportunities is a case in point. But user-centered commercials, especially those employing the narrative and visual capabilities of television, reinforce the product message with signals about life-styles. The promise is larger, and more ethically ambiguous, than the product. It is one thing to present a detergent as stronger, cheaper, or more convenient than its competitors. It is another to show children chanting "Ring around the collar!" at a housewife who has failed to use Wisk detergent.

Finally, advertising has become a symbol of our inner doubts about the affluent society. Earlier in this century, when most advertising dollars promoted products that were arguably necessities, concern about advertising ethics focused on the message not the product. Even in the Progressive Era, there were a few conservative moralists who suggested that advertising stimulated excessive consumption; these men and women feared advertising's effect on thrift and self-restraint. But now the doubters are everywhere. In a 1964 study of consumer views of advertising, nearly two out of three agreed that "advertising often persuades people to buy things they shouldn't buy."[49] Indeed, more than four-fifths of the businessmen who answered a 1971 questionnaire agreed with a similar statement.[50]

Today, worries about the impact of advertising on consumption indicate more than an ascetic frame of mind. The gap between wants and needs—or rather between wants and our notions of what people *should* need—looms large. It provokes us to wonder where our desires do come from, since they do not appear to derive from "objective" circumstances in the "real world," or from a spontaneous, autonomous will. This arouses the suspicion that advertising—a force emanating from a large, distant, and somewhat mysterious source—has itself created these desires. In other words, fears about advertising are also anxieties about ourselves and our styles of life. Do our possessions liberate us or oppress us? Does prosperity in fact mean freedom of choice? Does freedom of choice mean the imposition of alternatives defined and delineated by giant, impersonal organizations? To pose these questions is not to answer them. The purpose here is to explain the sources of some of the qualms Americans continue to have about advertising, not to vindicate or debunk them.

The popularity of Vance Packard's 1957 exposé, *The Hidden Persuaders,* can best be understood in light of these concerns. Unlike prior critics of advertising, Packard had little to say about advertising's wastefulness, its poor taste, or even its deceptiveness. Persuasion itself was the target. The loss of personal autonomy was the threat. "The most serious offense many of the depth manipulators commit, it seems to me," Packard concluded, "is that they try to invade the privacy of our minds."[51] The more recent books of Wilson Bryan Key, *Subliminal Seduction, Media Manipulation,* and

The Clam-Plate Orgy also speak to our fears about loss of personal control and dignity.[52] Key professes to find subliminal messages, often of a sexually suggestive nature, hidden in the designs of magazine and television advertisements.

Ironically, as public fears of manipulation and domination have grown, advertising experts have become more dubious about the extent of advertising's persuasive powers. Advertising leaders in the 1920s reflected the tendency of the era to believe that mass persuasion was virtually omnipotent. In their more exuberant moments, they were wont to claim the ability to manufacture tastes and engineer desires. More recently, however, advertising spokesmen have emphasized the difficulties of persuasion. Audiences, they have stated, are "obstinate"; consumers perceive ads selectively, tend to take from them only the messages that reinforce prior beliefs, confuse rival ads and brands, and forget quickly what ads have taught them. Eager to erase the label of hidden persuaders, advertising spokespeople sometimes even claim they do not persuade at all. This self-denial does not please George Lois, a flamboyant art director turned agency executive. He reports the following dialogue:

> I was on *The David Susskind Show* with some ad guys the other day, and he said, "Well, what is advertising supposed to do?" And one of them says, "It gives information." And that's really what most of them think it does, you know. . . .
> I told the guy, "You and I are in different businesses. I spray poison gas."[53]

But the profane image of advertising as gas warfare raises issues too unsettling for the industry to contemplate. Lois is in a small minority. The price of moral legitimacy for the advertising business today is the rejection, at least in rhetoric, of its own persuasive powers.

Ever since the mythic moment in 1904 when John E.

Kennedy vouchsafed to Albert Lasker the definition of advertising as "Salesmanship in Print," advertising people of all stylistic bents have agreed upon the purpose of the work: the task of advertising is to sell. The only legitimate measure of success is at the cash register. This credo unites advocates of hard-sell and soft-sell, exponents of quantitative research and believers in creative intuition, those who emphasize facts and those who push images. Indeed, it is a fundamental element of continuity in advertising from the beginning of the century until today.

Despite the enduring common purpose of selling, anyone who peruses advertisements of past years will immediately note how outmoded many seem. True, a few slogans and themes have persisted, but in general the advertisements of 1920 would be as jarringly out of place in today's newspaper as would the headlines and news stories from that year. Retrospective showings of "classic" television commercials at theaters, on cable TV, and on network television confirm that advertising styles change rapidly.

Part of the evanescence of advertisements results from what Daniel Boorstin calls their "self-liquidating" quality.[54] Advertising claims of yesterday lose their impact in the face of today's new promises. In its tritest form, the "self-liquidating" principle gives us the all-too-familiar "New! Improved! Bigger! Better!" campaigns which cannibalize their predecessors for the sake of novelty. Not too surprisingly, it is likely that this demand for something new strengthens the widely held belief that advertising is "a young man's game," with high turnover and meteoric career paths.

Advertisements also change along with customs and styles. The cycles of fashion that we observe in the stores and on the streets can also be found in advertisements: hemlines rise and fall, neckties alternate between wide and slim. More importantly, though, advertising absorbs shifting values and behavior. As women began to smoke in public, cigarette advertisers timorously allowed women to be seen saying, first, "Blow some [smoke] my way," then holding a cigarette, and finally actually smoking one. The sharp division between the male world of work and the female one at home has faded along with growing female labor force participation. Advertising agencies are avid producers and consumers of research on life-styles and are quick to craft their ads to make use of the social trends they spot. It is not surprising, then, that social historians have looked at advertisements as valuable indices of cultural change.

Advertisements also express changing tastes in graphic arts. Changes in execution can affect the perception of an advertisement quite as much as changes in verbal content. An arcane literature on the relative merits of different elements of advertising design has produced rules of thumb on the proper number of words in headlines, the readability of various type faces, the color preferences of men and women, and many other matters. But these rules exist to be broken as new trends, insights, and hunches take shape. For example, the hard-edged, bright-colored "psychedelic" art work of the late 1960s and early 1970s has largely disappeared. It would look hopelessly passé today.

Another reason for the evolution of advertisements can be found in the growing technical capacities of the media. At any given time, these capacities set limits on the persuasive techniques advertising people can employ. It is hard, for example, to sell foods in publications that do not offer color printing. Television is an ideal medium to show products in use to drive home their advantages. Outdoor advertising rarely gets more than a brief exposure, so that items requiring complex selling messages are excluded. But media capabilities themselves change to accommodate marketing needs. Magazines, for instance, can "bleed" illustrations so that they cover the entire page without white borders. There are now methods of showing large three-dimensional objects on billboards. In the last decade or so, some advertisers have even been able to offer "scratch and sniff" patches in print advertisements to convey their products' fragrances.

For all these reasons, then, advertisements change. In the final analysis, however, it is marketing function that determines advertising form. Advertising is designed to make people buy, but the way it works depends on the firm's marketing situation. If the advertising of 1920—let alone 1890—looks quaint, naive, or crassly dishonest, recall that the marketing context has been transformed in the intervening decades. Although the new marketing environment has many facets, the rise of market segmentation, the growth of services, the dominant position of the electronic media, and the more intense scrutiny of factual claims are among the major forces determining the advertising messages we receive.

It is impossible to give a full account of the impact these developments have had on advertising copy and design. Advertisements are far too diverse for any complete typology. Moreover, even though marketing needs mold advertising appeals, there is some autonomy, some genuine room for maneuver in translating strategy into advertisements. Yet there are three interrelated trends that bear analysis. These are the growth of user-centered advertising, the rise of dramatic or narrative forms, and the subordination of explicit product claims.

At the risk of overgeneralization, we might say that product-focused advertising flourished from the turn of the century until mid-century. Oligopolistic manufacturers of familiar consumer products tried to stake a claim to product superiority. In Michael Porter's terminology, differentiation was the leading generic strategy. The excruciating difficulties of finding advantages in what were essentially equivalent products posed incessant problems for the "creative" workers in advertising. In the 1950s, Rosser Reeves, the leading proponent of hard-sell campaigns, put it this way: "Our problem is—a client comes into my office and throws two newly minted half-dollars onto my desk and says, 'Mine is the one on the left. You prove it's better.'"[55]

Reeve's solution to the client's conundrum was the USP, the Unique Selling Proposition which, he asserted, all successful advertising must offer. Campaigns must show a specific benefit to the consumer, one that the competition does not provide and that is "so strong that it can move the mass millions."[56] As Reeves acknowledges, the USP doctrine harkens back to Kennedy's "Salesmanship in Print" formula. Both contrasted their advice with the static puffery that contained only tired superlatives or flat announcements. Both Reeves and Kennedy condemned irrelevant, bombastic, and pointless verbiage as useless. Finally, Reeves, like Kennedy, Claude C. Hopkins, John Caples, and other star copywriters of the first half of the century, directed his messages to the mass audience, not targeted market segments.

Advertising to differentiate a brand from its competitors, rather than to carve out a portion of the market, tended to be product-focused. These were the campaigns of secret ingredients, greater horsepower, new formulas, brighter washdays. Such advertising found a comfortable home in the mass circulation media of the era, in particular the general-interest magazines like the *Saturday Evening Post, Look,* and *Life.* The media fit the messages because the advertisers waged their market-share wars on a national scale, where almost all consumers were fair game. In the technical terminology of media research, reach was more important than frequency: "Try to reach more people, not the same people," wrote Reeves.[57]

The doctrine of the Unique Selling Proposition still holds

sway over much of American advertising. Reeves himself created some of the least loved but most effective advertising of the 1950s and 1960s for mass-marketed, frequently-purchased packaged goods. Where differentiation is the strategy, product-centered advertising may be the most effective. Moreover, as Herbert Krugman, a leading theorist of the psychology of advertising, has argued, some consumer behavior involves "low-involvement learning." Normally, marketers believe, consumers must proceed through a series of stages, from attention through interest through desire to action. Krugman contends that this hierarchy-of-effects model does not apply to low-cost products with few emotional connotations. For these low-involvement situations, mere exposure to advertising can be the stimulus that evokes a purchase response when the consumer sees the brand in the store. Behavior change can precede attitude change. This low-involvement learning would generally imply simple, repetitious, product-focused advertising messages. The point is to get the brand name embedded in the consumer's head and then to provoke the desired buying behavior.[58]

To some degree, advertising that touted the differences of almost identical brands was self-destructive. Too often for advertisers' comfort, campaigns were not truly memorable, the promise not really distinctive. There was too much "me too" in the product-centered campaigns. In retrospect, even some of the most prominent advertising men and women detested the blandness of the era of product-focused campaigns. Shirley Polykoff, who designed memorable campaigns for Clairol hair coloring, wrote, ". . . [I]n those days, big agencies were riddled with research and marketing types who specialized in weekly staff meetings of monumental monotony. . . . And most of the advertising of the fifties reflected this dullness."[59]

Focus strategies, based on segmenting markets, targeting

audiences, and positioning products, were behind many of the campaigns that typified the "new advertising" and the "creative revolution" of the 1960s. Even in the fifties, agency heads like David Ogilvy were convinced that USP advertising was inadequate. Ogilvy specialized in products and services with elite markets—Schweppes beverages, Hathaway Shirts, and Rolls-Royce, to name a few. These products needed not just a claim but an image, which Ogilvy supplied. Typically, his ads featured a dramatic visual symbol, such as the Hathaway Shirt model with his black eyepatch. They also used long textual passages, discussing the brand in a conversational tone but emphasizing high quality and exclusivity. The brand image Ogilvy cultivated also defined the consumer group targeted for his clients' products. Although product attributes were the manifest content of the most famous Ogilvy advertisements, benefits for a particular class of users were the implicit promise.

Other contemporary campaigns can be based on a focus strategy while featuring the product, not the user. The Volkswagen advertising of the 1960s, voted by practitioners and academics to be the best campaign of the last half-century, was entirely product-centered.[60] The cars were photographed dramatically out of context, on a blank page with a short text that discussed technical or other automotive features. Nevertheless, this was a classic segmentation campaign, based on the principle that there was a distinct group of consumers who wanted an alternative to big, gaudy American cars.

More characteristically, however, segmentation campaigns are user-focused and concentrate on consumer benefits rather than product attributes. They show people with whom the target audience can identify, people who represent a credible source of authority for them or who express their latent desires and dreams. Marketers home in on consumers

whose life-styles and personalities have been carefully pro-
filed. For example, one brewer recently introduced a "super-
premium" beer, Signature, aimed "for the executive not in
the middle but off to one side," noted *Advertising Age*.
"The Signature drinker is an 'independent thinker who is
more inclined to go out on his own and do his own thing.
...' He is 'a person who is less likely to be found working at
a large company and more likely to be found running his
own business,'" stated the brewer's marketing executive.[61]
Ads, then, match the consumer profile.

Service marketing also implies a shift to user-centered advertising. The most vivid service commercials of recent
years show consumers employing the service. Thus, for example, McDonald's leading themes are "We do it all for
you" and "You deserve a break today." American Telephone and Telegraph's campaign for long-distance phone
service is an effort to remove the psychological link between
long-distance calls and unexpected bad news. "A.T.&T.
wanted us to emphasize the *casual, positive* aspect," explained the agency creative group head for the "Reach Out
and Touch Someone" campaign.[62]

Related to the rise of user-centered advertising which
stresses consumer benefits is the growing importance of narrative and dramatic forms. Ads are more and more frequently used to tell stories. Of course these forms were never ab-
sent. As early as 1924, a text on copywriting commented on
the growing popularity of story advertisements.[63] The long-
running campaign for Listerine mouthwash warned of the
perils of halitosis (Listerine's own name for bad breath)
through lurid tales of lost romance and failed ambition. Other advertising in the 1920s also relied on personal, emotional-
ly charged narratives. Publicity for the Alexander Hamilton
Institute's home study programs warned of career disasters
and held out the promise of success for those who sub-

scribed. The classic story, "They laughed when I sat down to play," promoted mail order piano lessons with tales of social acceptance.

With the shift from product differentiation to market segmentation, however, there appears to be a change in the substance of advertising stories. What is striking to the reader of the older tales is the emphasis on social conformity and acceptance as the means of success. Today, the promises, either latent or manifest in some of the most notable advertisements, are self-fulfillment, escape, and private fantasy. Note, for example, the change in hair coloring advertisements. In the 1950s, Shirley Polykoff introduced the Clairol slogan, "Does she or doesn't she? Only her hairdresser knows for sure." Users would not suffer the embarrassment of discovery. Today, hair coloring is offered as a means of expressing one's true nature, of manifesting one's distinctiveness. Michelob beer commercials present wordless dramas, played in elegant, exotic, and somewhat sinister settings. The stories show the Michelob drinker outwitting a little man who is mysteriously pursuing him. The theme, for the beer and for the hero, is that Michelob is "one step ahead."

The electronic media have been a factor in the success of story-line advertisements. Commercial dialogue on the printed page can seem false and stilted but may come alive when performed on television or even radio. Television permits effective demonstrations of the product in use and its benefits for consumers, and dramatic commercial vignettes are often effective ways of staging these demonstrations. Thus, we have long-running campaigns with characters whose fortes are brewing coffee for neighbors, wiping up spilled liquids with paper towels, and squeezing toilet paper in grocery store aisles.

We may also surmise that the tighter regulatory environment has brought an increase in these advertising minidramas. Speaking directly to the audience, an advertisement can scarcely avoid making product claims that may require substantiation. If the message is delivered in a dramatic dialogue, with actors playing roles, it is easier to stick to subjective, and therefore largely unverifiable, personal reactions. The announcer who proclaims the nutritional value of a food product or the durability of a toy may incite a regulatory response; the mother giving those brands to her child in a story commercial is unlikely to provoke complaints about deception. Advertising industry spokespeople have often complained that excessive regulation will spark a return to vacuous puffery. Afraid to make substantive claims about their products, advertisers will, the argument goes, opt to say nothing.

But other forces as well have brought about this subordination of product claims. Even in the Progressive Era, advertising men sometimes adopted a drastically subjective view of the goods they promoted. The product was not the tangible substance but the benefits it provided the buyer. Such a viewpoint accords well with the theory of consumer demand in contemporary economic thought; buyers want the stream of services a product gives, and the product demand curve is derived from the true demand schedules for these services.[64]

The essence of a commodity, then, can be found not in what it is but in what it does, or rather in what consumers do with it. Much the same can be said of an advertisement. An ad is not a set of statements but a "package of stimuli" which "resonates with the information already stored within an individual. . . . Resonance takes place when the stimuli put into our communication evoke *meaning* in a listener or viewer. That which we put into the communication has no meaning in itself."[65] The speaker here is Tony Schwartz, responsible for one of the most powerful yet controversial commercials ever. In the 1964 presidential campaign,

Schwartz filmed a little girl counting the petals on a daisy; her image was then frozen as the countdown for a nuclear explosion began. At zero, the blast was shown, and Lyndon Johnson's voice intoned, "Either we must love each other or we must die." The film concluded with a visual reminder to vote for Johnson on Election Day. It is doubtful that any "reason-why" advertising, or a list of factual claims, could have had the persuasive impact of the "Daisy" advertisement.

Attempts to measure how much information advertisements convey are liable to methodological criticism. Even when facts are presented, they may (as in the case of an Ogilvy "brand image" ad) be there in order to develop a congruence between the target audience and the brand. Recent studies do indicate that, even using a very broad definition of information, advertisements contain few facts. Researchers allowed an ad to be classified as informative if it contained any one of fourteen "informational cues," such as price or value, packaging, taste, safety, or new ideas for use. By this liberal criterion, the researchers found that 86 percent of a sample of magazine ads were informative. Only 52 percent, however, contained more than one informational cue. More strikingly, a companion study of television advertising revealed that more than half of these commercials contained no informational cues whatsoever. Only 1 percent of the television advertisements offered information in three or more categories.[66]

Marketing strategies also affect the informational content of advertisements. Focus strategies, with their emphasis on user-centered appeals, may be most likely to subordinate product claims to "resonance." It is suggestive that, among the television commercials evaluated, ads appearing on weekend mornings and weekday afternoons were the least informational.[67] In these time periods, the audiences are likely to be narrowly defined (children and nonworking women), and segmentation campaigns are most suitable.

The evocative, resonating character of much contemporary advertising puts it in an ethical and epistemological limbo. Accustomed to judging messages as true or false, we lack the appropriate concepts for evaluating ads that are neither true nor false. Accustomed to extracting information from statements we see and hear, how do we analyze messages that contain no information? Advertising themes like "Coke Is It!" leave us unsure of how to reply. They preclude any dialogue between buyer and seller.

Will advertising continue to float in this limbo? A review of advertising's history offers no sure guide to its future, but it should help to place our expectations and hopes in a realistic context. Nearly a century ago national advertising arose to meet the needs of businesses that employed new technologies and sold to new mass consumer markets. Rather quickly, an advertising industry emerged that was capable of meeting these marketing requirements. Advertising practitioners developed professional standards and skills appropriate to the demands businesses placed upon them. By about 1920, the institutional arrangements that still characterize American advertising were already set in place. By then, too, an ideology of advertising had appeared. Its exponents portrayed advertising as a force that would reconcile social harmony with personal freedom of choice. Persuasion would replace coercion. The ideals of liberal individualism could be realized in a society dominated by large-scale enterprises.

As we have seen, the ideological vision remains unfulfilled today. National advertising continues to serve a corporate system whose workings inspire doubt, though not revolt. The advertising business itself is more solidly established than it once was, but undercurrents of anxiety and insecurity remain. The public sees advertising's ethical standards as sorely inadequate. In place of a harmonious, cooperative society, advertisements offer us token memberships in consumption communities which are created and dissolved for the profit of others.

Just as technological and organizational changes created a new kind of advertising in the late nineteenth and early twentieth centuries, the new structures of a postindustrial society may bring about another advertising revolution. The changes wrought in the last generation by new media, the rise of service industries, and the practice of market segmentation may only be harbingers of a more profound transformation. The advertising of the future might become a means of realizing humane and progressive values.

A quick sketch of the outlines of a possible future will inevitably do injustices to the complexity and diversity of futuristic visions.[68] At their most optimistic, they predict the decentralization of production and a return to smaller-scale units. An idyllic image of the craftsperson with a computer exemplifies this prophecy. Media may also become smaller in scale, more numerous, and diversified. On cable television, some predict, "narrowcasting" for specialized interest groups will replace broadcasting of lowest-common-denominator entertainment. The newspaper of tomorrow may consist of information selected by viewers to fit their interests and needs from data banks accessible on home computers. Interactive systems may allow consumers to examine, order, and pay for products at home, bypassing established channels of distribution. A wealthier and better educated public should be more demanding yet more appreciative of the quality and diversity of output new technologies will permit.

If these visionary possibilities are realized, current market segmentation activities will, in retrospect, look like embryonic forms of a more individualized and egalitarian kind of communications. Advertisers would be able to speak directly to the needs and concerns of their audiences. A dominant service sector would thrive by adapting to customer desires and involving buyers in the distribution process. The top-down flow of advertising messages would be altered because the public would have a wider range of media to choose from. There would be alternatives to messages that depersonalize and insult their intended audiences. These developments would make the paths between producers and consumers shorter and wider and would allow a two-way flow of communications. The marketing system could be a way to express and satisfy desires for individual growth and development. As the spatial and social distance between producers and consumers decreased, there would be more opportunities for communication as equals. Sellers and buyers would share information and therefore share power. This new advertising might be a genuinely democratic dialogue.

However, older prophecies that mass advertising would be the basis of a more free and harmonious society proved to be delusive. The futurists' hopes may be equally mistaken. In the first place, mass consumption has meant one thing for the wealthy but another for the poor. For those who have not shared in America's affluence, national advertising has been a mocking tease instead of an invitation to partake in the good life. Similarly, in a postindustrial America, the full benefits of innovations and the opportunities for new forms of egalitarian communications may be rationed to the well-off and well-educated. As Fred Hirsch pointed out, many of the most desirable goods and services in the coming decades will be "positional."[69] Their value will derive from or depend upon the fact that not everybody can have them—and not even American advertising can convincingly promise exclusivity for everybody. Second, advertising will continue to be subject to the vicissitudes of the business cycle and secular economic trends. The advent of the futurists' golden age may be postponed during an era of intense foreign competition, industrial decay, and stagflation. In such an epoch, the advertising of hard-pressed firms is more likely to be strident than sensible. Finally, the question of control is still crucial. The needs of profit-seeking businesses, not the imperatives of technology alone, will shape advertising in the future as they have in the past. Corporations will resist those innovations that decentralize their authority and embrace those that enhance their power. Of course they cannot entirely channel the flow of new technologies, but they can wield influence. Some recent developments do not bode well for future diversity. For example, some alarms have been raised about increased concentration and the entrance of several large communications conglomerates in the cable television field. We may soon be paying directly for the same kind of programming we now receive on commercial television and be subject to advertising on cable stations in the bargain. Large numbers of channels do not, in themselves, guarantee substantial variety, as the current state of the nation's 7,500 or so commercial radio stations would indicate. Advertisers continue to think of programs as mere vehicles for delivering advertising messages to finely-divided audience segments. Thus, the great attraction of proposals for a new springtime professional football league is that it will give television advertisers a few extra months to sell beer and pickup trucks and chain saws to eighteen-to-forty-nine-year-old male football addicts.

In sum, the futurists' predictions of a humane new advertising age, though beguiling, ultimately rest upon a technological determinism the historical record does not bear out.

Technological utopias tend to recede as we try to approach them. Innovations may be liberating, but they may also serve to reinforce centralized, remote, and unresponsive authority. If such a counterutopia is our more probable fate, advertising in the future may be little more than sleek, enticing packaging for shopworn corporate images of the good life.

NOTES

Chapter 1

1. Cited in *Printers' Ink,* 20 (25 August 1897): 42.

2. *Printers' Ink,* 91 (27 May 1915): 102.

3. James P. Wood, *The Story of Advertising* (New York: Ronald Press, 1958), pp. 45–46.

4. Quoted in Henry Sampson, *A History of Advertising from the Earliest Times* (London: Chatto and Windus, 1875), p. 201.

5. John W. Blake, "Blind Advertising Expenditure," in John Caples, ed., *Tested Advertising Methods* (New York: Harper, 1932), p. 2.

6. For a fascinating description of the production of a television commercial for American Telephone & Telegraph's long-distance service, see Michael J. Arlen, *Thirty Seconds* (New York: Farrar, Straus & Giroux, 1980).

7. U.S. Bureau of the Census, *Historical Statistics of the United States: Colonial Times to 1970* (Washington, D.C.: U.S. Government Printing Office, 1975), pp. 855–56; U.S. Bureau of the Census, *Statistical Abstract of the United States: 1981* (Washington, D.C.: U.S. Government Printing Office, 1981), p. 572.

8. There are, however, several significant books. The most detailed is Frank S. Presbrey, *The History and Development of Advertising* (Garden City, N.Y.: Doubleday, Doran, 1929); Wood (see note 3) is clear and readable, although not analytical. E. S. Turner, *The Shocking History of Advertising!* (New York: Dutton, 1953) is a more serious work than the title indicates. There are some fine specialized works, including Ralph M. Hower, *The History of an Advertising Agency,* rev. ed. (Cambridge: Harvard University Press, 1949); Otis A. Pease, *The Responsibilities of American Advertising* (New Haven: Yale University Press, 1958); Stuart Ewen, *Captains of Consciousness* (New York: McGraw-Hill, 1976). In a related area, the history of public relations, an excellent new book is Richard S. Tedlow, *Keeping the Corporate Image* (Greenwich, Conn.: JAI Press, 1979). Richard W. Pollay, ed., *Information Sources in Advertising History* (Westport, Conn.: Greenwood Press, 1979) has some useful essays and is invaluable for its bibliography.

Notes

9. Cited in David Ogilvy, *Confessions of an Advertising Man* (New York: Atheneum, 1963), p. 59.

10. Marshall McLuhan, *The Mechanical Bride* (Boston: Beacon Press, 1967), first pub. 1951; Erving Goffman, *Gender Advertisements* (Cambridge: Harvard University Press, 1979). Other works in this category include Jules Henry, *Culture Against Man* (New York: Random House, 1963), chap. 3; Varda Langholz Leymore, *Hidden Myth* (New York: Basic Books, 1975); Judith Williamson, *Decoding Advertisements* (London: Marion Boyars, 1978). A sophisticated commentary on those who object to advertising's effects is Michael Schudson, "Criticizing the Critics of Advertising: Towards a Sociological View of Marketing," *Media, Culture and Society*, 3 (1981): 3–12.

11. Daniel J. Boorstin, "Advertising and American Civilization," in Yale Brozen, ed., *Advertising and Society* (New York: New York University Press, 1974), see p. 13 for definition. See also Boorstin, *The Americans: The Democratic Experience* (New York: Random House, 1973), pp. 137–48 and part 2, and "Welcome to the Consumption Community," *Fortune*, 76 (September 1967): 118ff.

12. *Printers' Ink*, 101 (13 December 1917): 148.

13. *Altruism in Action—Concerning a Literature Which Compels Action* (Chicago: Lord & Thomas, 1911), pp. 12, 24–25.

14. Truman A. DeWeese, *Keeping a Dollar at Work* (New York: *New York Evening Post*, 1917), p. 45.

15. Quoted in James H. Young, *The Toadstool Millionaires* (Princeton, N.J.: Princeton University Press, 1961), p. 101.

16. John Broadus Watson was a vice president of the J. Walter Thompson advertising agency. He dedicated his landmark *Behaviorism* (New York: People's Institute, 1925) to Stanley B. Resor, the agency's president.

Chapter 2

1. For a succinct statement of this approach, see Harold Demsetz, "Two Systems of Belief about Monopoly," in Harvey J. Goldschmid et al., eds., *Industrial Concentration: The New Learning* (Boston: Little, Brown, 1974), pp. 164–84; see also John S. McGee, *In Defense of Industrial Concentration* (New York: Praeger, 1971).

2. Carter Goodrich, *Government Promotion of American Canals and Railroads* (New York: Columbia University Press, 1960), pp. 270–71.

3. Fred Bateman and Thomas J. Weiss, "Market Structure Before the Age of Big Business: Concentration and Profits in Early Southern Manufacturing," *Business History Review*, 49 (Autumn 1975): 312–36. Richard K. Vedder and Lowell E. Gallaway, "The Profitability of Antebellum Manufacturing: Some New Estimates," *Business History Review*, 54 (Spring 1980): 92–103, find lower profit rates than do Bateman and Weiss.

4. Robert Wiebe, *The Search for Order* (New York: Hill & Wang, 1966).

Notes

5. Robert J. Coen, a vice president at McCann-Erickson, has revised and continued Weld's series. His most recent estimates of advertising expenditures can be found in "200 Years of U.S. Advertising," *Advertising Age*, 5 July 1976, p. 1; a note, "About These Estimates" on p. 41 of this article presents a brief explanation of how the series was derived. U.S. Bureau of the Census, *Historical Statistics of the United States Colonial Times to 1970* (Washington, D.C.: Government Printing Office, 1975), pp. 855–56, is a convenient source for the figures prior to Coen's modifications.

6. Claude C. Hopkins, *My Life in Advertising* (New York: Harper and Brothers, 1927), p. 15.

7. National Advertising Co., *America's Advertisers* (New York: Arno Press, 1976), p. 3, first published 1893.

8. For a knowledgeable discussion of the methods and difficulties of estimating advertising volume, see Neil H. Borden, *The Economic Effects of Advertising* (Chicago: Richard D. Irwin, 1944): 887–916.

9. *Printers' Ink,* 16 (30 September 1896): 6; 39 (16 April 1902): 37; 46 (17 February 1904): 42–44; 48 (17 August 1904): 34; Paul T. Cherington, *Advertising as a Business Force* (New York: Doubleday, Page, 1913), p. 69; *Associated Advertising,* 7 (September 1916): 50.

10. J. George Frederick, *Masters of Advertising Copy* (New York: Frank-Maurice, 1925), p. 32.

11. *Printers' Ink,* 104 (19 September 1918): 10.

12. Borden, *Effects of Advertising*, pp. 61–65.

13. Mark S. Albion and Paul W. Farris, *Appraising Research on Advertising's Economic Impacts,* Report No. 79-115 (Cambridge: Marketing Science Institute, 1979), pp. 19–23; data on distribution costs in Harold Barger, *Distribution's Place in the American Economy Since 1869* (Princeton, N.J.: Princeton University Press, 1955), p. 70.

14. Data reprinted in J. Frederic Dewhurst and Paul W. Stewart, *Does Distribution Cost Too Much?* (New York: Twentieth Century Fund, 1939), p. 394.

15. Earnest E. Calkins and Ralph Holden, *Modern Advertising* (New York: D. Appleton, 1905), p. 13.

16. Daniel Nelson, *Managers and Workers* (Madison: University of Wisconsin Press, 1975), pp. 5–8.

17. Alfred D. Chandler, Jr., *The Visible Hand* (Cambridge: Harvard University Press, 1977), pp. 240–44; my sketch of the rise of big business draws heavily on Chandler's work.

18. U. S. Bureau of the Census, *Historical Statistics of the United States,* pp. 666, 684–85.

19. Harry Tipper, *The New Business* (New York: Doubleday, Page, 1914), p. 13; Tipper et al., *Advertising: Its Principles and Practice* (New York: Ronald Press, 1915), pp. 4–6; *Printers' Ink,* 18 (20 January 1897): 26.

20. William G. Panschaar, *Baking in America*, vol. 1, *Economic Development* (Evanston, Ill.: Northwestern University Press, 1956), pp. 47, 178.

21. An intriguing history of this industry can be found in Claudia B. Kidwell, *Cutting a Fashionable Fit,* Smithsonian Studies in History and Technology, no. 42 (Washington: Smithsonian Institution Press, 1979).

Notes

22. Julian L. Simon, *Issues in the Economics of Advertising* (Urbana, Ill.: University of Illinois Press, 1970), pp. 41–51.

23. Personal income figures from Simon Kuznets et al., *Population Redistribution and Economic Growth: United States 1870–1950*, vol. 2, *Analysis of Economic Change* (Philadelphia: American Philosophical Society, 1960), p. 185; urban population calculated from U.S. Bureau of the Census, *Historical Statistics of the United States*, pp. 24–37; newspaper advertising from U.S. Census Office, *Twelfth Census, 1900*, vol. 9, *Manufactures, Part III* (Washington: U.S. Census Office, 1902), pp. 1056–58; and U.S. Bureau of the Census, *Fourteenth Census of the United States*, vol. 10, *Manufacturers, 1919* (Washington: Government Printing Office, 1923), p. 576.

24. *Advertiser's Gazette*, 4 (April 1870): 95. "Letterbooks," General, Volume E-16, E. C. Allen Collection, Harvard Graduate School of Business Administration Manuscript Division; Asher quoted in Boris Emmet and John E. Jeuck, *Catalogues and Counters* (Chicago: University of Chicago Press, 1950), p. 65.

25. *Printers' Ink*, 41 (3 December 1902): 28; 42 (12 March 1903): 32; *New York Times*, 24 June 1915, p. 12.

26. David Potter, *People of Plenty* (Chicago: University of Chicago Press, 1966), p. 172; Simon, *Economics of Advertising* pp. 167–70.

27. Jeffrey James and Stephen Lister, "Galbraith Revisited: Advertising in Nonaffluent Societies," *World Development*, 8 (1980): 88–89.

28. Data for this study come from Crowell Publishing Company, *National Markets and National Advertising 1922* (New York: Crowell Publishing Co., 1923), pp. 52–53, 60.

29. Current figures in *Advertising Age*, 11 September 1980, pp. 1, 48.

30. These firms were found by inspecting *America's Advertisers*, see n. 7, this chapter.

31. *Interbrand Choice, Strategy and Bilateral Market Power* (Cambridge: Harvard University Press, 1976), pp. 24–5. Philip Nelson, in a series of articles, distinguishes between search and experience goods in a somewhat different fashion. See his "Information and Consumer Behavior," *Journal of Political Economy*, 78 (March-April 1970): 311–29; "Advertising as Information," *Journal of Political Economy*, 81 (July-August 1974): 729–45, and "The Economic Consequences of Advertising," *Journal of Business*, 48 (April 1975): 213–41.

32. William Cahn, *Out of the Cracker Barrel* (New York: Simon and Schuster, 1969) is the main source; see also Chandler, *Visible Hand*, pp. 334–35.

33. *Printers' Ink*, 32 (18 August 1900): 30.

34. The best source on Eastman is Reese V. Jenkins, *Images and Enterprise* (Baltimore: Johns Hopkins University Press, 1975), pp. 66–187. See also Carl Ackerman, *George Eastman* (Boston: Houghton Mifflin, 1930).

35. Ackerman, *Eastman*, p. 78.

36. Jenkins, *Images and Enterprise*, p. 157; National Advertising Co., *America's Advertisers*, p. 441.

37. Jenkins, *Images and Enterprise*, p. 178; *Printers' Ink*, 28 (26 July 1899): pp. 14–15.

38. *Fame*, 1 (June 1892): 117; *Printers' Ink*, 29 (1 November 1899): 30.

Notes

39. U.S. Bureau of Corporations, *Report of the Commissioner of Corporations on the Tobacco Industry,* vol. 1 (Washington: Government Printing Office, 1909), p. 51.

40. Duke quoted in N. M. Tilley, *The Bright-Tobacco Industry: 1860-1929* (Chapel Hill: University of North Carolina Press, 1948), p. 557.

41. P. Glenn Porter, "Origins of the American Tobacco Company," *Business History Review,* 43 (Spring 1969): 59-76, gives a brief overview of these changes. See also Chandler, *The Visible Hand,* pp. 290-91.

42. U.S. Bureau of Corporations, *Report . . . on the Tobacco Industry,* vol. 3 contains voluminous data on advertising costs, sales revenues, and profits.

43. *American Tobacco Company et al.* vs. *United States, Brief for the United States,* U.S. Supreme Court, October Term, 1909, p. 193.

44. Arthur F. Marquette, *Brands, Trademarks and Goodwill: The Story of the Quaker Oats Company* (New York: McGraw-Hill, 1967), pp. 50-51.

45. *Printers' Ink,* 24 (24 August 1898): 34.

46. Quoted in Russell B. Adams, *King C. Gillette, The Man and His Wonderful Shaving Device* (Boston: Little Brown, 1978), pp. 18-19.

47. Ibid., p. 56.

48. Ibid., p. 85.

49. J. Owen Stalson, *Marketing Life Insurance* (Cambridge: Harvard University Press, 1942), pp. 269-70.

50. Morton Keller, *The Life Insurance Enterprise, 1885-1910* (Cambridge: Harvard University Press, 1963), pp. 67-68.

51. Brochure in Northwestern Mutual Life Folder, Vertical File, The College of Insurance Library, New York, New York.

52. R. Carlyle Buley, *The Equitable Life Assurance Society of the United States 1859-1964,* vol. 1 (New York: Appleton-Century-Crofts, 1967), pp. 397, 403.

53. National Advertising Co., *America's Advertisers,* part 2, p. 117.

54. Stalson, *Marketing Life Insurance,* pp. 802, 821.

55. *Insurance Monitor,* in Earl C. May and Will Oursler, *The Prudential* (Garden City, N.Y.: Doubleday, 1950), pp. 118-21.

56. Albert E. Haase, "Ideas that Advertising Turned into Big Business," *Printers' Ink Monthly,* 14 (March 1927): 86.

57. *Printers' Ink,* 57 (18 November 1906): 26; 51 (31 May 1905): 32-33.

Chapter 3

1. Ralph L. Nelson, *Merger Movements in American Industry 1895-1965* (Princeton, N.J.: Princeton University Press, 1963), pp. 67-68.

2. This is a key conclusion of Alfred D. Chandler, *The Visible Hand* (Cambridge: Harvard University Press, 1977). See, in particular, pp. 372-76 and 503-12.

3. *Printers' Ink,* 29 (8 November 1899): 3-4; and (20 December 1899): 4. Harry Tipper et al., *Advertising: Its Principles and Practice* (New York: Ronald

Notes

Press, 1915), p. 54; John Lee Mahin, "Who Pays for Advertising?" in his *Lectures on Advertising* (n.p.: n.d. [1915?]), p. 6.

4. Nicholas Kaldor, "The Economic Aspects of Advertising," *Review of Economic Studies,* 18 (1949-1950): 14, 13.

5. Joe S. Bain, *Barriers to New Competition* (Cambridge: Harvard University Press, 1956), pp. 114-43, 201-04.

6. For reviews of the literature, see Albion and Farris, *Appraising Research on Advertising's Economic Impacts,* Report No. 79-115 (Cambridge: Marketing Science Institute, 1979), pp. 126-38; James M. Ferguson, *Advertising and Competition: Theory, Measurement, Fact* (Cambridge: Ballinger, 1974), pp. 15-20, 73-84; Julian L. Simon and Johan Arndt, "The Shape of the Advertising Response Function," *Journal of Advertising Research,* 20 (August 1980): 11-28.

7. Richard Schmalensee, "Brand Loyalty and Barriers to Entry," *Southern Economic Journal,* 40 (April 1974): 583; Harold Demsetz, "Accounting for Advertising as a Barrier to Entry," *Journal of Business,* 52 (July 1979): 345-60.

8. Stanley I. Ornstein, *Industrial Concentration and Advertising Intensity* (Washington, D.C.: American Enterprise Institute, 1977); Willard F. Mueller and Richard T. Rogers, "The Role of Advertising in Changing Concentration of Manufacturing Industries," *Review of Economics and Statistics,* 62 (February 1980): 89-96; Allyn D. Strickland and Leonard W. Weiss, "Advertising, Concentration and Price-Cost Margins," *Journal of Political Economy,* 84 (October 1976): 1119; J. A. Henning and H. Michael Mann, "Advertising and Concentration: A Tentative Determination of Cause and Effect," in Robert T. Masson and P. David Qualls, eds., *Essays on Industrial Organization in Honor of Joe S. Bain* (Cambridge: Ballinger, 1976), pp. 143-54.

9. *Advertiser's Magazine,* 1 (October 1873): 3.

10. *Printers' Ink,* 48 (24 August 1904): 14; 44 (5 August 1903): 28.

11. William A. Shryer, *Analytical Advertising* (Detroit: Business Service Corp., 1912), p. 47.

12. Daniel Starch, *Advertising: Its Principles, Practice and Technique* (Chicago: Scott, Foresman, 1914), pp. 51-52, 172.

13. Scrapbook H-6, Baker Chocolate Company Papers, Harvard Graduate School of Business Administration Library, Manuscript Division; *Printers' Ink,* 51 (31 May 1905): 33; 64 (8 July 1908): 16. The phrase "reputation monopolies" comes from Dorothea Braithwaite, "The Economic Effect of Advertisement," *Economic Journal,* 38 (March 1928): 33.

14. Alfred D. Chandler, Jr., "The Structure of American Industry in the Twentieth Century: An Historical Overview," *Business History Review,* 43 (Autumn 1969): 273, 292-93.

15. See Demsetz, "Two Systems of Belief about Monopoly," in Harvey J. Goldschmidt et al., eds., *Industrial Concentration: The New Learning* (Boston: Little, Brown, 1974) for this approach.

16. William S. Comanor and Thomas A. Wilson, *Advertising and Market Power* (Cambridge: Harvard University Press, 1974), p. 242.

17. Nelson, "Economic Consequences of Advertising"; Albion and Farris, *Advertising's Economic Impacts,* pp. 61-64.

Notes

18. Lee Benham, "The Effect of Advertising on the Price of Eyeglasses," *Journal of Law and Economics,* 40 (October 1972): 337–52.

19. Lewis E. Atherton, *The Pioneer Merchant in Mid-America,* University of Missouri Studies, 14 (April 1939): 122; Ralph M. Hower, *History of Macy's of New York 1858–1919* (Cambridge: Harvard University Press, 1946), pp. 269, 274.

20. *Fame,* 1 (April 1892): 35; *Printers' Ink,* 37 (6 November 1901): 42; 48 (6 July 1904): 12–13; 44 (8 July 1908): 12–13.

21. Joseph H. Appel, *Growing Up with Advertising* (New York: Business Bourse, 1940), pp. 148ff.; *Printers' Ink,* 100 (13 September 1917): 121–22; *Associated Advertising,* 7 (October 1917): 11.

22. *Printers' Ink,* 42 (4 March 1903): 28; 48 (21 September 1904): 26; Mahin, "Advertising, The Highest Form of Commercial Achievement" and "Does Advertising Add Value to Merchandise?" in *Lectures on Advertising.* p. 5–6.

23. See Record Group 122, File 7222-36-1, National Archives, Washington, D.C. (Hereafter, Record Group 122 will be cited as RG 122.)

24. RG 122, File 7222-55-1, National Archives.

25. RG 122, File 7222-68-1, National Archives.

26. Bureau of Corporations, *Report,* vol. 3, pp. 158, 164.

27. For valuable commentaries on the gap between economists and marketing specialists, see Porter, *Interbrand Choice,* pp. 1–5; Louis W. Stern and Torger Reve, "Distribution Channels as Political Economies: A Framework for Comparative Analysis," *Journal of Marketing,* 44 (Summer 1980): 52–64; Dan Horsky and Subrata K. Sen, "Interfaces Between Marketing and Economics: An Overview," *Journal of Business,* 53 (July 1980): S5–S12.

28. *Printers's Ink,* 90 (11 February 1915): 3.

29. Glenn Porter and Harold C. Livesay, *Merchants and Manufacturers* (Baltimore: Johns Hopkins University Press, 1971), is the best source on these changing relationships. On Jacksonian wealth, see Edward Pessen, *Riches, Class and Power Before the Civil War* (Lexington, Mass.: D.C. Heath, 1973).

30. *Advertising,* 2 (June 1897): 63.

31. Information on these and other firms with retailing operations can be found in the various sections of RG 122, File 7222, National Archives.

32. Thomas C. Cochran, *The Pabst Brewing Company* (New York: New York University Press, 1948), p. 199.

33. Walter S. Hayward and Percival White, *Chain Stores: Their Management and Operation* (New York: McGraw-Hill, 1922), p. 318; Paul H. Nystrom, *The Economics of Retailing,* 2nd ed. (New York: Ronald Press, 1919), p. 275.

34. *Printers' Ink,* 80 (22 August 1912): 46–47.

35. *Printers' Ink,* 78 (1 February 1912): 61.

36. *Journal of Commerce* reprinted in *Printers' Ink,* 29 (27 September 1899): 30; Paul T. Cherington, *Advertising as a Business Force* (New York: Doubleday, Page, 1913), p. 207.

37. United States Industrial Commission, *Report of the Industrial Commission on the Relations and Conditions of Capital and Labor,* vol. 7 (Washington, D.C.: Government Printing Office, 1901), p. 714.

Notes

38. The relationship of technological and market changes to vertical integration is carefully analyzed in Alfred D. Chandler, *The Visible Hand,* (Cambridge: Harvard University Press, 1977), and Porter and Livesay, *Merchants and Manufacturers.*

39. RG 122, File 7222-80-1 (Parker Pens); File 7222-70-1 (Cluett, Peabody); File 7222-64-1 (Western Clock), National Archives.

40. RG 122, File 7222-57-1 (Pacific Coast Borax); File 7222-57-1 (Parke-Davis), National Archives.

41. Harold Barger, *Distribution's Place in the American Economy Since 1869* (Princeton, N.J.: Princeton University Press, 1955), p. 57.

42. Advertising data compiled from Crowell Publishing Company, *National Markets and National Advertisers 1929* (New York: Crowell Publishing Co., 1930); distribution channels data in U.S. Bureau of the Census, *Fifteenth Census of the United States, Distribution of Sales of Manufacturing Plants* (Washington, D.C.: Government Printing Office, 1932).

43. On the Proprietary Association, see James H. Young, *The Medical Messiahs* (Princeton, N.J.: Princeton University Press, 1967), p. 24; one example of druggists' complaints is in *Printers' Ink,* 20 (7 July 1897): p. 4; chain store figures from U.S. Bureau of the Census, *Historical Statistics of the United States Colonial Times to 1970* (Washington D.C.: Government Printing Office, 1975), p. 847.

44. *Printers' Ink,* 39 (23 April 1902): 47.

45. *Printers' Ink,* 81 (14 November 1912): 98; 79 (18 April 1912): 92–93; *Advertising and Selling,* 21 (May 1912): 35–36.

46. *Printers' Ink,* 81 (14 November 1912): 98; 100 (13 September 1917): 83–88; 61 (11 December 1907): 24; *Advertising and Selling,* 25 (June 1915): 36.

47. *Printers' Ink,* 51 (14 June 1905): 32; Curtis Publishing Company, *National Advertising: The Modern Selling Force* (Philadelphia: Curtis Publishing Co., n.d.), p. 14.

48. Nebraska survey in *Printers' Ink,* 88 (13 August 1914): 42; Paul T. Cherington, *The First Advertising Book* (New York: Doubleday, Page, 1916), p. 83.

49. *Printers' Ink,* 77 (23 November 1911): 72–73; Cherington, *Advertising as a Business Force,* p. 35.

50. Lawrence C. Lockley, *Vertical Cooperative Advertising* (New York: McGraw-Hill, 1931), pp. 4–5; *Printers' Ink,* 12 (6 February 1895): 20; Daniel Starch, *Principles of Advertising* (Chicago: A. W. Shaw, 1923), pp. 882–83.

51. *Printers' Ink,* 82 (27 March 1913): 106; 94 (6 July 1916): 20; *New York Times,* 27 June 1916, p. 9.

52. *Printers' Ink,* 80 (19 September 1912): 42ff. reports survey. Cherington, *First Advertising Book,* ch. 8, offers advice on dealer helps.

53. Lockley, *Vertical Cooperative Advertising,* pp. 75–113 and 171; on Robinson-Patman, see Morton J. Simon, *The Law for Advertising and Marketing* (New York: W. W. Norton, 1956), pp. 413ff.

54. *Printers' Ink,* 96 (6 July 1916): 84–99; Crisco example in *Advertising and Selling,* 21 (August 1911): 43.

55. Telser "Why Should Manufacturers Want Fair Trade?" *Journal of Law and Economics,* 3 (October 1960): 86; Claudius T. Murchison, *Resale Price*

Notes

Maintenance, Columbia University Studies in History, Economics and Public Law, 82, 2 (1919), p. 22.

56. *The Outlook,* 24 May 1913, in RG 122, File 7222-36-1, National Archives.

57. A convenient summary of the early legal history of price maintenance can be found in U.S. Federal Trade Commission, *Report of the Federal Trade Commission on Resale Price Maintenance* (Washington, D.C.: Government Printing Office, 1945), pp. 17–38; Murchison, *Resale Price Maintenance,* p. 28.

58. *Printers' Ink,* 83 (5 June 1913): 74; 89 (24 December 1914): 72.

59. RG 122, File 7222-45-1, numbers 15 and 21 (Eastman); File 7222-95-21, p. 4 (Gillette); File 7222-80-1, pp. 1–2 (Parker); File 7222-73-1, number 20 (Eaton, Crane and Pike); National Archives.

60. Federal Trade Commission, *Report on Price Maintenance,* pp. 17–38; Edwin R. A. Seligman and Robert A. Love, *Price Cutting and Price Maintenance: A Study in Economics* (New York: Harper and Brothers, 1932), chaps. 3 and 4.

61. RG 122, File 7222-48-1 (Dr. Miles), National Archives.

62. RG 122, File 7222-89-1 (apparel); File 7222-97-1 (stoves); File 7222-107-1 (caskets); 7222-57-1 (Borax); File 7222-62-1 (Van Camp); File 7222-85-1 (Cudahy), National Archives.

63. On Fair Trade League membership, see W. H. S. Stevens, "Resale Price Maintenance as Unfair Competition," *Columbia Law Review,* 19 (June 1919): 278; and Federal Trade Commission, *Report on Price Maintenance,* p. 44. Objectives in *Printers' Ink,* 84 (3 July 1913): 13.

64. *Advertising and Selling,* 22 (June 1912), p. 78; William Woodhead, President, Associated Advertising Clubs of America, to Honorable Joseph E. Davies, 13 October 1913, RG 122, File 1370-7, National Archives.

65. Federal Trade Commission, *Report on Price Maintenance,* p. 45.

66. Surveys reported in U.S. Congress, House Committee on Interstate and Foreign Commerce, 64th Congress, 1st Session, *Regulation of Prices* (Washington, D.C.: Government Printing Office, 1916), pp. 90, 195. Wholesalers' views can be found here and in U.S. Congress, House Committee on Interstate and Foreign Commerce, 63rd Congress, 2d and 3d Sessions, *Hearings on H.R. 13305 to Prevent Discrimination in Prices and to Provide for Publicity of Prices to Dealers and the Public* (Washington, D.C.: Government Printing Office, 1915). See also 64th Congress, 2d Session, *Hearings on H.R. 13568 to Protect the Public Against Dishonest Advertising and False Pretenses in Merchandising* (Washington, D.C.: Government Printing Office, 1917).

67. Chamber of Commerce of the United States of America, "Referendum Number Thirteen," *Special Bulletin,* 2 June 1916, in RG 122, File 7225-9-1, Exhibit 1, National Archives; U.S. Federal Trade Commission, *Resale Price Maintenance,* House Document 546, Part 1, 70th Congress, 2d Session (Washington, D.C.: Government Printing Office, 1929), pp. 36, 62, 78; Federal Trade Commission, *Report on Resale Price Maintenance,* part 2, *Commercial Aspects and Tendencies* (Washington, D.C.: Government Printing Office, 1931), pp. 27–28, 169–70, 182–83.

68. *Hearings on H.R. 13568,* p. 194.

Notes

69. *Regulation of Prices,* p. 43.

70. *New York Times,* 27 December 1913, p. 8; Cherington, *Advertising as a Business Force,* p. 404; Federal Trade Commission, *Resale Price Maintenance* (1931), p. 11.

71. *Printers' Ink,* 97 (21 December 1916): 122; on the relationship of wartime conditions to price cutting, see *Printers' Ink,* 100 (9 August 1917): 142; Ewald T. Grether, *Price Control Under Fair Trade Legislation* (New York: Oxford University Press, 1939), p. 260.

72. Telser, "Why Should Manufacturers Want Fair Trade?" p. 95; B. S. Yamey, *The Economics of Resale Price Maintenance* (London: Sir Isaac Pitman, 1954), pp. 33–34; chain store growth in President's Conference on Unemployment, *Recent Economic Changes in the Unites States* (New York: Johnson Reprint, 1966), pp. 362, 373, first published 1929; "wheel of retailing" concept in Malcolm P. McNair, "Significant Trends and Developments in the Postwar Period," in A. B. Smith, ed., *Competitive Distribution in a Free High-Level Economy and Its Implications for the University* (Pittsburgh: University of Pittsburgh Press, 1958), pp. 17–18. See also Stanley C. Hollander, "The Wheel of Retailing," *Journal of Marketing,* 25 (July 1960): 37–42.

73. Robert L. Steiner, "A Dual-Stage Approach to the Effects of Brand Advertising on Competition and Price," in John F. Cady, ed., *Marketing and the Public Interest,* Report No. 78-105 (Boston: Marketing Science Institute), p. 143; and Steiner, "Toward a New Theory of Brand Advertising and Price," in Gordon E. Miracle, ed., *Sharing for Understanding, Proceedings of the American Academy of Advertising* (1977), pp. 29–37.

74. *Printers' Ink,* 51 (28 June 1905): 37.

75. MacMartin, *Advertising Campaigns* (New York: Alexander Hamilton Institute, 1916), pp. 1, 3–4.

Chapter 4

1. Frank Presbrey, *The History and Development of Advertising,* (New York: Greenwood Press, 1968), p. 625, first published 1929.

2. *V. B. Palmer's Businessmen's Almanac for the Year 1849,* p. 55; *Historical Statistics of the United States,* p. 810; Greeley quoted in George P. Rowell, *Forty Years an Advertising Agent* (New York: Printers' Ink Publishing Co., 1906), p. 295.

3. Rowell, *Forty Years,* p. 28.

4. Ibid., p. 323.

5. Cited in Donald L. Holland, "Volney B. Palmer: The Nation's First Advertising Agency Man," *Pennsylvania Magazine of History and Biography,* 98 (July 1974): 359.

6. *Printers' Ink,* 3 (24 December 1890): 686.

7. *V. B. Palmer's Almanac,* p. 55.

8. Ralph M. Hower, *The History of an Advertising Agency,* rev. ed. (Cambridge: Harvard University Press, 1949), p. 13.

Notes

9. *Advertiser's Gazette,* 5 (October 1871): 71; this forerunner of *Printers' Ink* contained many ads for Rowell's newspaper lists.

10. For an overview of the history of J. Walter Thompson, see *Advertising Age,* 35 (7 December 1964): section 2, 1–202. Hower, *History of an Advertising Agency,* p. 16; Presbrey, *History of Advertising,* pp. 272, 281.

11. Rowell, *Forty Years,* pp. 137, 190; *Advertiser's Gazette,* 5 (April 1871): 408; 5 (October 1871), p. 49.

12. Hower, *History of an Advertising Agency,* p. 50.

13. See *Printers' Ink,* 4 (13 May 1891): 634–35 for an "old-timer's" reminiscences about the profitability of space brokerage.

14. *Printers' Ink,* 139 (21 April 1927): 17–18.

15. Rowell, *Forty Years,* p. 370 and pp. 370–75 for Ripans story.

16. Kenneth H. Myers, Jr., *SRDS: The National Authority Serving the Media-Buying Function* (Evanston, Ill: Northwestern University Press, 1968), p. 40 lists seven; I have encountered one other.

17. Hower, *History of an Advertising Agency,* pp. 91–92.

18. Rowell, *Forty Years,* p. 306.

19. *Mercantile Agency Reference Book,* 67 (January 1885) for data on credit ratings.

20. Comments from R. G. Dun & Co. Reports, Baker Library, Harvard Graduate School of Business Administration, Boston, Massachusetts. Dauchy, v. 373, p. 1463, 1201I; Burr, v. 440, p. 604; Thompson, v. 389, pp. 2189, 2400/ a53; Erickson, v. 381, p. 200a/169; Bates and Locke, v. 439, pp. 600, 600c.

21. *Fame,* 1 (November 1892): 288–89; *Printers' Ink,* 7 (28 December 1892): 876.

22. *Art in Advertising,* 9 (October 1894): 278, 282.

23. John Manning, cited in Earnest Elmo Calkins and Ralph Holden, *Modern Advertising* (New York: D. Appleton, 1905), p. 26.

24. See Rowell, *Forty Years,* pp. 258–67.

25. Ed Roberts, ed., "Beggars, Peddlers and Advertising Men: An Anecdotal History of BBDO," unpublished manuscript at Batten Barton Durstine & Osborn, New York, p. 40.

26. *Fame,* 1 (October 1892): 247; Chalmers L. Pancoast, *Trail Blazers of Advertising* (New York: Frederick H. Hitchcock, 1926), p. xiii; Nathaniel C. Fowler, *Fowler's Publicity,* 3rd ed., (Chicago: Publicity Publishing Co., 1904), ch. 9; Charles A. Bates, *The Art and Literature of Business* (New York: Bates Publishing Co., 1909), p. 35, first published 1902.

27. *Advertiser's Gazette,* 4 (April 1870): 90.

28. *American Advertiser Reporter,* new series 5 (8 July 1891): 222.

29. Rowell, *Forty Years,* p. 98; resolution in *Printers' Ink,* 76 (31 August 1911): 38.

30. Hower, *History of an Advertising Agency,* pp. 27, 55, 232, 536; *Advertising Guide,* 2 (June 1877): rear cover page.

31. Agency totals from *Wilson's Business Directory 1869–1870,* and 32 (1879–1880); *The Trow City Directory Co's Formerly Wilson's Business Directory of New York City,* 42 (1889); *Trow's Business Directory of Greater New York, 1899,* vol. 2.

Notes

32. Rowell, *Forty Years*, pp. 74–75, 446.

33. *Printers' Ink*, 7 (18 February 1893): 258–59; *American Advertiser Reporter*, new series 5 (29 April 1891): 139.

34. *Printers' Ink*, 32 (8 August 1900): 27.

35. *Advertiser's Gazette*, 4 (July 1870): 177; *Printers' Ink* 76 (31 August 1911): 34–35; 1 (1 May 1889): 508; E. C. Allen Collection vols. LB-1, LB-2, LB-3, Manuscript Collections, Baker Library, Harvard Graduate School of Business Administration, Boston, Massachusetts.

36. Edwin Emery, *History of the American Newspaper Publishers Association* (Minneapolis: University of Minnesota Press, 1950), p. 37; *Printers' Ink*, 9 (12 September 1893): 293; 4 (3 June 1891): 742; Calkins and Holden, *Modern Advertising*, p. 173.

37. *Printers' Ink*, 24 (10 August 1898): 38 for this scornful characterization.

38. *Advertiser's Gazette*, 6 (October 1872): 14.

39. Presbrey, *History of Advertising*, p. 309 for salary estimate; *Advertising and Selling*, 9 (24 August 1927): 46 for insurance story.

40. *Printers' Ink*, 26 (11 January 1899): 3.

41. A good summary of changes in newspaper technology is found in Alfred McClung Lee, *The Daily Newspaper in America* (New York: Macmillan, 1937), pp. 97–132.

42. Ibid., p. 749.

43. *Printers' Ink*, 27 (21 June 1899): 26.

44. Fowler, *Publicity*, p. 192; *Printers' Ink*, 10 (31 January 1894): 116.

45. *Profitable Advertising*, 1 (June 1891): 5–6; *Printers' Ink*, 8 (1 March 1893): 320; 37 (30 October 1901): 28.

46. Hower, *History of an Advertising Agency*, pp. 76, 79; *Advertising*, 1 (January 1896): 5; John Gunther, *Taken at the Flood*, (New York: Popular Library 1961), pp. 48–49.

47. Curtis Publishing Co., *National Advertising: The Modern Selling Force* (Philadelphia: Curtis Publishing Co. 1910[?]), p. 23; Roberts, "Beggars, Peddlers and Advertising Men," pp. 13–14.

48. Presbrey, *History of Advertising*, pp. 98–101 for the Millais episode; *Printers' Ink*, 26 (4 January 1899): 34; Roberts, "Beggars, Peddlers and Advertising Men," pp. 13–14.

49. Hower, *History of an Advertising Agency*, pp. 72–77.

50. Curtis Publishing Co, *National Advertising: The Modern Selling Force*, p. 23; Henri, Hurst, and McDonald, *The Functions of the Modern Advertising Agency* (Chicago: Henri, Hurst and McDonald, 1917), p. 36.

51. Henri, Hurst, and McDonald, *Functions of the Modern Advertising Agency*, p. 12.

52. Calkins and Holden, *Modern Advertising*, pp. 173–74; *Printers' Ink*, 61 (11 December 1907): p. 24; 81 (10 October 1912): 83–84; *The Ayer Idea in Advertising* (Philadelphia: N. W. Ayer & Son, 1912), p. 35; *Forty Years of Advertising* (Philadelphia: N. W. Ayer & Son, 1909), pp. 53–54; *Modern Merchandising* (Chicago: Mallory, Mitchell & Faust, 1915), foreword.

53. *Printers' Ink*, 92 (8 July 1915): 79–80; Roy S. Durstine, "Advertising

Notes

Agency Service in the United States," in John Clyde Oswald, ed., *The Advertising Yearbook for 1924* (New York: Doubleday, Page, 1925), pp. 90–91.

54. Mac Martin, *Advertising Campaigns* (New York: Alexander Hamilton Institute, 1917), p. 116.

55. Oliver E. Williamson, *Markets and Hierarchies: Analysis and Antitrust Implications* (New York: Free Press, 1975), pp. 20–40 presents a theoretical framework; see also Oliver E. Williamson, "The Vertical Integration of Production: Market Failure Considerations," *American Economic Review*, 61 (May 1971): 112–23.

56. *Printers' Ink,* 8 (28 June 1893): 755–61; National Advertising Co., *America's Advertisers* (New York: Arno Press, 1976), p. 412, first published 1893.

57. *Printers' Ink,* 87 (14 May 1914): 10–12.

58. *Printers' Ink,* 4 (4 March 1891): 310; Gunther, *Taken at the Flood,* pp. 56–57, 62–65; Claude C. Hopkins, *My Life in Advertising* (New York: Harper and Brothers, 1927), p. 94.

59. American Association of Advertising Agencies, *Advertising in America* (New York: American Association of Advertising Agencies, 1918), p. 8.

60. S. Wilbur Corman, "How an Advertising Department Should Function in its Relations With the Advertising Agency," Address delivered at Annual Meeting of Association of National Advertisers, n.d., p. 3.

61. Seth Brown, *Advertising Agency Relations* (Chicago: Seth Brown Publishing Co., 1912), pp. 8–9.

62. 1873 convention discussed in *Printers' Ink,* 76 (31 August 1911): 35; 1 (1 May 1889): 591 ff; Emery, *History of Newspaper Publishers,* pp. 37–38; *Printers' Ink,* 10 (7 March 1894): 272; Rowell, *Forty Years,* pp. 441–42.

63. George Britt, *Forty Years—Forty Millions* (New York: Farrar & Rinehart, 1935), p. 101; Frank Luther Mott, *A History of American Magazines: 1885–1905* (Cambridge: Harvard University Press, 1957), p. 611; opposition to Munsey in *Printers' Ink,* 25 (9 November 1898): 43; *Profitable Advertising,* 8 (15 November 1898): 282–83.

64. James W. Young, *Advertising Agency Compensation* (Chicago: University of Chicago Press, 1933), pp. 32, 34.

65. Young, *Agency Compensation,* pp. 34–35, 7–10; *Printers' Ink,* 83 (22 May 1913): 74–75.

66. *Thirteenth Annual Meeting of the American Trade Press Association* (New York: American Trade Press Association, 1902), pp. 18–20; Young, *Agency Compensation,* p. 37.

67. *Printers' Ink,* 104 (19 September 1918): 77.

68. *Printers' Ink,* 80 (4 July 1912), pp. 66–67; Young, *Agency Compensation,* p. 40; Edward J. Baur, "Voluntary Control in the Advertising Industry," (Unpublished Ph.D. dissertation, University of Chicago, 1942), chap. 8; see also Albert E. Haase, *Advertising Agency Compensation: Theory, Law, Practice* (n.p.: Association of National Advertisers, 1934).

69. On Curtis, see Young, *Agency Compensation,* p. 35; Hower, *History of an Advertising Agency,* p. 409; Haase, *Compensation: Theory, Law, Practice,* pp. 181–84.

Notes

70. Morton J. Simon, *The Law for Advertising and Marketing* (New York: W. W. Norton, 1956), pp. 42*ff*, is a detailed source; see also Haase, *Compensation: Theory, Law, Practice*, pp. 71-90.

71. The case is in 99 N.Y. Supp. 522; 50 N.Y. Misc. 539. For commentary, see Haase, *Compensation: Theory, Law, Practice*, pp. 73-74.

72. 170 Mo. App. 490, 156 S.W. 737 for *Kastor* v. *Elders;* 83 N.Y. Misc. Rep. 404, 145 N.Y.S. 145 for *Clarke* v. *Watt;* Simon, *Law for Advertising*, pp. 24, 64-65: Haase, *Compensation: Theory, Law, Practice*, p. 88.

73. Cited in Young, *Agency Compensation*, p. 41.

74. Ibid. p. 98.

75. Haase, *Compensation: Theory, Law, Practice*, p. 53.

76. Hower, *History of an Advertising Agency*, p. 340.

77. Brown, *Advertising Agency Relations*, p. 27.

78. *Modern Merchandising* (Chicago: Mallory, Mitchell & Faust, 1915), n.p.; Harold W. Dickinson, *Crying Our Wares* (New York: John Day, 1929), pp. 4-5; William E. Woodward, *The Gift of Life* (New York: E. P. Dutton, 1947), p. 175.

79. *The Speculative Preparation of Plans, Copy or Art Work in the Solicitation of Business* (New York: American Association of Advertising Agencies, 1920); Haase, *Compensation: Theory, Law, Practice*, p. 211; Jerry Della Femina, *From Those Wonderful Folks Who Gave You Pearl Harbor* (New York: Pocket Books, 1971), pp. 64-68.

80. Haase, *Compensation: Theory, Law, Practice*, pp. 203, 209; Young, *Agency Compensation*, pp. 59-60 for complaints about unneeded services. These complaints grew more vociferous in the 1950s and 1960s.

81. William H. Boyenton, *Audit Bureau of Circulations* (Chicago: Audit Bureau of Circulations, 1952), p. 6; Charles O. Bennett, *Facts Without Opinion* (Chicago: Audit Bureau of Circulations, 1965), p. 6.

82. *Printers' Ink*, 14 (1 January 1896): 38; Rowell, *Forty Years*, p. 266; Bennett, *Facts, Without Opinion*, pp. 12-13.

83. Cited in Mott, *History of American Magazines*, pp. 15-16.

84. *Printers' Ink*, 4 (29 April 1891): 567-69; *Profitable Advertising*, I (July 1891): 45-56; 8 (15 October 1898): 236; Rowell quoted in Bennett, *Facts Without Opinion*, p. 17.

85. *Printers' Ink*, 86 (5 March 1914): 44, for lack of interest; agency hostility in for example, *Printers' Ink*, 39 (16 April 1902): 18; membership in Bennett, *Facts Without Opinion*, p. 21.

86. *Printers' Ink*, 74 (19 January 1911): 182; 81 (3 October 1912): 82.

87. Bennett, *Facts Without Opinion*, pp. 25-52; see also Kenneth H. Myers, "ABC and SRDS: The Evolution of Two Specialized Advertising Services," *Business History Review*, 34 (Autumn 1960): 310.

88. Curtis Publishing Co, *National Advertising*, p. 22.

89. For use of "advertising attorney," see, for example, *Profitable Advertising*, 1 (March 1892): 308; *Printers' Ink*, 28 (5 July 1899): 26.

90. *Associated Advertising*, 7 (April 1916): 28; *Ad Club News*, 2 (9 July 1917): 2; *Associated Advertising*, 9 (July 1918): 18; *Printers' Ink*, 96 (28 September 1916): 81-85; *Associated Advertising*, 9 (August 1918): 18.

Notes

91. *Printers' Ink,* 41 (29 October 1902): 42; Calkins and Holden, *Modern Advertising,* p. 6; Calkins, *The Business of Advertising,* pp. 336–37; Associated Advertising Clubs of America, *Seventh Annual Convention of the AACA, Boston, August 1–4, 1911* (Boston: Pilgrim Publicity Association, n.d.), p. 223; *Associated Advertising,* 4 (November 1913), p. 15.

92. *Advertising in America: What Agency Service Is* (New York: American Association of Advertising Agencies, 1918), pp. 12–16.

93. For Ayer, see Hower, *History of an Advertising Agency,* p. 503; for Batten, Roberts, see pp. 23, 51, 175–77.

94. Hower, *History of an Advertising Agency,* pp. 590–91; for Thompson, see *Advertising Age,* 25 (7 December 1964): 36. For Lord & Thomas, see Gunther, *Taken at the Flood,* p. 41.

95. The Thompson organization chart and standardization plans can be found in J. Walter Thompson Company Archives, R.G. 5, U.S.A. and International Offices: Committee on Standardization, 1:1, 1919.

96. *Printers' Ink,* 124 (6 September 1923): 4.

97. Charles Wilson Hoyt, *Training for the Business of Advertising* (New York: George B. Woolson, 1922), pp. 56–57.

98. Data tabulated from *Who's Who in Advertising* (Detroit: Business Service Corp., 1916), based on the sixty who worked at general agencies listed on pp. 88–89; *The Advertising Man of Detroit* (New York: Advertising Federation of America, 1930), pp. 25, 41–47; John L. Rogers, ed., *Who's Who in Advertising 1931* (New York: Harper & Brothers, 1931), tabulations based on random sample which yielded ninety-six subjects.

99. Martin Mayer, *Madison Avenue, U.S.A.* (New York: Pocket Books, 1959), p. 12; Rogers, *Who's Who in Advertising 1931,* p. xv.

100. Associated Advertising Clubs of America, *Seventh Annual Convention of the A.A.C.A., Boston, August 1–4, 1911* (Boston: Pilgrim Publicity Association, n.d.); *Printers' Ink,* 95 (29 June 1916): 195; Helen Woodward, *Through Many Windows* (New York: Harper & Brothers, 1926), pp. 348–49.

101. *Advertising and Selling,* 27 (17 December 1936), p. 35; William A. Sutton, "Sherwood Anderson: The Advertising Years," *Northwest Ohio Quarterly,* 22 (Summer 1950): 120–57; Sherwood Anderson, *A Story Teller's Story,* Ray Lewis White, ed. (Cleveland: Case Western Reserve University, 1968), p. 215; Ray Lewis White, ed., *Sherwood Anderson's Memoirs* (Chapel Hill: University of North Carolina Press, 1969), pp. 396, 415–17.

102. James Rorty, "It Has Happened Here: The Memoirs of a Muck-Raker," unpublished typescript, James Rorty Papers, University of Oregon Library, Eugene, Oregon, chap. 10, pp. 10–11.

103. Andrew Turnbull, *Scott Fitzgerald* (New York: Charles Scribner's Sons, 1962), p. 92; Charles A. Fenton, *Stephen Vincent Benét* (New Haven: Yale University Press, 1958), p. 78; Millicent Bell, *Marquand: An American Life* (Boston: Little, Brown-Atlantic Monthly Press, 1979), p. 113.

104. E. T. Gundlach, *Old Sox on Trumpeting* (Chicago: Consolidated Book Company, 1927).

105. *Printers' Ink,* 112 (29 July 1920): 10, 12.

Notes

Chapter 5

1. For advertising men's views, see H. J. Kenner, *The Fight for Truth in Advertising* (New York: Round Table Press, 1936) and Frank Presbrey, *The History and Development of Advertising* (Garden City, N.Y.: Doubleday, Doran, 1929), pp. 531–40. The "white light of truth" phrase is from *New York Times,* 23 June 1915, p. 22.

2. There are some indications of the monetary losses. Americans spent nearly $75 million on proprietary drugs in 1904; few, if any, of these drugs did what they promised. In 1912, the Chief U. S. Postal Inspector estimated that his agency had caught "swindling promoters" who, the previous year, had obtained about $77 million. U. S. Bureau of the Census, *Biennial Census of Manufactures: 1921* (Washington: 1924), p. 746; *Printers' Ink,* 77 (25 January 1912): 22.

3. *Advertiser's Gazette,* 6 (October, 1872): 9.

4. Drug promoter quoted in James H. Young, *The Toadstool Millionaires* (Princeton, N.J.: Princeton University Press, 1961), p. 101.

5. The phrase is from Oliver Wendell Holmes, Sr. See Young, *Toadstool Millionaires* p. 67.

6. Kenner, *Fight for Truth* p. 7; Joseph H. Appel, *The Business Biography of John Wanamaker* (New York: Macmillan, 1930) p. 104; Appel, *Growing Up with Advertising* (New York: Business Bourse, 1940), pp. 94–98; Presbrey, *History and Development,* p.332.

7. Appel, *Business Biography,* p. 108.

8. Presbrey, *History and Development,* pp. 234, 531; *Printers' Ink,* 8 (15 February 1893): 246–47.

9. "Medical Advertisements not Accepted," volume 0-4, E. C. Allen Collection, Harvard Business School, Baker Library. One useful source of information on Allen is George P. Rowell, *Forty Years an Advertising Agent* (New York: Printers' Ink Publishing Co., 1906), pp. 201–04.

10. "Letterbooks," General, Volume E-5, p. 149, October 21, 1887; pp. 507–08, November 22, 1887; p. 749, December 17, 1887; p. 642, July 15, 1889; E. C. Allen Collection.

11. Volume 0-4, January 17, 1888, E. C. Allen Collection.

12. Edward Bok, *The Americanization of Edward Bok* (New York: C. Scribner's Sons, 1921), pp. 166, 199, 201–02, 340; Presbrey, *History and Development,* pp. 354, 477, 481; *Printers' Ink* XX (18 August 1897): 11; *Advertising,* 2 (August, 1897): 85.

13. Ed Roberts, "Beggars, Peddlers and Advertising Men: An Anecdotal History of BBDO," unpublished manuscript at Batten, Barton, Durstine & Osborn, New York, 1964; Ralph M. Hower, *The History of an Advertising Agency,* rev. ed., (Cambridge: Harvard University Press, 1949), p. 91.

14. For an example of a reproach to a publisher who complained about losses from excluding false advertising, see *Printers' Ink,* 65 (21 October 1908): 31–32.

15. *Printers' Ink,* 16 (16 September 1896), p. 26; 14 (8 January 1896): 42; 27 (26 April 1899): 24; 10 (11 April 1894): 432; 11 (24 October 1894): 688.

Notes

16. *Fame,* 1 (June, 1892): 99; *Printers' Ink,* 4 (29 April 1891): 580; 18 (24 March 1897): 34; 26 (18 January 1899): 35; 24 (10 August 1898): 38.

17. *Printers' Ink,* 21 (15 February 1897): 42; 8 (7 August 1895): 34.

18. *Printers' Ink,* 1 (15 July 1888): 19; Daniel Boorstin, *The Image* (New York: Harper & Row, 1964) first pub. 1961, pp. 211–28; see also his *The Americans: The Democratic Experience* (New York: Random House, 1973), esp. pp. 137–48, and "Advertising and American Civilization," in Yale Brozen, ed., *Advertising and Society* (New York: New York University Press, 1974), pp. 11–23.

19. Tabulation of advertisers in *Profitable Advertising,* 8 (15 December 1898): 302; Ayer statistics in Hower, *History of an Advertising Agency,* p. 590; *Printers' Ink,* 24 (10 August 1898): 34.

20. *Biennial Census of Manufactures: 1921,* p. 746; *Printers' Ink,* 24 (6 July 1898): 44; 42 (25 February 1903): 30; 46 (16 March 1904): 42; and 46 (30 March 1904): 45.

21. Samuel H. Adams, "Liquozone," *Collier's,* 36 (18 November 1905): 20; Derrick account in *Printers' Ink,* 51 (21 May 1905): 28; For Richardson, see Samuel H. Adams, "Preying on the Incurables," *Collier's* (13 January 1906): 18–19; for Coleman, see Samuel H. Adams, "The Fundamental Fakers," *Collier's* (17 February 1906): 22.

22. Earnest W. Calkins and Ralph Holden, *Modern Advertising* (New York: D. Appleton, 1905), p. 5; Rowell, *Forty Years* pp. 401–02.

23. Good accounts of the origins of the legislation are to be found in Young, *Toadstool Millionaires,* chaps. 13–14, and Oscar E. Anderson, Jr., *The Health of a Nation: Harvey W. Wiley and the Fight for Pure Food* (Chicago: University of Chicago Press, 1958), chaps. 7–9.

24. *Printers' Ink,* 56 (11 July 1906): 27; 56 (19 September 1906): 28; 57 (19 December 1906): 30.

25. James H. Young, *The Medical Messiahs* (Princeton, N.J.: 1967), esp. p. 37, for the problems of enforcement.

26. *Printers' Ink,* 74 (16 February 1911): 73–74; *Associated Advertising* 6 (January, 1915): 20–24 and 5 (November, 1914): 16.

27. Advertising Appropriations in Advertising Department, Crowell Publishing Company, *National Markets and National Advertising 1922* (New York: 1923), p. 53; *McKittrick Directory of Advertisers,* vol. 2 (1900–1901) and vol. 12 (1911) for agency information.

28. Mahin policy in Hower, *History of an Advertising Agency,* pp. 602–03; ibid. pp. 92–93 for Ayer policy.

29. John Lee Mahin, "The Commercial Value of Advertising," *Lectures on Advertising* (n.p.: [1915?]), p. 20.

30. *Printers' Ink,* 10 (2 May 1894): 544; 19 (21 April 1897): 32.

31. *Printers' Ink,* 47 (27 April 1904): 40; 58 (6 March 1907): 28; Curtis code in Daniel Starch, *Advertising: Its Principles, Practice and Technique* (Chicago: Scott, Foresman, 1914), p. 101; *Printers' Ink,* 88 (20 August 1904): 40; Lord & Thomas ad in 96 (20 July 1916): 43; Kewanee Boiler Company in 88 (30 July 1914): 3.

32. *Printers' Ink,* 48 (6 July 1904): 12–13, *Associated Advertising,* 8 (Octo-

Notes

ber, 1917): 11; *Printers' Ink* 13 (18 September 1895): 34; John Lee Mahin, "Does Advertising Add Value to Merchandise?", *Lectures on Advertising*, (n.p.: n.d. [1915?]) p. 6; Mahin, *Advertising: Selling the Consumer* (n.p.: 1919), p. 249.

33. *Printers' Ink*, 48 (21 September 1904): 26.

34. *Printers' Ink*, 85 (16 October 1913): 100.

35. Kenner, *Fight for Truth*, p. 19; attendance figures in Associated Advertising Clubs of America, *Seventh Annual Convention of the AACA. Boston. August 1-4, 1911* (Boston: n.d.), p. 87; *Advertising and Selling*, 21 (September, 1911): 80.

36. Appel, *Growing Up with Advertising*, p. 148; Kenner, *Fight for Truth*, pp. 23-24 for popularity of Appel speech; *Seventh Annual Convention*, p. 28.

37. *Seventh Annual Convention*, pp. 182-83.

38. For the status of legal sanctions against dishonest advertising, see Kenner, *Fight for Truth*, pp. 5ff. and Clowry Chapman, *The Law of Advertising and Sales*, 2 vols., (Denver: Clowry Chapman, 1908), esp. vol. 1, chap. 7.

39. The model statute can be found in Presbrey, *History and Development*, p. 537 among other places; on failure of earlier laws, see Nims in *Printers' Ink*, 77 (16 November 1911): 17, 22.

40. *Printers' Ink*, 77 (30 November 1911): 20.

41. *Printers' Ink*, 77 (30 November 1911): 76, 79-80; Kenner, *Fight for Truth*, p. 34; *Printers' Ink*, 115 (16 June 1921): 44.

42. For advertising men's opposition to weaker bills, see *Printers' Ink*, 83 (8 May 1913): 96-97; 90 (4 March, 1915): 66; Portland, Or. Ad Club *Spotlight*, 3 (14 February 1917): 2.

43. *Printers' Ink*, 91 (15 April 1915): 72-73; Davies Speech in *New York Times*, 21 June 1915, p. 11; Kenner, *Fight for Truth*, p. 65; *Printers' Ink*, 95 (29 June 1916): 18; Hurley speech in *New York Times*, 30 June 1916, p. 3; *Printers' Ink*, 98 (8 February 1917): 112.

44. Kenner, *Fight for Truth*, p. 31; *Advertising and Selling*, 22 (June, 1912): 11; *Associated Advertising*, 5 (November, 1914), pp. 28-29; Kenner, *Fight for Truth*, pp. 48-49.

45. *Printers' Ink*, 77 (21 December 1911): 78; 88 (2 July 1914): 114-15.

46. Activities of the Minneapolis Vigilance Bureau and its successor, the Minneapolis Better Business Bureau of Minneapolis, can be traced in the papers of the Better Business Bureau of Minneapolis, Minnesota Historical Society, St. Paul, Minn. For work on the passage of the Model Statute, see Box 1. (The Collection is hereafter cited as Minneapolis Better Business Bureau Papers.)

47. Minneapolis Better Business Bureau Papers, Box 1; other paid secretaries by mid-1916 were in Milwaukee, Boston, Spokane, Indianapolis, Kansas City, Chicago, Buffalo, and Des Moines, according to *Printers' Ink*, 95 (29 June 1916): 19-20; 1921 situation in *Printers' Ink*, 115 (16 June 1921): 48.

48. *First Annual Report of the Vigilance Bureau of the Minneapolis Advertising Forum*, March 1, 1914 to March 1, 1915, pp. 1, 3; *Second Annual Report . . .*, March 1, 1915 to March 1, 1916; *Third Annual Report . . .*, March 1, 1916 to March 1, 1917, pp. 4-7.

49. *Annual Reports* contain information on complaints and prosecutions.

50. Cleveland Advertising Club *Torch*, 7 (18 June 1917): 4; *Spotlight*, 3 (23

Notes

June 1917): 2; *Spotlight,* 3 (22 November 1916): 2; *Spotlight,* 3 (21 February 1917): 2.

51. *Torch,* 7 (5 March 1917): 3; *Spotlight,* 3 (27 September 1916): 2; *Spotlight,* 7 (5 June 1918): 4; *Oregon Voter,* 9 (30 June 1917): 468 for circus story, reprinted from article by Samuel H. Adams in *New York Tribune; Torch,* 8 (29 June 1918): 1; *Torch,* 8 (18 May 1918): 2: Minneapolis Better Business Bureau Papers, Boxes 5 and 6; Kenner, *Fight for Truth,* pp. 69, 73*ff.*

52. "National Vigilance Committee Confidential Bulletin No. 10" and "National Vigilance Committee's Plan of Work," Minneapolis Better Business Bureau Papers, Box 1; Kenner, *Fight for Truth,* p. 71.

53. Milton Handler, "False and Misleading Advertising," *Yale Law Journal,* (November 1929): 45–46.

54. The moralistic tone of the campaign can perhaps best be seen in the lay sermons preached at churches in the cities where the Associated Advertising Clubs' conventions were held. The 1912 sermons are reprinted conveniently in the *Eighth Annual Convention of the Associated Advertising Clubs of America* (n.p.: 1912), pp. 1–65. At the 1915 convention, delegates sang, to the tune of "My Country 'Tis of Thee," the following:

> My emblem 'tis of thee,
> Emblem of AAC
> Of Truth I sing,
> Our credo glorious
> Makes Truth victorious;
> Truth reigning over us
> Will freedom bring.
>
> God grant our emblem grace
> To hold its noble place,
> Truth exalting.
> Upheld with earnest pride
> Publish it far and wide
> Truth for which martyrs died
> Of Truth we sing.
> (Kenner, *Fight for Truth,* p. 58)

55. *Printers' Ink,* 87 (9 April 1914): 104; Kenner, *Fight for Truth,* pp. 44–45.

56. *Spotlight,* 7 (23 October 1918): 2; New York *Advertising Club News,* 1 (25 October 1915): 2.

57. Pittsburgh decision reported in *Advertising Club News,* 1 (3 January 1916): 2; National Advertising Commission head quoted in Edward J. Baur, "Voluntary Control in the Advertising Industry," (Ph.D. diss., University of Chicago, 1942), p. 77; Moses in *Editor and Publisher,* 49 (1 July 1916): 4.

58. Frank Armstrong to Ira B. Henthorn, 18 February 1918, Minneapolis Better Business Bureau Papers, Box 5.

59. "White light of truth" phrase in *New York Times,* 23 June 1915, p. 22.

60. Larrabee in *Printers' Ink,* 283 (14 June 1963): 11. It is suggestive that many of the businessmen prosecuted had apparently Jewish surnames. Anti-

Notes

Semitic stereotypes occasionally surfaced. A Mr. Chance, speaking from the floor at the 1916 AACW Newspaper Department session, explained his organization's approach to the false advertiser: "We appeal to his selfishness if not his morals—you can't get by with that on the average 'kike'—you can't do it, *Editor and Publisher,* 49 (1 July 1916): p. 12. Richard Waldo of the *New York Tribune* told a Boston gathering that New York businessmen failed to cooperate on truth in advertising because "there is a large Hebraic element in the community and they are afraid to trust each other." On the other hand, men with Jewish surnames were leaders in vigilance work in many cities. Since there were prominent Jewish businessmen in Mr. Waldo's audience, his remark "was greeted in cold silence," *Editor and Publisher,* 49 (31 March 1917): p. 12.

61. Neal cited in *Printer's Ink,* 88 (2 July 1914): 80–81; Waldo to AACW Convention in *Editor and Publisher,* 49 (1 July 1916): 7; Handler, "False and Misleading Advertising," pp. 28–29, for judge's opinion and mail fraud analysis.

62. The Wrigley case can be followed in Minneapolis Better Business Bureau Papers, Box 1. In particular, see National Vigilance Committee Confidential Bulletin 16, 19 March 1914; Harry D. Robbins to "Dear Sir", 24 March 1914; National Vigilance Committee Confidential Bulletin 19, 7 May 1914.

63. Donnelly case in Minneapolis Better Business Bureau Papers, Box 4, including G. M. Husser to J. C. Armstrong, 19 July 1917; Armstrong to C. F. French, 24 July 1917; Houston to Armstrong, 31 July 1917. Hart, Schaffner, Marx case in Boxes 4 and 5; J. C. Armstrong to Henry P. Williams, Advertising Manager, Hart, Schaffner and Marx, 12 October 1917.

64. Armstrong to Houston, 8 August 1917, Minneapolis Better Business Bureau Papers, Box 4.

65. Vigilance Bureau, *First Annual Report,* p. 4; *Minneapolis Journal,* 13 January 1913, clipping in Minneapolis Better Business Bureau Papers, Box 1; Fort Worth paper cited in *Editor and Publisher,* 49 (17 June 1916): 21; Samuel H. Adams, *The Adams Articles* (New York: Tribune Association, 1916), pp. 21, 36.

66. Kenner, *Fight for Truth,* p. 207; *Printers' Ink,* 98 (1 March 1917): 95; Minneapolis Vigilance Bureau, *Third Annual Report,* p. 5; *Editor and Publisher,* 49 (30 December 1916): 32; *Torch,* 10 (21 April 1919): 4.

67. "Tramps and beggars" phrase in *Editor and Publisher,* 49 (1 July 1916): 7; *Printers' Ink,* 95 (11 May 1916): 109; *Editor and Publisher,* 49 (25 November 1916): 18; *Printers' Ink,* 95 (15 June 1916): 119–120 and (29 June 1916): 6–8.

68. On fact-opinion distinction, see, e.g., *Printers' Ink,* 90 (4 March 1915): 66; on difficulties of legal action, see Handler, "False and Misleading Advertising," citing opinions, esp. pp. 29, 32–34. Correspondence in the Minneapolis Better Business Bureau Papers frequently indicates worries about the difficulty of prosecutions.

69. Among the main critiques of advertising in the twenties and thirties are: James Rorty, *Our Master's Voice* (New York: John Day, 1934); Max Radin, *The Lawful Pursuit of Gain* (Boston: Houghton Mifflin, 1931); Ralph Borsodi, *The Distribution Age* (New York: D. Appleton, 1927). Discussion of these and other critiques and the industry's generally weak response can be found in Otis Pease, *The Responsibilities of American Advertising* (New Haven: Yale Uni-

Notes

versity Press, 1958), chap. 4; see also Stuart Ewen, *Captains of Consciousness* (New York: McGraw-Hill, 1976), esp. pp. 202–07, and Stephen Richard Shapiro, "The Big Sell: Attitudes of Advertising Writers about their Craft in the 1920's and 1930's." (Ph.D. diss., University of Wisconsin, 1969).

70. The argument here is based on extensive examination of the era's advertising. Information on the beginnings of Woodbury's Soap and Cadillac advertisements can be found in Julian Lewis Watkins, *The 100 Greatest Advertisements: Who Wrote Them and What They Did,* rev. ed. (New York: Dover, 1959), pp. 23, 49. Hopkins discusses his campaigns in *My Life in Advertising* (New York: Harper and Brothers, 1927), esp. chaps. 7, 13, 14.

71. Basic patterns of life insurance marketing are covered in J. Owen Stalson, *Marketing Life Insurance* (Cambridge: Harvard University Press, 1942); investment-oriented ads can be found, for example, in *Harper's,* 101 (June-November, 1901); "cannibalism" phrase quoted in R. Carlyle Buley, *The Equitable Life Assurance Society of the United States,* 2 vols (New York: Appleton-Century-Crofts, 1967), vol. 1, p. 99.

72. Morton Keller, *The Life Insurance Enterprise 1885–1910* (Cambridge: Harvard University Press, 1963), chaps. 15–17 discusses and interprets the Armstrong Commission and its impact.

73. Stalson, *Marketing Life Insurance,* p. 551; Spencer L. Kimball, *Insurance and Public Policy* (Madison, Wisconsin: University of Wisconsin Press, 1960), p. 122; distinction between buyer-oriented and product-oriented appeals in Darrell B. Lucas and Stuart H. Britt, *Advertising: Psychology and Research,* (New York: McGraw-Hill, 1950), pp. 156ff.

74. Equitable advertising in Equitable Life Assurance Society Archives, New York, New York; Mutual Benefit Life ad in Mildred Stone, *Since 1845* (New Brunswick, Rutgers University Press, 1957), pp. 125–26.

75. For some perspectives on professionalization, see Howard M. Vollmer and Donald L. Mills, eds., *Professionalization* (Englewood Cliffs, N.J.: Prentice-Hall, 1966). Among sociologists who stress the creation of ethical restraints in professionalization are Bernard Barber, "Some Problems in the Sociology of the Professions," *Daedalus,* 92 (Fall 1963): 669–88, and Talcott Parsons, *Essays in Sociological Theory,* 2d ed. (New York: Free Press, 1954), pp. 34–49. Magali Sarfatti Larson, *The Rise of Professionalism* (Berkeley, California: University of California Press, 1977) maintains (to oversimplify a rich and complex argument) that corporate capitalism demanded and facilitated professionalization and that professional ethics tend to reinforce rather than challenge class inequalities.

76. Harper in *Printers' Ink,* 283 (14 June 1963): 54; Neil Borden, *The Economic Effects of Advertising* (Chicago: Richard D. Irwin, 1944), p. 6; *Printer's Ink,* 81 (21 November 1912): 90–91.

77. John K. Galbraith, *The New Industrial State* (Boston: Houghton Mifflin, 1967), p. 325; Giancarlo Buzzi, *Advertising: Its Cultural and Political Effects,* trans. B. David Garmize (Minneapolis: University of Minnesota Press, 1968), p. 14.

78. Paul Baran and Paul Sweezy, *Monopoly Capital* (New York: Monthly Review Press, 1966), p. 121; Rorty, *Our Master's Voice,* pp. 353, 177, 358–59. See also Ewen, *Captains of Consciousness.*

Notes

Chapter 6

1. Charles Austin Bates, *Good Advertising* (New York: Holmes Publishing Company, 1896), p. 22; *America's Advertisers*, p. 432.
2. Crowell Publishing Co., *National Markets and National Advertising 1923* (New York: Crowell, 1923), p. 86.
3. Cited in R. Carlyle Buley, *The Equitable Life Assurance Society of the United States*, vol. 1 (New York: Appleton-Century-Crofts, 1967), pp. 397, 403.
4. Nathaniel C. Fowler, Jr., *Fowler's Publicity* (New York: Publicity Publishing Co., 1897), p. 862; negative appraisal in *Printers' Ink*, 28 (26 July 1899): 27.
5. See, for example, Earnest E. Calkins, *The Business of Advertising* (New York: D. Appleton, 1915), p. viii.
6. If it is conducted by researchers with an awareness of and sensitivity to changing business and marketing conditions, content analysis can be very instructive. The research projects of C. Roland Marchand and Richard W. Pollay, which entail large-scale content analyses, appear very promising. For other examples, see S. M. Dornbusch and L. C. Hickman, "Other-Directedness in Consumer-Goods Advertising," *Social Forces*, 38 (December 1959): 98–101; Bruce W. Brown, *Image of Family Life in Magazine Advertising 1920–1978* (New York: Praeger, 1981); Jib Fowles, *Mass Advertising as Social Forecast* (Westport, Conn.: Greenwood Press, 1976).
7. *Advertiser's Gazette*, 5 (January 1871): 312; 4 (July 1870): 149.
8. *Advertiser's Gazette*, 4 (July 1870): 175.
9. *Advertiser's Magazine*, 1 (October 1873): 3.
10. Halstead quoted in Alfred M. Lee, *The Daily Newspaper in America* (New York: Macmillan, 1937), p. 327.
11. *Printers' Ink*, 7 (26 October 1892): 532; 8 (18 January 1893): 15–16.
12. Cited in *Printers' Ink*, 24 (28 September 1898): 16–17.
13. *Printers' Ink*, 48 (24 August 1904): 14.
14. Roberts, "Beggars, Peddlers and Advertising Men: An Anecdotal History of BBDO," unpublished manuscript, p. 2.
15. *Printers' Ink*, 25 (26 October 1898): 42; 15 (8 April 1896): 42.
16. Fowler, *Publicity*, p. 343.
17. *Printers' Ink*, 24 (3 August 1898): 8; William A. Shryer, *Analytical Advertising* (Detroit: Business Service Co., 1912), p. 70; Harry L. Hollingworth, *Advertising and Selling* (New York: D. Appleton, for the Advertising Men's League of New York City, 1913), pp. 107–08.
18. Hollingworth, *Advertising and Selling,* p. 64, citing Walter Dill Scott; Daniel Starch, *Advertising* (New York: Scott, Foresman, 1914), p. 40.
19. Harry D. Kitson, "Minor Studies in the Psychology of Advertising," *Journal of Applied Psychology*, 5 (March 1921): 12.
20. Calkins and Holden, *Modern Advertising* (New York: D. Appleton, 1905), p. 326.
21. *Printers' Ink*, 24 (28 September 1898): 25–26; 25 (12 October 1898): 24–26.

Notes

22. *Printers' Ink,* 41 (29 October 1902): 39.

23. Starch, *Advertising,* p. 231.

24. John Gunther, *Taken at the Flood* (New York: Popular Library, 1961), pp. 55–56.

25. Cited in introduction to John E. Kennedy, *Intensive Advertising* (New York: Associated Business Publications, 1940), first pub. 1910, p. 7.

26. Kennedy, *Intensive Advertising,* esp. pp. 9 and 20.

27. Walter D. Scott, *The Psychology of Advertising* (Boston: Small, Maynard, 1908), p. 94.

28. *Printers Ink,* 59 (7 February 1906): 34.

29. For a discussion of rationalist and nonrationalist concepts in advertising thought, see Merle Curti, "The Changing Concept of 'Human Nature' in the Literature of American Advertising," *Business History Review,* 41 (Winter 1967): 335–57.

30. Shryer, *Analytical Advertising,* p. 45.

31. Scott, *Psychology of Advertising,* pp. 80–81.

32. Scott, *The Theory of Advertising* (Boston: Small, Maynard, 1903), p. 47. For a good discussion of developments in the psychology of advertising, see David P. Kuna, "The Concept of Suggestion in the Early History of Advertising Psychology," *Journal of the History of the Behavioral Sciences,* 12 (1976): 347–53; see also Kuna, "Early Advertising Applications of the Gale-Cattell Order-of-Merit Method," *Journal of the History of the Behavioral Sciences,* 15 (1979): 38–46.

33. Hollingworth, *Advertising and Selling,* p. 28.

34. George B. Hotchkiss, *Advertising Copy* (New York: Harper & Bros., 1925), p. 77; Harry Tipper, Harry L. Hollingworth, George Burton Hotchkiss, and Frank Alvah Parsons, *Advertising: Its Principles and Practice* (New York: Ronald Press, 1915), p. 186.

35. Hollingworth, *Advertising and Selling,* pp. 346–47.

36. Walter D. Scott, *The Psychology of Advertising,* rev. ed. (Boston: Small, Maynard, 1921). pp. 27–28.

37. Scott, *Psychology of Advertising* (1921), p. 24; *Printers' Ink,* 42 (1 January 1903): 25.

38. Tipper, et al., *Principles and Practice,* pp. 150, 155.

39. *Printers' Ink,* 4 (18 February 1891): 260.

40. *Printers' Ink,* 97 (16 November 1916): 124–25.

41. Scott, *Psychology of Advertising* (1921), pp. 124–25; Tipper et al., *Principles and Practice,* p. 222.

42. Harry D. Kitson, "Minor Studies in the Psychology of Advertising: Negative Suggestion in Advertising," *Journal of Applied Psychology,* 6 (March 1922): 66–68.

43. *Printers' Ink,* 12 (9 January 1895): 44.

44. *Fame,* 1 (March 1892): 24.

45. Scott, *Theory and Practice,* p. 24.

46. Starch, *Advertising,* p. 172.

47. Ibid.

Notes

48. George Burton Hotchkiss and Richard B. Franken, *The Leadership of Advertised Brands* (New York: Doubleday, Page for the Associated Advertising Clubs of the World, 1925), pp. 42–43.

49. Shryer, *Analytical Advertising*, pp. 79, 110.

50. Ibid.

51. Starch, *Advertising*, p. 178.

52. *Printers' Ink*, 30 (31 January 1900): 26; *Ad Club News*, 2 (4 March 1918): 3.

53. Herbert N. Casson, *Ads and Sales* (Chicago: A. N. McClurg, 1911), p. 81.

54. *Printers' Ink*, 86 (8 January 1914): 109–10.

55. *Printers' Ink*, 44 (2 September 1903): 26.

56. Fowler, *Publicity*, p. 720.

57. For these views, see *Printers' Ink*, 8 (3 May 1893): 550–51; 24 (24 August 1898): 16; Joseph H. Appel, *Growing Up with Advertising* (New York: Business Bourse, 1940), p. 127; Scott, *Theory and Practice*, pp. 77–78; Tipper et al., *Principles and Practice*, pp. 277, 209.

58. Fowler, *Publicity*, p. 725.

59. Claude C. Hopkins, *My Life in Advertising*, (New York: Harper and Brothers, 1927), pp. 116, 22, 178–79, 185, 174, and Hopkins, "Some Lessons I Have Learned in Advertising," in J. George Frederick, *Masters of Advertising Copy* (New York: Frank-Maurice, 1925), p. 117.

60. Hopkins, *My Life In Advertising*, pp. 6, 201, 206.

Chapter 7

1. Bergin quoted in *Advertising Age*, 8 February 1982, p. 82; for background, see Peter W. Bernstein, "Coke Strikes Back," *Fortune*, 103 (1 June 1981): 30–36; J. C. Louis and Harvey Z. Yazijian, *The Cola Wars* (New York: Everest House, 1980).

2. *Beverage World*, 100 (March 1982): 17; *Leading National Advertisers Ad $ Summary*, January-December 1981, p. 46; by contrast, Coke spent about $182,961 in national magazine advertising in 1920. See *National Markets and National Advertising 1922* (New York: Crowell Publishing Company, 1923), p. 71.

3. *Beverage Industry*, 12 March 1982, p. 13.

4. For a broader perspective on this, see Alfred D. Chandler, Jr., *The Visible Hand* (Cambridge: Harvard University Press, 1977), part 5.

5. *Advertising Age*, September 10, 1981, p. 8. Food producers are listed in the following categories: food; gum and candy; soft drinks. Chemicals are listed in: chemicals; soaps, cleansers (and allied); toiletries, cosmetics.

6. Louis W. Stern and Adel I. El-Ansary, *Marketing Channels* (Englewood Cliffs, N.J.: Prentice-Hall, 1977), p. 104

7. Ibid., pp. 38–39, 53.

8. Albert D. Lasker, *The Lasker Story—As He Told It.* (Chicago: Advertising Publications, 1953), p. 72.

9. Beer market shares in *Beverage Industry, 1982 Annual Manual*, p. 52; cigarettes in *Marketing and Media Decisions*, 16 (October 1981): 172.

Notes

10. Wendell R. Smith, "Product Differentiation and Market Segmentation as Alternative Marketing Strategies," *Journal of Marketing*, 21 (July 1956), reprinted in James F. Engel, Henry F. Fiorillo, and Murray A. Cayley, eds., *Market Segmentation: Concepts and Applications* (New York: Holt, Rinehard and Winston, 1972), p. 33.

11. Ronald E. Frank, "Market Segmentation Research: Findings and Implications," reprinted in Engel, et al., *Market Segmentation,* p. 132.

12. See Chandler, *The Visible Hand,* part 4, for an overview of the integration of mass production and mass distribution.

13. Alfred P. Sloan, Jr., *My Years With General Motors* (New York: Macfadden-Bartell, 1965), pp. 65, 69, 265.

14. Joel Dean, *Managerial Economics* (Englewood Cliffs, N.J.: Prentice-Hall, 1951), p. 476.

15. Theodore Levitt, "Exploit the Product Life Cycle," *Harvard Business Review*, 43 (November-December 1965): 81–94.

16. U.S. Bureau of the Census, *Historical Statistics of the United States: Colonial Times to 1970* (Washington, D.C.: 1975), p. 137; *New York Times*, 18 May 1982, p. D1.

17. Theodore Levitt, "The Industrialization of Service," *Harvard Business Review*, 54 (September-October 1976): 63–74.

18. Michael E. Porter, *Competitive Strategy* (New York: Free Press, 1980), p. 37.

19. For Ayer, see Ralph M. Hower, *The History of An Advertising Agency,* rev. ed. (Cambridge: Harvard University Press, 1949), p. 591, 593. Thompson data from J. Walter Thompson Company Archives, RG 5 U.S.A. and International Offices: Committee on Standardization, 1919; and RG 3 JWT History: Scrapbooks: (JWT Company Portfolio Comprising Figures and Facts), c. 1924; and *An Intimate Picture of the World's Largest Advertising Agency, 1935;* 1970 and 1980 figures calculated from *Advertising Age,* 22 February 1971, 1ff., and 18 March 1981, pp. 1, 8.

20. Quoted in Martin Mayer, *Madison Avenue U.S.A.* (New York: Pocket Books, 1959), p. 98.

21. See, for example, *Wall Street Journal,* 2 March 1982, pp. 1, 15.

22. *Advertising Age,* 9 March 1981, p. S12.

23. Association of National Advertisers, *Current Advertiser Practices in Compensating Their Advertising Agencies* (New York: Association of National Advertisers, 1976), pp. 10, 37.

24. For a good discussion of the situation at the time of the consent decrees, see Spencer Klaw, "Advertising: The Battle of Fifteen Percent," *Fortune,* 54 (October 1956): 142ff. A retrospective commentary is Donald R. Holland, "The Great Tradeoff," *Advertising Age,* 6 July 1981, p. 41.

25. *Current Practices in Agency Compensation,* pp. 3. 19; *Advertising Age,* 18 May 1981, p. 64.

26. Edward Buxton, *Promise Them Anything* (New York: Stein and Day, 1972), p. 245.

27. "Here Come the Super Agencies," *Fortune,* 100 (27 August 1979): 46.

28. *Advertising Age,* 3 May 1982, p. M2.

Notes

29. *Advertising Age,* 8 June 1981, pp. 3 *ff.*

30. Edward Buxton, *Creative People at Work* (New York: Executive Communications, Inc., 1975), p. 43.

31. *Advertising Age,* 5 December 1977, pp. 51–52.

32. For an instructive and lively account of the FTC's early experience, see Richard S. Tedlow, "From Competitor to Consumer: The Changing Focus of Federal Regulation of Advertising, 1914–1938," *Business History Review,* 55 (Spring 1981): 35–58.

33. *Kalwajtys* v. *FTC,* 237 F.2d 654 (7th Cir. 1956).

34. Cited in American Academy of Advertising Panel on Advertising and Government, *Advertising and Government Regulation,* Marketing Science Institute Report No. 79-106 (Cambridge: Marketing Science Institute, 1979), p. 11.

35. James P. Neelankavil and Albert B. Stridsberg, *Advertising Self-Regulation* (New York: Hastings House, 1980), p. 130.

36. Priscilla La Barbera, "Advertising Self-Regulation: An Evaluation," *Michigan State University Business Topics,* 28 (Summer 1980): 58.

37. Neil H. Borden, *The Economic Effects of Advertising* (Chicago: Richard D. Irwin, 1942), p. 3.

38. Raymond A. Bauer and Stephen A. Greyser, *Advertising in America* (Boston: Division of Research, Harvard University Graduate School of Business Administration), p. 72; *Advertising Age,* 23 May 1977, pp. 4, 102.

39. Ronald D. Anderson, Jack L. Engledow, and Helmut Becker, "Advertising Attitudes in West Germany and the U.S.: An Analysis over Age and Time," *Journal of International Business Studies,* 9 (Winter 1978): 37.

40. *New York Times,* 20 September 1981, p. 35.

41. Christopher Gale, "Truth in Advertising: The Consumer View," D.B.A. diss., Harvard Graduate School of Business Administration, 1970, p. I:1.

42. John T. Lucas and Richard Gurman, *Truth in Advertising* (New York: American Management Association, 1972), p. 3.

43. Cited in Ivan L. Preston, *The Great American Blow-Up* (Madison: University of Wisconsin Press, 1975), p. 173.

44. David Ogilvy, *Confessions of an Advertising Man,* paperback ed. (New York: Ballantine, 1971), p. 84.

45. U.S. Federal Trade Commission, *Federal Trade Commission Staff Report on Television Advertising to Children,* February, 1978, p. 14.

46. Ibid. p. 17, citing *Advertising Age,* 19 July 1965.

47. Ethel G. Bedford, "Specialization of Deceptive Practices in Advertising Directed at Socio-Economic Market Segments," in Fredric Stuart, ed., *Consumer Protection from Deceptive Advertising,* Hofstra University Yearbook of Business, series 10, vol. 3 (1974), pp. 351–83.

48. Cited in Leigh R. Isaacs, "Psychological Advertising: A New Area of FTC Regulation," *Wisconsin Law Review,* 1972, p. 1104.

49. Bauer and Greyser, *Advertising in America,* p. 109.

50. Stephen A. Greyser and Bonnie B. Reece, "Businessmen Look Hard at Advertising," *Harvard Business Review* (May-June 1971), reprinted in *Harvard Business Review, Ethics for Executives,* part 2, p. 113.

Notes

51. Vance Packard, *The Hidden Persuaders* (New York: Pocket Books, 1978), p. 229. See also Michael Schudson, "Criticizing the Critics of Advertising," *Media, Culture and Society,* 3 (1981): 3-12.

52. Wilson Bryan Key, *Subliminal Seduction,* (Englewood Cliffs, N.J.: Prentice-Hall, 1973), *Media Sexploitation* (Prentice-Hall, 1976), and *The Clam-Plate Orgy* (Prentice-Hall, 1980).

53. Quoted in Jonathan Price, *The Best Thing on TV: Commercials* (New York: Penguin Books, 1978), pp. 78, 80.

54. Daniel J. Boorstin, "Advertising and American Civilization," in Yale Brozen, ed., *Advertising and Society* (New York: New York University Press, 1974), pp. 18-20.

55. Quoted in Mayer, *Madison Avenue,* p. 53.

56. Rosser Reeves, *Reality in Advertising* (New York: Knopf, 1961), pp. 47-49.

57. Ibid. p. 125.

58. For a recent restatement of the Krugman theory, see his "Memory without Recall, Exposure without Perception," *Journal of Advertising Research,* 17 (August 1977): 7-12.

59. Shirley Polykoff, *Does She ... Or Doesn't She?* (Garden City, N.Y.: Doubleday, 1975), p. 72.

60. *Advertising Age,* 30 April 1980, p. 130.

61. *Advertising Age,* 3 May 1982, p. 12.

62. Michael J. Arlen, *Thirty Seconds* (New York: Farrar, Straus & Giroux, 1980), p. 13.

63. George Burton Hotchkiss, *Advertising Copy* (New York: Harper and Brothers, 1924), p. 185.

64. Kelvin Lancaster, *Consumer Demand: A New Approach* (New York: Columbia University Press, 1971).

65. Tony Schwartz, *The Responsive Chord,* paperback ed. (New York: Anchor Books, 1974), pp. 24-25.

66. Bruce L. Stern, Dean M. Krugman, and Alan Resnik, "Magazine Advertising: An Analysis of Its Information Content," *Journal of Advertising Research,* 21 (April 1981): 39-44; Alan Resnik and Bruce L. Stern, "An Analysis of Information Content in Television Advertising," *Journal of Marketing,* 41 (January 1977): 50-53.

67. Resnik and Stern, "An Analysis of Television Advertising," p. 52.

68. For some of the most popular and influential recent theories, see Alvin Toffler, *The Third Wave* (New York: William Morrow, 1980); Christopher Evans, *The Micro Millennium* (New York: Viking Press, 1979); Daniel Bell, "The Social Framework of the Information Society," in Tom Forester, ed., *The Microelectronics Revolution* (Cambridge: MIT Press, 1981), pp. 500-49.

69. Fred Hirsch, *The Social Limits to Growth* (Cambridge: Harvard University Press, 1976).

INDEX

A & P, 90, 98
account executives, 165
accounts: as ad man's personal property, 164-165; competitive, 163-164
Adams, Samuel H., 195, 196
adulteration, 196
"advertisability," 46
advertisements: size of, 235
advertiser service, 142
advertising: and acculturation, 258; and affluence, 38-39; as barrier to entry, 65-66, 70; barter for, 23; behaviorism in, 14; campaign concept of, 140-141, 244; and centralization of power, 58; commentary on social implications of, 10-11; consumer distrust of, 272-273, 282-283; and consumer welfare, 70-77; content analysis of, 230-231; cumulative impact of, 245-246; data on, 21-29; dishonest, 185, 187, 191-196, 202-207, 215, 233, 277;

early, 4, 34, 232; effectiveness of, 47; effects on industry, 62-111; as element of business strategy, 40-41; ethics of, 184-226; evanescence of, 284; expenditures, see expenditures; future of, 294-298; growth of, 6, 30; as herald of democracy, 11; as history, 3; history of, 9-10; human interest, 241-242; and industrial concentration, 65-67; industry's demand for, 18-61; inner conflicts of, 182; as investment, 68-69; local, 9; and mass production, 5; mentality of, 180; modern, 6-7; national, see national advertising; newspaper, see newspaper advertising; oral, 4; outdoor, 157; as "package of stimuli," 292; as prostitution, 180-181; radical analyses of, 224-225; "reason why," 237-240, 242; rejected, 188-

327

Index

Index

Index

Index

Index

J. B. Williams Company, 281
Johns, William, 178
Johnson, Lyndon B., 293
Johnson, Samuel, 4
Johnston, William, 122
Jones, Lewis B., 51
Jordan Marsh, 103
Journal of Commerce, 84
Judd, Orange, 187
The Jungle (Sinclair), 196
J. Walter Thompson Agency,
    59, 118, 124–125, 156, 164–
    165, 175, 176, 189–190, 199,
    265–267; advertiser services
    of, 141–142, 177

Kaldor, Nicholas, 64–65
Kastor v. Elders, 161
Keller, Morton, 57–58
Kellogg, 42
Kellogg, W. K., 75, 96
Kennedy, John E., 149, 238–
    239, 245, 254, 283–284
Kenner, H. J., 203, 208, 210–
    211
Kewanee Boiler Company,
    200
Key, W. B.: *The Clam Plate
    Orgy,* 283; *Media Manipu-
    lation,* 282; *Subliminal Se-
    duction,* 282
K-mart, 257

Ladies' Home Journal, 137,
    149, 156, 228; muckraking
    in, 196; self-censorship of,
    190
Larrabee, C. B., 215
Lasker, Albert, 119, 139, 179,
    199, 238, 284
LeBon, Gustave, 247
Leverhulme, W. H. (1st Vis-
    count), 10
Levitt, Theodore, 263
liberal ideology, 15
life insurance: advertising of,
    221–223, 229; marketing
    strategies for, 57–60
Lincoln, Abraham, 31, 242
Liquozone, 194–195
Literary Digest, 235
Locke, David, 125–126
Longfellow, Henry W., 134
Lord & Thomas, 13, 139, 194,
    199, 200, 238; growth of,
    176
Lowney Chocolate and Cocoa
    company, 75
Lydia Pinkham's tonic, 198

Macy's, 73, 90, 103
Madison Avenue, 165; client
    power on, 266; move to,
    175; speculative presenta-
    tions on, 166; as "Ulcer
    Gulch," 271–272
magazine advertising, 43–45
magazines, mass circulation:
    advent of, 137; and commis-
    sion system, 155–156, 162;
    size of advertisements in,
    235
Mahin Agency, 198
Mahin, John L., 74, 199, 201
mail order advertising, 37–38,
    137; limiting conditions for,
    80–81; marginal, 121
manufacturers and national

Index

advertising, 77–108

Mapes, Emery, 171

marketing channels, 256–257

marketing of services, 262–263

marketing research: consumer reliance on advertising, 47; development of, 142–144; rudimentary, 10, 141

marketing strategies, 245–248; of American Tobacco, 53–54; of Eastman Kodak, 50–52; of Gillette, 56–57; of life insurance companies, 57–60; of Nabisco, 48–51; of Progressive Era, 48–61; of Quaker Oats, 55

market segmentation, 13, 259; era of, 252–298

market structure, 63–70

Marlboro, 258

Marquand, John P., 180–181

Marshall Field, 90, 103

Marx, Karl, 15, 225

mass consumption, 11–12

mass production, 248–249; and advertising, 5; and consumer education, 33; and diversification, 260–261

Masters of Advertising Copy (Frederick), 27

Maxwell-Chalmers, 42

McCann-Erickson Advertising Agency, 21–22, 253, 266

McCann, H. K., 148

McClure's, 137, 156

McKinney, Harry N., 48, 124

McLuhan, Marshall, 10

McManus Agency, 221

media: growth of, 8–9; matching advertisers with, 113; new, 133, 136

Mellin's Food, 198

Mercantile Agency Reference Book, 124

merger wave (1898–1902), 63

Merrimack Textile Mill, 32

Metropolitan Life, 59

Millais, John, 140

Miller-Tydings Act (1937), 105

minidramas, 291–292

Minneapolis Ad Forum, 206, 208, 209

Minneapolis Journal, 217

"mixed regimen," 106–107

Modern Advertising (Calkins and Holden), 195

Molière, 41

Moses, Bert, 203, 214

muckraking, 196

Munsey, Frank, 137; attempt to break commission system, 155–156

Munsey's Magazine, 155–156

Mutual of New York, 57, 222

Nabisco (National Biscuit Company), 42, 75; account competing with, 164; forward integration of, 84; marketing strategy of, 48–50; substitution peril to, 88

NAD/NARB system (National Advertising Division/National Advertising Review Board), 275–276

national advertising: and consumer welfare, 108–111;

335

Index

national advertising *(continued)* creating new products, 50; dealer cooperation with, 91–94; invention of, 31; large-scale practitioners of, 41–46; lead taken by, 30; manufacturers, distributors, and, 77–108; and marketing strategies, 48–61, 245–248; modern, 252–255; rise of, 62–63; transformations of, 8–9; and urbanization, 34–38

National Advertising Commission, 214

National Advertising Records, 86

National Baptist, 119

national markets, 5

National Outdoor Advertising Bureau, 157

Navin, Thomas, 45

Neal, Jesse H., 215

newspaper advertising: antebellum, 4–5; first, 4; and urbanization, 37

newspaper directories, 129–130

newspapers: circulation announced by, 169; and commission system, 162; growth of, 113

New York Daily Tribune, 119, 215; ads rejected by, 188

New York Herald, 188

New York Life Insurance Company, 57, 222

New York Stock Exchange, 219

The New York Times, 104, 190

Nichols-Shepard Company, 141

Niles, S. R., 116

Nims, H. D., 204–205, 208

N. W. Ayer and Son, 48, 80, 119, 124, 128–129, 138, 141, 143, 164, 176, 238, 265; accounts turned down by, 191, 198; patent medicine accounts of, 193–194

Nystrom, Paul, 103

Ochs, A., 190

Ogilvy & Mather, 279

Ogilvy, David, 279, 289

Oneida Community Plate, 47

open contract, 129

opportunism, 147

oral advertising, 4

Ornstein, Stanley, 67

outdoor advertising, 157

Pabst Brewing Company, 82

Pacific Coast Borax, 85

packaging, 50

Packard, Vance: *The Hidden Persuaders,* 282

Painter, William, 55–56

Palmer, Volney B., 114–117

Pandolfo, Samuel, 212

Parke Davis, 85

Parker Pens, 85, 97

Park Row, 119–120

patent medicines, 186–187,

Index

Index

manufacturers' direct sales to, 85

segmentation campaigns, 289–290

service marketing, 262–263

sex appeal, 221, 228

Sherwin-Willaims Paint Company, 81

Shryer, William A., 68, 240, 245, 246

Sidener, Merle, 207

Siegel-Cooper, 135

Simon, Julian: *Issues in the Economics of Advertising*, 38

Sinclair, Upton: *The Jungle*, 196

Sloan, Alfred P., 261

Smith, Wendell R., 259

space jobbers, 117

special agents, 130–132

speculative presentations, 165–166

Standard Oil, 148, 199

Starch, Daniel, 68, 237, 245, 246

Steiner, Robert, 106–108

Stephens-Ashurst Bill, 102–103

stereotyping, 136

Stevens, R. B., 102

Strong, E. K., 241

Studebaker, 42

substitution peril, 87–90

suburbanization, 257

Sudler & Henessey, 267

suggestion, 240–241

suicide, 180–181

Sullivan, Mark, 196

Sweezy, Paul, 225

Swift, 42

Swift, Gustavus, 79

Telser, Lester, 95, 105

Texaco, 33

Tipper, Harry, 33–34

toadstool millionaires, 187

Tobacco Trust, 53–54

trademarks, 69

trusts: biscuit, 49; formation of, 63; need to advertise, 64; tobacco, 53–54

truth: definitions of, 219–220; irrelevant, 221; uncertainty over, 278

truth in advertising movement, 184, 188, 191–192, 202–212, 273–274; boundaries of, 212–226

TWA, 166

Uneeda Biscuit, 48–51

Union Carbide, 70

Unique Selling Proposition, 287–288

United Cigar Stores, 54

urbanization, 34–38

U. S. Rubber, 42, 256

U. S. Steel, 70

values: of advertising men, 15–16; and content analysis, 230

Van Camp, 88, 99

Veblen, Thorstein, 225

vertical integration, 78, 85–86; perils of, 83–84

Victor Talking Machines, 47

Index

Vivarin, 281
Volkswagen advertising, 289

Waldo, Richard, 204, 215
Walter Baker Chocolate, 60, 69
Wanamaker, John, 10, 89
Wanamaker's, 73–74; ad copy written for, 134–135, 187–188
Ward, Artemas, 73, 125, 149, 192, 234, 236, 244
Washington Evening Star, 169
W. Atlee Burpee Seed Company, 80
Weissenberger, S. A., 210
Welch's Grape Juice, 60
Weld, L. D. H., 21–25
Westinghouse, 70
Whittier, Edwin, 100–101
Who's Who in Advertising, 177–179

Wiebe, Robert, 20
Wiley, Harvey, 196, 206
Williamson, Oliver, 145, 147
Willys-Overland, 42
Wilson, Thomas A., 71–72
women, advertisers' image of, 247–248
Woodbury, John H., 227
Woodbury Soap, 221, 227–228
Woodward, Helen R., 179–180
World War I, 6; advertising volume during, 30; and social persuasion, 12
Wrigley, W., Jr., 216
Wundt, Wilhelm, 239

Young and Rubicam, 265, 267
Young, James H., 197

ZuZu cookies, 49